George Matheson

Growth of the Spirit of Christianity

From the First Century to the Dawn of the Lutheran Era: Volume II.

George Matheson

Growth of the Spirit of Christianity
From the First Century to the Dawn of the Lutheran Era: Volume II.

ISBN/EAN: 9783337100957

Printed in Europe, USA, Canada, Australia, Japan

Cover: Foto ©Lupo / pixelio.de

More available books at **www.hansebooks.com**

GROWTH

OF THE

SPIRIT OF CHRISTIANITY

FROM THE FIRST CENTURY

TO

THE DAWN OF THE LUTHERAN ERA

BY THE

REV. GEORGE MATHESON, M.A. B.D.

AUTHOR OF
'AIDS TO THE STUDY OF GERMAN THEOLOGY'

VOLUME II.

EDINBURGH
T. AND T. CLARK, 38 GEORGE STREET
1877

THE GROWTH OF THE SPIRIT OF CHRISTIANITY

CHAPTER XXIII.

THE CHURCH UNDER NEW GUARDIANSHIP.

WE must now retrace our steps, to consider the character of that new power which was destined to interrupt the progress of mankind. We mentioned incidentally in the previous chapter, that Pepin, the father of Charlemagne, had obtained the concurrence of the Bishop of Rome in the organization of a political revolution. The significant fact here is, that Pepin should have deemed such a concurrence to be of the slightest value,—that in an age when might was right, and the physically strongest were the survivors, he should have esteemed the sanction of a Roman bishop to be a source of additional power. It is one of those facts which, though insignificant in themselves, are yet like the quivering of the leaves, indicative that a wind is blowing. If the sanction of a Roman bishop could in the eighth century lend weight to a political revolution, we cannot resist the conclusion, that in the eighth century the representative monarchy of the Roman See must have been already beginning to harden into the absolute sovereignty of Papal dominion. Of course, we do not suppose that the Church had ever formally signed away its freedom. We cannot put our finger upon any date, and say it was then that the spirit of Christianity relinquished its birthright; the greatest revolutions of history are produced, not by deliberate acts, but by a determinate process. And such a process was undoubtedly being accomplished here. It seems to us that the method by which the Bishop of Rome passed from the royal representative into the despotic sovereign of the Church, was precisely analogous to the method by which image representation passed into image worship,—analogous to it, and at the same time parallel with it. The image at first was valued because it stood for some other object; it ultimately came to be valued for some inherent power which it was believed to possess. The Bishop of Rome, in like manner, was originally an object of reverence, because, being ruler of the most prominent see of Christendom, he was taken as the representative of Christendom. Gradually, however, the virtues which attached to him vicariously came to be imputed personally; and by slow and insensible degrees the Church began to look in the Bishop of Rome for those manifestations of spiritual power which he ought to have derived only as a gift from itself. We must not suppose that the transition was effected by any outward force or power of physical terror. We have only to remember the circumstances of those early mediæval centuries, and it will all seem to us very natural. The barbarians of the North could not appreciate the existence of an invisible and an abstract power; they must see it individualized. The Roman bishopric represented to them the power of God in the world; there was only a step between representation and incarnation. If all images shared in the nature of the objects which they symbolized, why should not the principle be carried out here also? If the Roman See centralized the divine will, why should it not centralize the divine power? if it expressed the ultimate voice of the Church, why should it not dispense with all other voices? Such was the intuitive reasoning by which the age of opening mediævalism passed into the contemplation of Rome as a sovereign authority. The men of that day required no outward force, and received no outward force, to accustom them to such a contemplation; they reached it as a legitimate conclusion from defective premises, and they were aided in reaching it by that materialising tendency which is incidental to certain stages of the school-life. Rome was assuredly coming rapidly into a second empire; but as yet its empire depended exclusively upon its spiritual power.

It is not difficult to see, that had no power been added to this, it would have died in the course of nature. The natural growth of Christian intelligence would ere long have deprived the Roman bishopric of any exclusive privileges, if these privileges had not been secured by material armour. But now the time had come when the material armour was to be placed above the spiritual, and the authority of Rome was to be established by weapons which no intellectual culture could blunt or break. That political revolution which placed Pepin on the throne of France enabled the bishop of the seven hills to take his first step in the ascent to the throne of the world. The concurrence of Rome in the elevation of Pepin made that monarch its debtor, and it was not long ere the debt was paid. The payment was made in the form of a temporal possession: Ravenna was conquered from the Lombards, and delivered over, as a permanent inheritance, to the Roman See. That gift was only the prelude to others. Thick and fast the temporal donations to the chair of St. Peter came crowding in, and before the century closed it had already a claim to rank amongst the secular powers of the earth. It is from this epoch of temporal dominion that we date the true rise of the Papacy, —from the time when the rule of fatherhood was merged in the sway of kinghood, and when the idea of spiritual reverence was covered by the feeling of outward terror. Henceforth the Bishop of Rome disappears from history, and the Roman pontiff arises in his room; henceforth the idea of a representative government in the Church gradually fades away, and the notion of an absolute monarchy becomes day by day more definite. Not even yet, indeed, did the Papacy aspire to political independence; it was still content to acknowledge its subjection to imperial rule; but it began to claim, in no measured accents, the empire of the ecclesiastical world, and the concession of such an empire logically implied political absolutism. Let it once be granted that the Roman pontiff was sovereign of the Church, it could soon be proved that he was sovereign of the State as well; for was not the extent of the Church commensurate with the extent of the world? and were not all the kingdoms of the earth only provinces of the kingdom of God? These gigantic pretensions the Papacy as yet did not broach; nay, it was probably as yet unaware that such pretensions were really involved in its present attitude; but when it aspired to temporal dominion over the thoughts of the ecclesiastical world, it started upon a course which could have no consistent pause until it had reached the summit of empire, and made the kings of the earth its tributaries.

It is curious to observe how soon the altered circumstances of the Papacy produced an altered tone. Scarcely had the Roman bishop, or as we may now say, the Pope, assumed the sword of temporal dominion, when he assumed the air of imperious command. Supported by the authority of Pepin, he issued to all the churches an order for uniformity in worship, and demanded that they should take as their standard of uniformity that mode of celebration which prevailed at Rome. In this decree there were compressed the most prominent characteristics of Papal Catholicism. There was the struggle towards unity, as a starting-point; there was the identification of unity with uniformity, which is a very different idea; there was the announcement that this unity or uniformity must be regulated after one individual type; and there was the declaration that the will of this one individual was a sufficient reason to the Christian Church for the adoption of any standard of worship. These were bold assumptions, yet they met with little opposition. It is worthy of remark that the only quarter from which opposition came was Italy. There were several Italian churches which determinedly refused the decree of uniformity, and, unconquered either by threats or by promises, persisted in preserving their individual peculiarities. Was there not to be heard, even at this early period, a murmur in the valleys ?—the mutterings, faint and low, of those dissentient voices which ere long were to swell into one great chorus in the Protestant reaction of the Waldenses.

Thus far Rome had met with little resistance. But now there came that temporary interruption which in the former chapter we have tried to portray, and which threatened at one time to extinguish the life of hierarchical dominion. The Mohammedan wave, after overwhelming Asia, and breaking against the shores of Greece, had allowed its echoes to be heard in the North and West of Europe. We have seen how France and Britain had been especially stirred by the reverberations of the storm. It seemed as if the breezes from the East had wafted into these nations the seeds of Eastern life—had inspired them with a new principle of being, and roused them into a sense of patriotic fervour and of national responsibility. It seemed for a moment as if the heart of Christendom were about to fall back upon its primitive instincts—to abandon the ceremonious ritual and the material image, and to seek direct instruction from the portraiture of the written word. And when — in spite of the retrogressive example of Greece, in spite of the crushing policy of Irene, in spite of the condemnation pronounced by the second Nicene Council — the French Church, with the authority of Charlemagne, proceeded to condemn the worship of the image, even the least sanguine might be excused for looking forward to a new day. The decision of that Council of Frankfort was perhaps the most critical moment in the life of the incipient Papacy. Its existence was trembling in the balance. Its whole life depended on the continuance of the value which had been attached to image representation. The Pope aspired to be the visible image of the theocracy; take away the necessity for such representation, and his power must fall to pieces. The blow appeared to have been struck which was to check these pretensions in the germ; and the life of that Papal See which had but just begun, was ready, in its hour of birth, to vanish away.

All at once it was saved by one of those strange turns of fortune which, to him who looks only at isolated events, often seem the product of accident. In the very moment of his advance, Charlemagne beat a retreat. Without any apparent reason, without experiencing any increase of outward obstacles, at the very instant when the field of reformation had opened to his view, he commanded the march to halt, and the preparations to be stayed. Had matters ended here, humanity might still have reaped some advantage from those labours which his reign had already accomplished; but this tergiversation was only the beginning of an entire change of policy. Not content with commanding a retreat, Charlemagne passed over into the camp of the enemy. His youth had displayed the vigorous reformer; his age exhibited the aspect of the blind devotee. How are we to account for such a transition? Did it proceed from the sobering effect of years? Did it originate in a moment of remorse for the cruelties of a life spent much in war and slaughter? Did it spring from one of those sudden and violent changes of religious conviction which are occasionally, though not frequently, found in human nature? We do not believe it had its ground in any of these sources. To our mind, the change in the religious attitude of Charlemagne had its root in a profound policy. We believe it was at this time that there first entered into his mind that thought which a few years later found expression in a great historical act; we mean the idea of reviving the Western empire. In the absence of any definite information, we are, of course, thrown back upon conjecture, yet it seems to us highly probable that this idea was first suggested to Charlemagne by the Roman pontiff. The suggestion might have come in such a form as this: You are seeking to institute a renaissance, to establish an empire on the basis of culture and civilisation; it is well, but why should you seek to do so by revolting from the institutions of the past? why not find its accomplishment in the resurrection of that past itself? Would it not be possible to establish an empire whose culture and civilisation would be compatible with all this existing hierarchical system? Instead of advancing into the future, let us go back into the past; let us revive the Western empire of the Cæsars, as a counterpoise to the Eastern dominion of the Greeks; let us unite the Christian hierarchy to that civilisation of an older time, which presents to hierarchical worship so many and so strong resemblances. This we believe to have been the spirit of the Papal suggestion. We know, as a matter of history, that a few years later it actually dominated the mind of Charlemagne; and there is no improbability in the supposition that it may have entered his mind now. If it did, it will account for his whole conduct. There was suddenly presented to him a new object of ambition — an object not inconsistent with his dreams of a renaissance, and yet altogether consistent with fidelity to the established faith—an object whose attainment would really prove a source of greatness, and which yet would involve no divorce from the associations of bygone days. He felt that a resurrection of the Roman empire would invest his name with almost a classic glory; he perceived, at the same time, that to accomplish this aim, the Papacy would be eminently necessary. The Roman States were bound together by a tie stronger than that which could be formed by any despot's chain—the tie of religious brotherhood. They were united as one family in the household of one father, and the father of that household was the pontiff himself; this was the centre of their alliance, this was the ground of their union. Any conqueror who would perpetuate that union must accept the existing association, must ally himself with those religious ideas which constituted the Roman brotherhood. And a man so far-seeing as Charlemagne was not slow to perceive this. He desired to see the empire of the Cæsars rise in his person into resurrection life, but he knew that without its present religious atmosphere it would immediately crumble again into corruption. He desired, therefore, that the revival of ancient Rome should be a revival into living religious forms; that while it was a resurrection of the secular past, it should find its incorporation in the sacred present; that while it rose with the culture of the Augustan age, it should receive the impress of the mediæval hierarchy. Charlemagne must be its head, but the pontiff must continue to be the heart of its life.

These magnificent designs were not destined to lie long in abeyance. Not later than six years after the Protestant attitude assumed by the Council of Frankfort, there was transacted, before the eyes of astonished Europe, a very remarkable spectacle. Charlemagne stood in the city of the Cæsars, and by his side stood the Bishop of that city. It was a meeting of the unities—the unity of secular power, and the unity of religious life. On the one side, was the man who held in his hand the sceptre of continental Europe, who, partly by inheritance and partly by the fortune of war, had extended his sway over one of the largest empires which has ever fallen to the lot of earthly potentate; on the other, was the man who professedly represented the Prince of Peace, but who had weapons in reserve more powerful than those of war,—the man who, from the claim to be successor to the chair of St. Peter, had advanced his pretensions step by step to the claim of almost theocratic power. Looking at these two potentates as they stood confronting the world, the men of that day might have thought the strength of the emperor the more enduring; in reality, it was only more pretentiously displayed. The Roman pontiff was even then by far the more formidable authority, though as yet he did not know it, nor would Charlemagne have admitted it. The very purpose of their meeting had in it some prophecy of Papal greatness. The secular monarch came to be crowned Emperor of the West, to be officially proclaimed restorer of the dynasty of Cæsar, but the crown was to be placed on his head by the hand of the Roman pontiff. If the act, in its present interpretation, indicated the willingness of the Pope to serve the Emperor, it pointed symbolically and prophetically to an event which was even now looming in the future—to that time when the chair of St. Peter would claim to be the crowner of all kings, the source of all regal authority, and the fountain of all secular power. Charlemagne had in the meantime the pre-eminence, yet, had he possessed a deeper insight into the laws of history, he might have applied to himself the words of the Baptist in the wilderness, and said of his sacred rival, 'He must increase, but I must decrease.'

Let us now survey the position in which the Papacy had been placed by this memorable coronation. Charlemagne retained to himself the supreme power over Rome and the surrounding districts, yet he left to the pontiff a delegated authority, only inferior by reason of its being delegated. This fact alone formed an important step in Papal advancement. It was not merely that the temporal possessions of the Pope were increased numerically; it was much more. By this act of Charlemagne the temporal power of the pontiff was for the first time legalised. Hitherto it had been a growing fact, but not a recognised law. Hitherto it had derived its existence almost entirely from the religious fears of men, and the superstitions incidental to a primitive age. But when Charlemagne recognised the Papal headship, he stamped his temporal power with his own imprimatur, he put his seal upon it, and made it legal. Henceforth it was to stand upon an entirely new footing. It was no longer to be dependent for its subsistence on the craven fear of the multitude, or the ignorant superstition of a community; it was to present itself to the world as one of the world's own institutions, made by its own laws, and deriving its rights from its own titles. A power thus supported was independent of the special caprices of human nature. It was no longer the product of a particular age, nor was it any longer to derive its strength from the weakness of that age; it had obtained a charter from the world, and it held its right by the authority of kings.

And what all this time was the situation of Christianity's school-life? How was this affected by the elevation of a new authority? It had experienced a change of masters, and at the same time a change of guardians. Its first schoolmaster had been the abbot; but the abbot, as we have seen, had been only a preparatory teacher. His office had been to harmonize the spirit of Christianity with the idea of monarchy; accordingly the monastery had been constructed after the similitude of a little kingdom, and the mind of the Church had been specially trained to obedience. The little kingdom was now to be merged in the greater,—the abbot was to surrender the keys to the Pope, and the school-life was to find in the Pope a more potent and a more authoritative teacher. How thorough had been that monastic training by which the Church had been prepared for submission to authority, was manifested by the ease with which the transference was effected. There was a time when the Christian Church would have recoiled with horror from submission to any individual authority; there came a time, again, when even the Church of mediævalism was constrained to assert its birthright. But here was a transition moment between the old and the new; the old thirst for liberty was quenched, and the thirst for a new freedom had not yet come. The spirit of Irenæus, the spirit of Cyprian, the spirit of Augustine, was no more. The heart of Christendom had been corrupted by its contact with the world, and the school-life of the Christian Church had already strayed from many of the warm impulses of its childhood. It yielded to Papal dominion without a struggle; it surrendered its birthright without a blow. If we ask why, we need not look far for the answer. The school-life was already in harmony with the mind of the new schoolmaster. Emerson, in his work on representative men, has said of Napoleon Bonaparte that he was accepted by the men of his age, because the men of his age were themselves Napoleons. The same may be affirmed of this mediæval world. The men of that age had become worldly, and therefore they fell in with the purposes of the world. The dream of Papal dominion had a fascination for the heart of Christendom, because the heart of Christendom was already beginning to become a heart of stone. The old pagan ideal was reviving within it, and the resurrection of the Western empire fanned the flame. The new schoolmaster promised to the pupil a short road to greatness; he would train the mind of the Church for the possession of an empire independent of the caprices of human will,—an empire which would rule by imperative command, and reduce the spirits of men into the attitude of mechanical instruments. And the mind of Christendom was allured by the prospect; it was a dream which addressed the present bent of its nature, and therefore gave it joy. It entered eagerly into the project, it identified itself with its schoolmaster, and it professed its willingness to rise or fall with the success or failure of the Papal scheme of ambition.

But the temporal power of the Pope brought to the school-life of Christianity not only a change of masters, but a change of guardians. Hitherto the guardian of the Church had been the State; the guardian of the Church was now to be a power delegated by the State,—a power not wholly ecclesiastical, nor yet wholly civil, but bordering upon both. The State still retained a potential jurisdiction, but that jurisdiction it rarely exercised. Indeed, there were circumstances looming in the future which made it inevitable that the delegated guardianship of the Papacy should ere long pass into an absolute guardianship—circumstances which were to depress the strength of the civil power, and give to the ecclesiastical force a preponderating influence. In order to elucidate these, we must pursue a little farther the thread of our historical narrative.

The revival of the Western empire promised to resuscitate the authority of kings. It appeared for a time to have arrested that progress of feudalism which had been steadily advancing with the advance of the Northern barbarians, and it bade fair to restore the imperial dignity to that lofty position which it had occupied in classic days. Yet it was soon to be seen on how frail a tenure such a hope was built. The power of Charlemagne was really a power which emanated from himself; his empire did not give it to him, he gave it to his empire. The submission of his vassals was not the result of fear, but of admiration; the minds of these primitive Germans, like the minds of their modern successors, yielded that homage to individual intellect which they never yielded to individual authority. It was speedily to be made manifest that the empire without Charlemagne would experience the fate of the body without the soul. Its very vastness prevented it from being enduring; it was held together by a master hand, but the withdrawal of that hand must cause its dissolution. And the hand was now about to be withdrawn. In the height of his splendour, in the fulness of his years, in the blaze of his fame, Charlemagne passed away, and with him passed the glory of that Carlovingian race, of which his father had been but the founder; its life seemed to have exhausted itself in the overflowing richness of this one life, and those who followed in the train had not their due share of vigour. Charlemagne, as we have said, had two natures in him—that of the barbarous age, and that of the incipient renaissance; the masculine roughness, and the feminine tenderness. The former died with him, the latter he bequeathed to his posterity. His son Louis, who succeeded him in the empire, succeeded him also in the softer side of his character. His name has come down to us with the designation of 'The Meek;' and it is probable that to that rude age the surname was a mark of contempt. Had he lived a few centuries later, he would probably have been canonised; had he lived during the revival of letters, he would certainly have been extolled as a patron of learning; but living at the period in which he did, he was like a man born out of his place and time. He had not come into the inheritance of that sterner part of his father's nature, which had attracted and captivated the fierce Northern hordes. He was a man for days of piety, a king for times of peace; but not a suitable chief for a season of war and bloodshed. Accordingly the death of Charlemagne was to the new Western empire what the sacking of imperial Rome was to the old—a lifting of the chain, which left the nations free. Those tribes which had begun to bask in the sunshine of civilisation went back again into the cold. Step by step the unity of the mighty empire melted away; and that which once had formed a continent of united power, was parted into islands of individual ambition. New swarms of barbarians came pouring from the North, to prey upon the borders of the empire; and the sea as well as the land now entered on the war. From Denmark and from Norway there were streaming over the ocean two bands of rugged warriors, who, after exhausting the adventures of the shore, had sought a new dominion on the deep. Denmark poured forth the Danes, Norway sent out the Normans; the former harassed England, and the latter devastated France. Both had in some respects an analogous success. The one rolled back the civilising work of the great Alfred; the other crushed what remained of the renaissance of Charlemagne: the one obtained a lodgment on the shores of Britain; the other secured a possession in the kingdom of France: the one became amalgamated with the Saxon blood; the other ultimately united both with Frank and Saxon, and contributed still further to cement the relative interests of these great nations. But the great effect of these inundations from the North, whether by land or sea, was to increase and confirm the tendency to feudalism; and the tendency to feudalism undoubtedly pointed in the direction of a depression of regal authority. The feudal system bore a strong resemblance to the solar system; it had a central sun, a body of revolving planets, and a company of attending satellites,—the first represented by the king, the second by the barons, and the third by the vassals of the barons. Theoretically, the king was supreme; to him all the barons swore fealty, and bound themselves to assist him in times of war. But in times of peace it was very hard to tell where the supremacy really lay. In the sense that one was independent of another, there was no supremacy; the analogy to the solar system held pre-eminently good here. As in that system the destruction of the less would involve the shaking of the greater, so in feudalism there was a principle of mutual attraction, which made the existence of the kingly power dependent on the existence of the vassal. The baron was bound to assist his sovereign by no other law than that which obliged the vassal to assist the baron; and neither sovereign nor baron was on his side free from obligation to his inferior. The king could legally take no step without consulting the barons; the barons could legally take no step without consulting their vassals; and the extremes of social life were thus knit together by a bond of mutual dependence. No doubt, there was often a very great discrepancy between the law and the practice. In mediæval times, a sovereign of commanding military talents was frequently a despot, and not seldom a successful despot; yet he was so, not by reason of the constitution, but by reason of the personal respect entertained for his warlike genius; this was in that age the sure passport to .fealty. But the constitution of feudalism itself pointed towards the advance of political and social liberty. It was directly opposed to monopoly; was theoretically irreconcilable with the despotism of the few over the many. It contained in germ a recognition of the rights of individual men; and it was thus far in strict harmony with the Christian spirit, which, on its social side, is the spirit of human brotherhood. The advance of feudalism was a step in the progress of freedom. It broke the arbitrary power of kings, it annulled the supremacy of individual over national will, and in some sense it subordinated the power of the State to the united power of the community.

Such was, in our view, the influence which led to the relaxation of that guardianship which, since the days of Constantine, the State had claimed over the Church. And as the guardianship of the State relaxed, that of the Papacy became daily more strict and vigilant; the power which had originally been delegated, aimed at being self-supporting. There happened during this period two incidents within the Church which greatly contributed to further the tendency of outward circumstances. The first was the broaching, by Pascasius Radbert, of that doctrine of transubstantiation, which has become so integral a part of the Catholic communion. It was an attempt to re-create within the Church that presence of the Master which the exclusive contemplation of His divinity had banished from the world. If the power of restoring this presence could be proved to reside with the hierarchy, it would clearly confer upon that hierarchy an influence and an authority which must render it invincible. As yet the view of Radbert was by no means universally accepted;—it was opposed by Bertram, it was opposed by Erigena, it was opposed by many of the most eminent bishops of that day;—nevertheless, the very suggestion of such a theory pointed to great possibilities of ecclesiastical domination. The second of these incidents which contributed to exalt the new guardianship was even more directly Papal. Not long after the effort of Pascasius Radbert, there appeared a series of documents, purporting to be of very ancient date, and professing to establish legally the Roman claim to absolute dominion. The name of Isidore of Seville was attached to them, and hence they have come down to us with the designation of the Isidorian decretals. Some of them were compiled from contemporary literature, and some of them were deliberate forgeries. Their genuineness was doubted by many Latin bishops of that day; their spuriousness is not at all doubted by any Roman Catholic of ours; nevertheless, they served in their generation an important purpose, and suggested ideas which had more influence over the mind than the source whence they sprang. They contemplated three objects, each rising conspicuously above the other. The first was the elevation of the Papacy into the centre of clerical dependence; this was, in point of fact, almost already accomplished. The second was the complete separation of the Papacy from the existence of the civil power; the first step of that process had also begun to be accomplished. The third, and most extravagant aim, was the erection of the Papacy into one all-embracing empire, of which Church and State were alike the tributaries and dependants; the fulfilment of this design was still in the future. The Papacy had thus committed itself to a theory, had adopted a political creed, perhaps the boldest ever devised by individual ambition. It seems very strange that for so long a time it should have rested there,—that, having formulated such a lofty plan, it should still have made no immediate effort to realise it. One would naturally have expected that the Roman bishopric, having once acknowledged its pretensions in thought, would have lost no time in carrying them into action,—that having once expressed its ambition in theory, it would have proceeded forthwith to manifest it in practice. Instead of that, it is an indisputable fact that the period immediately succeeding the publication of these decretals is a period of declining energy. The Papacy seems to have acted towards the State as Charlemagne had acted towards the hierarchy: it advanced to battle, and immediately retreated. It proclaimed itself to be the centre of church-life, it declared its right to a separate existence from the State, it predicted the coming of a day when it should make the State itself its vassal, and then it folded its hands and sank to rest. Never had its power been more formidable than in the middle of the ninth century; never was its power more contemptible than at the opening of the tenth: the mountain apparently had brought forth the mouse, the lofty pretensions had issued in a life grovelling in the dust. Is there any explanation of an order of events so strange and so unnatural, any mode of accounting for this seeming reversal of the ordinary course of actions? In answering that question, we must take into account another element. Worldly ambition formed only one of the factors which constituted the idea of the Papacy; in addition to that there was a strong sense of worldly possession. These sentiments are not only different, but in some measure conflicting in their influence: ambition spurs on, and is therefore energising; the sense of possession impels to rest, and is therefore ultimately enervating. There is a time in individual life, there is a time in the life of a nation, when the world obtains so strong a mastery over the heart as to limit its action to the gratification of the hour. The stage of worldly ambition is never the stage of deepest corruption; the period of deepest corruption is that in which the future disappears from view in the all-absorbing consciousness of the delights of the moment. And such a period was coming to the Christian Church.

A season was approaching in which the school-life under the world's guardianship was to become the world's coadjutor; a season in which the Christian intellect and the Christian heart were to be so overmastered by the allurements of the day and hour, that all aspirations, even temporal aspirations, were to die. Papal Rome for a time was to rest in the joy of its possessions, and abandon itself to the seductions of the passing scene. Its dream of empire was to be curtained for a time by the mist of a worldliness deeper and denser still; a worldliness in which the sensuous was to triumph over the aspiring, and in which the rapture of voluptuous ease was to eclipse the vision even of future imperial glory. It was entering upon that period which historians have generally stamped by the name of the Dark Ages. We do not believe that it lasted so long as to merit such a name,—it might all be comprehended in a single age,—yet if a period drags heavily through history, in proportion to its corruptness and its barrenness, it may be allowed to rank as the longest and the dreariest portion of ecclesiastical annals; long because uneventful, dreary because seeming to arrest the march of Christian development. That it did arrest that march we do not for a moment believe; that the united life of Christendom ever paused is contradicted by all the facts of experience. As we have already said, it was the mission of the spirit of Christianity to permeate the secular as well as the sacred; and in order to permeate the secular, it was necessary it should know the world. It is difficult to see how, either in individual life or in national life, worldly knowledge can be purchased without an admixture of temporary worldly corruption; for the knowledge of such corruption is itself an essential part of that experience which human life must gain,—we cannot avoid the fire until we have felt that it burns. The Dark Ages contributed their share to the education of the Christian spirit; contributed by an underground process, and in an apparently adverse way, yet not the less conspired to farther the universal end. In the meantime, however, the wave of human energy, which is ever to some extent the wave of human progress, was receding fast; receding, doubtless, only to roll forward upon the shore with redoubled impetus, yet exhibiting for the present a spectacle of painful retrogression. The State-power was losing day by day that concentrated unity which had made it strong. The Papacy was strengthening day by day, but it was growing lethargic in its strength. The mind of the Christian Church, passing through its stage of pupilage, was taking its tone from the schoolmaster, and sinking into the apathy of self-indulgence. A day of busy life was wearing to its close, a day of more activity still was about to dawn; but between them was to intervene a season of repose,—the night was coming in which no man could work.

Before, however, this first day went down, it left behind it one monument which survived the night. This century, barren as it was in immediate results, and disappointing as it was in the fulfilment of its promises, bequeathed to the mediæval world one gift, which must be pronounced a boon: it was during this period that the first female convent was planted in Europe. No Protestant will deny, that to such an age as this such an institution was of unspeakable advantage; it was as if the mind of Christendom were anticipating its approaching decline, and making provision for the evil to come. The ideal of mediæval greatness was woman; the full glory of humanity was represented here. Surely it was of infinite importance that this ideal should be kept unspotted, and that the idea of womanhood should be allowed to preserve its virgin bloom. There were days coming in which such preservation must be difficult in the extreme; days of sensuous corruption, in which the eye was to dominate the soul, and the pleasures of sense were to obliterate the delights of man's spiritual being,—in which the Church itself was to speak the language of the world, and strive after conformity with temporal aims and joys. In such a world the ideal of womanhood must perish unless protected from the blast; the flower must fade unless preserved by artificial warmth. The convent was that receptacle into which the tender plant was to be conveyed until the snows of winter were overpast. Here—far from the din of battle, far from the haunts of revelry, far from the scenes where man forgets his manliness and co-ordinates himself with the beast of the field—there were to be stored up the seeds of a purer life, and the prophecies of a milder day. Here, in remote seclusion from the busy crowd, there were to spring forth lives more busy still; more helpful, more hopeful, more full of genuine work, more rich in Christian promise; bearing the burden of others' sorrow, and carrying the weight of others' sin, and keeping lit through the darkness the lamp of Christ-like purity. That they shared in the religious errors of their day, that they partook in the mistaken notion that physical prostration can generate inward holiness, that they saw through a glass darkly what they might have beheld face to face,—all this is patent and indisputable. But though they could not create a purer light, they walked purely in their own; though they could not transcend the limits of their age, they touched its very boundary-line. Catholicism has assigned to many of them the name of saint; to us it seems sufficient praise that they represented the best humanity of their time. Catholicism has woven around their memory prodigies of outward wonder, legends of miraculous power, resting on no higher basis than the imagination of a fond enthusiasm; but were they as true as they are fictitious, they would to us have no glory, by reason of that all-excelling glory which, though unappreciated, is really there—the turning of the water into wine, the revelation of strength in the midst of weakness.

CHAPTER XXIV.

THE CHURCH BECOME THE WORLD.

IN the first year of the tenth century, died Alfred of England, the best and the greatest of the Saxon kings; and with him went out the last gleam of the renaissance of Charlemagne. As the sunlight sometimes lingers in solitary splendour on a single peak, when its beams have departed from all surrounding objects, even so had the light of this great intellectual revival lingered on the shores of Britain after it had faded from all other shores. With the death of Alfred it lost its home here also, and set amidst the shadows of foreign warfare and intestine strife. The labours of Alfred for the moral regeneration of his country had been many and valuable; but perhaps his noblest work had been the attempt to establish in England the system of trial by jury.* In that effort there was a recognition of the rights of man, and therefore to some extent a defence of individual freedom. Unfortunately, it proved only an attempt; with the life of its projector, the newly-initiated system, sinking into disuse, virtually passed away. On the threshold of the Dark Ages,

---

* The fact is now disputed, doubtless the system was only rudimentary.

the feature which immediately and prominently arrests us is a very grotesque standard of criminal jurisprudence,—a standard which it is worth while pausing to contemplate, not for the sake of its absurdity, but because it furnishes the key to that entire world of materialism into which the spirit of Christianity had entered.

We said in the former chapter that the period called the Dark Ages was essentially lethargic. In nothing was the lethargy more conspicuously shown than in the unwillingness to sift the evidence of crime. That a man accused of any breach of law, must be acquitted or condemned according to the testimony of outward witnesses or outward circumstances, is a principle in our days so axiomatic, that one finds it difficult to conceive a time in which it was not operative. Yet such a time was the Dark Ages. The modern process of legal justice would have involved too much labour, would have taxed too severely the energies of men whose minds were bent upon repose. To such an age, moreover, it would have been wasted labour. The men of that day had a short and easy method, which could dispense with all legal investigation; a method by which, without inquiring into the circumstances of the case, or the character of the accused, they could obtain the direct verdict of Heaven itself. Trial by jury was only a human mode of arriving at a conclusion; there were divine modes of decision, much more expeditious, and far more easy: there was trial by cold water, trial by hot water, trial by fire, trial by the cross, and trial by single combat.

If a man were thrown into the water, with his right foot tied to his left arm, his guilt or innocence could be determined by his sinking or floating. If he were made to thrust his hand into a boiling caldron, the same result could be reached according to the amount of scalding. If he desired to prove his integrity, he could be challenged to walk on red-hot ploughshares, or to hold a burning ball in his hand, or to carry a red-hot coal in his bosom. If he wished to refute the accusation of an adversary, the matter could easily be decided between them; both could hold out their arms in the form of a cross, and he who could longest retain the position should be awarded the palm. Or if he conceived himself to have suffered injury at the hands of another, the sword would determine whether his complaint were just; if in battle he vanquished his enemy, the result would prove that on his side lay the justice of the strife. These were the substitutes which the Christendom of that age proposed for trial by jury. As we have said, it is not their absurdity which makes them interesting as historical facts. In this respect they are not peculiar. They belong to the same class as auguries, portents, omens, and signs; they are really analogous to the practice of casting lots, and with that practice their absurdity must rise or fall. If there were any evidence that divine will would manifest itself in a way proposed by human agency, these modes of determining guilt or innocence would perhaps be the most satisfactory in existence; the grotesqueness lies in the theological assumption that divine will can be so manifested. But what makes the observation of these methods a matter of interest to the historian, is the fact that they all point to one common goal: the regress towards paganism. There is one feature which distinguishes every one of them, and that is the subordination of the moral to the physical. The tests are all physical tests; they are measures, not of the standard of moral character, but of the weight of the body, the strength of the nerves, the ability to endure pain, the dexterity of the hand, and the general firmness of the constitutional temperament. This is in strictest conformity with the spirit of paganism; a spirit which, as we have seen, deified human strength, and estimated the greatness of man by his muscular powers and physical capacities. There is only one of the tests which has the slightest pretension to a moral bearing, and that is the trial by single combat. Experience seems to prove that the best man, the man of the most balanced mind, makes the bravest and the most stedfast soldier; and that the success of outward war depends not wholly on the outward arm. Yet it is certain that this view of the subject was beyond the reach of that darkened age, and that the trial by combat had to its generation no higher significance than the determination by lot of Heaven's will. If we inquire whence proceeded this retrogressive movement? if we ask why a Church, into whose members had been breathed a spirit of life, should have voluntarily and deliberately retraced its steps back to those elements of death from which it had been set free? the answer must be sought in the very brilliancy of these events which we have been recently contemplating. We do not believe that the regress into paganism was an accident; we do not believe that it proceeded entirely from ecclesiastical corruption, though it assuredly tended to deepen that corruption; we do not even believe that the earliest thought of it originated with the Church at all. It seems to us that the thought was suggested in that hour in which the power of the State, and the not less worldly power of the Papacy, combined to re-establish the empire of the West, to renew the sceptre of the Cæsars. Here was a grand imagination,—an imagination not unworthy of a Charlemagne, and not unfraught with possibilities of high enthusiasm, yet an imagination which had its root and ground exclusively in the past. The mind of Christendom was carried backwards,—the stream was diverted from its channel, and made to flow in a contrary direction. Where a man's treasure is, there his heart will be; where his Eden lies, thither his steps will bend. The ideal of a glorified past, was to the heart of Christendom a more effectual barrier to all progress than it had ever encountered in its days of heathen persecution. When it beheld the climax of its splendour in a surmounted stage of its development, when it looked for the consummation of its desires to the obtaining of an object which it had passed by as worthless on the way, there was no small reason to dread that the prospect of its future would pale. We have said that the idea of a revived Western empire was to Charlemagne no unworthy imagination; there was about it a breath of classic poetry, which gave it life and power; but the times were changed, and the mind of the world was changed with them. Charlemagne had desired a Christianized Roman empire, a cultured materialism; and as long as Charlemagne lived, that object had been partially secured. But now the culture had passed away, and the materialism alone remained; the fresh spirit of the renaissance was gone, and there were left only those beautiful forms in which from time to time it had enshrined itself, but from which it had now for ever departed. The men of this generation had no counterpoise to their materialism; it was, without exception, the most realistic period this world has ever seen. Never throughout human history has literature been so barren; never in the annals of the world has the spirit of Christianity been so severed from the spirit of culture. The age of Cædmon, the age of Bede, the age of Alcuin, was no more, and the places which they had left had remained vacant. There were many excellent schools, but they were planted by Mohammedanism; there were many distinguished teachers, but they came from the Crescent, not from the Cross. Amongst European nations, Spain alone showed symptoms of intellectual vitality, because amongst European nations Spain alone had bowed submissive to the Saracen yoke. There was one respect, indeed, in which the educational impulse imparted by Charlemagne continued true to itself even now. We have seen that in that bygone day the education of the people had been fostered by kings, had descended to the doors of the villages from the gates of the imperial palace. Royalty was still faithful to its high vocation. The Greek emperors, once foremost in religious reform, now sought to be foremost in reviving the drooping life of Christian intelligence. Otho of Germany, not undeservedly surnamed 'the Great,' aimed, in the true German spirit, to vivify into warm aspiration the languishing heart of his country, and to raise an intellectual power which should dispute the empire with the physical world. But it was all in vain; the pitcher was broken at the fountain. Royalty might plan, but royalty was no longer in direct sympathy with the heart of Christendom, nor was there any longer a channel of communion between the people and the throne; 'there had sprung up a new people which knew not Joseph.' They wanted no more corn from Egypt; they had received another governor, and for the present they were better pleased with him. The State had transferred the guardianship of its subjects, in so far as these subjects were Christians, and it was precisely in that aspect that they were most valuable to a nation. It had placed them under the authority of a new power,—a power equally worldly, though not equally sincere,—and thereby it had voluntarily lost its right to their sympathies, and broken the bridge of communication which had once given them a passage to the hearts of kings. It was this breaking of the bridge, this change of guardianship, this transference of authority, which prevented the designs of royalty from bearing fruit with the people. Still, as in the days of Charlemagne, was culture esteemed in high places; but the connecting road had been destroyed which had linked the high to the low. The people looked up to the heights, but desired not to reach them; they were content to stand afar off, and allow the love of learning to abide within the palace walls.

And the result of this absence of a popular literature was the absence of any counterpoise to the predominance of the physical. This has been called the iron age; to us it seems rather to have been an age of stone. Iron is hard, rough, stern, even cruel; but it is energetic, and contains, under certain conditions, the properties of magnetism. This age was hard, rough, stern, and cruel; but not energetic, not magnetic in its sympathies. It was cold, stolid, inert, incapable of high impulses, and a stranger to enthusiasm for the beautiful; it was an age of stone. The only occasions in which it seemed to rise above itself was when it expressed itself in stone; all the poetry of which it was susceptible concentrated itself in its architecture. Here the physical imagination lavished itself upon a physical element; and having found a congenial object, it produced something not wholly unworthy. It is possible that the magnificent cathedrals of that day owed half their origin to the Mohammedan impulse. Wherever Mohammedanism planted its foot, it planted the love of architectural beauty. Spain literally blazed with palaces, and the grandeur of its cities has been unsurpassed in modern days; one feels almost startled to hear, at so uncultured a time, of the paved streets of Cordova, brilliantly illuminated with continuous night lamps for a distance of seven miles. That the Mohammedan influence which had beautified the architecture of Spain should have exerted an indirect bearing upon the construction of Christian edifices, can surprise no man who remembers the many points of contact which the Crescent presented to the Cross. Yet the magnificence of the Christian architecture of this period was not wholly referable to Mohammedan sources. It seems to us that it was the beginning of that union of the masculine North with the feminine South, which we have already pointed out to be the goal of European civilisation. Here the Gothic and the Italian mind may be said to have begun their ceremony of marriage, to have taken the first step in that united life-journey, which was to last as long as culture should endure. In that marriage were represented and vindicated the rights of both parties. The Gothic mind contributed the stone, the strength, and the massiveness of form; the Italian mind contributed the symmetry and the features of a more luxurious beauty; the union of the two constituted the noblest effort, nay, the only effort, which that age of listless apathy made towards the appropriation of beauty.

And yet we doubt if even here the men of that day deserve full credit. They raised magnificent buildings; yet it seems to us that, in the very act of raising them, they became members of that class whom Matthew Arnold has comprehended under the name of Philistines. They were not seeking the beautiful for its own sake, but for the sake of its mercantile value. The mercantile value of beauty consisted on this occasion in its fancied power to propitiate the saints of heaven. Every church was dedicated to a saint, and the magnificence of the edifice made the gift more valuable. It secured for the donor the patronage of that celestial being to whom he had offered it. It held out the prospect, not only of patronage for the future, but of expiation for the past. It promised him the prayers, the intercessions, the helpful offices of that great spirit whom he had honoured by so costly a presentation, and it therefore touched a chord in something which stood to him for the possession of a religious nature. Even his architectural beauty was thus only a road to his self-interest; he sought it not as the poet seeks it, from the buoyancy of bounding aspiration, but from the sense of craven fear, which impelled him to contrive some offering which Heaven might accept in lieu of personal piety. In one sense, there is comedy in this, yet for our part we are more impressed with its tragedy. There is an awful depth of conscious helplessness, which drowns all our laughter. Here is a generation of human beings who have taken it for granted that there is no possible communion between the human and the divine, who have shut out the hope of earth embracing heaven, and have sought to content themselves with a less aspiring aim. And yet they cannot so content themselves. They bring under contribution all the forms of the universe, that they may fill up the void in their hearts; and all the forms of the universe leave them vacant still. All the saints of the calendar are exhausted in vain, and they cry out for more saints. Priest and monk are besieged by importunate suppliants to add to the list of celestial helpers, and the additions are so numerous that law interferes to restrain them. Long pilgrimages are undertaken to lay the hands upon some fancied relic, which perhaps may carry a healing efficacy to the soul. The bone of a dog, or the bone of a disentombed pagan, is believed to be the arm of St. James or the skull of St. Cyprian, is purchased at an immense price, and borne through the streets with the ceremony of gorgeous ritual and solemn procession. There is, indeed, an intense solemnity in the transaction, but the solemnity lies in something which that generation does not see. It is not in the pageant, it is not in the relic,—these belong to the comedy of the scene; it is in the contemplation of that terrible unrest which could prompt such a pageant, and inspire such a relic, in the sense of that awful abyss which the human heart had created within itself; an abyss which, having refused to be filled by God, was making efforts, as frantic as they were vain, to be bridged over by the thought of communion with His creatures. That is, to our mind, the real tragedy of this period; not its wars, not its crimes, not its brutalities, not its social degradations, but its feverish and maddening struggles to find a passport into rest without goodness and without God. In its magnificent cathedrals there were tapers that burned at noonday; it was a striking symbol of its position in the spiritual universe, a grand, though unconscious, satire on the meanness and inadequacy of that artificial light which the spirit of the Dark Ages had preferred to the natural.

And where was all this time the guardian of the school-life? where was that power which the State had placed over the Church to be the guide of its tender years? The guardian had sunk lower than the pupil, and the lord was morally beneath the disciple. Never before had the Papacy exhibited a degradation so deep, a corruption so ignoble; never again, we believe, did it exhibit it until the days immediately preceding the outburst of the Lutheran Reformation. Upon the whole, we believe the earlier corruption to have been the worse of the two: the Papacy of the Reformation had its vices mellowed by culture; the Papacy of the Dark Ages was vice undisguised and unrefined. It is from no hostile hand that we receive the record; we have the testimony of Muratori, we have the testimony of the best Catholic writers. The pontiffs of that day were the creatures of the Tuscan rulers, and the Tuscan rulers were in general the creatures of abandoned women. The tenth century alone numbered 28 popes; their reigns were all short, their lives were nearly all scandalous. Their immoralities, their debaucheries, their cruelties, their utter absorption in the pursuit of self-interest, their complete alienation from the principle of religious life, were such as to render them marked men, even in an age distinguished for its worldliness, its selfishness, its irreligion. Men do not like to see their own vices reflected in their rulers; nay, it is a law of our nature, that we despise most in others that which we know to be a weakness in ourselves. Accordingly the Papacy of this period was despised; the contemptibility of its vices was equalled by the contemptibility of its influence. One instance may stand for all. The Synod of Rheims deposed Archbishop Arnolf, without even consulting the pontiff, and when confronted by his opposition, met it with defiance; the mere occurrence of such an act is powerfully suggestive. It shows us that the Papacy of this age had been arrested in its ascent to meridian power; but it shows us more: it demonstrates that the secret of its power had all along been the belief in its sanctity. The fact is worth observing, because it has been overlooked by some historians. Mr. Draper has maintained that the Papacy owed its influence to political power. No one who reads these pages will suspect us of being advocates for the Papacy, yet we cannot, in candour, accept such a solution. What gave the political power to the Roman See? What enabled a frail human being, by the mere word of his mouth, to summon the armies of Europe to his standard, and bend the will of kings to his command? It was the belief that in that being there resided a power of abstinence from worldly temptations, a rigid austerity that could stand apart from the crowd in its rush after the pleasures of the hour, an asceticism which, to the unrestrained licence of that time, stood in the place of the highest sanctity. We cannot at this moment remember any instance in which the exercise of great Papal authority was not accompanied by the outward form of great Papal piety; nor do we remember any instance in which the absence of Papal piety was not accompanied by the absence of the world's respect and veneration. Why should the position of the pontiff have at this epoch been so low? There was no outward cause which could reasonably account for its depression. A century before, it had been the organizer of revolutions and the crowner of kings; 'wherefore now was none so poor as do it reverence?' It was because this power had itself ceased to be reverential, because it had lost that outward form of virtue which even those without virtue like to see, and because it had adopted that air of worldliness which even the worldly disrespect in the garb of a sacred profession. It had fallen from its power over the human will, because it had fallen from its power over the human heart; and it had received, in the estimation of men, that inferior place, which it had chosen for itself when it sacrificed its sacred calling to the allurements of the passing hour.

It will not surprise us, that when the religious life was so weak in its centre, the missionary spirit of its members should have been but weakly diffused; a bad fatherhood seldom makes a good brotherhood. The missionary zeal of this period seems to have been limited to the Eastern Church, and to have been limited within that church to the heretical sect of the Nestorians; the labours of that sect were crowned with real success, and by their efforts the light of Christianity was carried for a time into the heart of the Chinese empire. In the West, the conversion of nations was identical with their conquest by foreign kings. That a conquered kingdom should adopt the religion of the conqueror, was assumed to be as much in the course of nature, as that the subjects of such a kingdom should become thenceforth the subjects of the conqueror. Accordingly, the path pursued by conversion was at this period parallel with the path formerly pursued by education; it came from the sovereign to the people. When the monarch embraced Christianity, Christianity became immediately the religion of the nation; the whole difficulty lay in the conversion of kings; these could not be subjugated by force, could not be influenced by authority higher than their own, and therefore their minds had to be reached through another channel. Strange to say, that channel was the last through which, in so turbulent an age, one would naturally have dreamed of subjugating the will of royalty; it was the influence of woman. Two nations during the Dark Ages were added to European Christendom—Poland and Russia; but the rulers of both those countries were converted by their wives. The events were not strange from being anomalous; on the contrary, this had been a common experience in history since the days of Clovis in France, and of Ethelbert in England. But the frequency of an occurrence does not make it less remarkable, if there be anything remarkable in it. The strangeness of this occurrence lies not in its infrequency, but in its nature. That in a martial age,—when men lived by conquest, and ruled by the terror of their name, when self-help was deemed the essence of heroism, and arbitrary independence the mark of highest greatness, —the still small voice of woman should have turned aside the thunders of self-will, and bent the spirit of her lord submissive to her own; this is a phenomenon which needs explanation. The explanation lies in that Christian ideal of greatness which we have shown to be the leading feature of mediævalism,—that ideal which, in opposition to pagan culture, took for its basis the highest type of womanhood, and which no regress into pagan culture could altogether obliterate or destroy. If we reiterate this fact, it is only because it reiterates itself; it permeates the mediæval world like an atmosphere, we can no more escape from it than we can escape from the air we breathe. The Dark Ages, in proportion as they divorced the soul from the immediate vision of the divine, were forced to bring more and more into prominence the thought of the Virgin Mother; it was now that for her they devised the rosary and the crown. We have seen that they mistook the object of their reverence, we have seen that they went out of their way to find the treasure which was lying at their door. Yet, miserable as was the mistake, and defective as was the substitute, it was still a partial remedy for something more defective than itself. At the very least, the apotheosis of the Virgin Mother diffused a milder current through the bitter atmosphere of the age, and imparted some glow of warmth to that world so rigid and so cold. The elevation of the ideal woman cast a radiance over all women, gave them a hallowed place in naturally unhallowed hearts, and invested them with a potent influence over lives that were a law to themselves. It gave them an authority greater than the power of the sword, and made them in reality the first sovereigns of the world; they turned the minds of those whose hands wielded the sceptre.

We have now reviewed the leading aspects of that period which historians have called the Dark Ages; we have not spared its vices, nor sought to extenuate its errors. Yet whoever carefully studies the history of this period, will discern seeds of life floating through the darkness. It is a doctrine of modern science, that the worst forms of disease are themselves organic germs; in the spiritual world also, we frequently find it so. Many circumstances of this age which indicate its errors and imperfection, point at the same time to the prophecy of a higher life. There are two incidents which have specially arrested our attention, because they seem to enfold a nobler possibility of greatness than we should naturally have been disposed to look for in such a world; the one points to the memory of the past, the other to the anticipation of the future. The first is the institution of a festival in remembrance of departed souls, accompanied by an exhortation to the living to pray for the happiness of the dead. We do not appreciate the theology which underlies such a mandate, but we do appreciate in the mandate the dawning of something like a spirit of unselfishness. To look back upon the memory of the departed, to consider the friends of other days, to keep a place in our hearts for the relics of the past as well as for the engrossments of the present, is undoubtedly a step in advance over the undivided love of the seen and temporal; and we hail in this generation any outburst of enthusiasm which could lead it, even for a moment, from the thought of the meretricious hour to contemplate the memory of those bygone days, whose glories it had been content to abandon.

The second circumstance pointed not to the past, but to the future; it was the promulgation, and the general acceptance, of a belief that the end of the world was approaching. It was now well-nigh a thousand years since the human race had first listened to the tidings of 'glory to God' and 'goodwill to man.' There was an unaccountable expectation that the conclusion of the thousand years would be the close of earthly history, and that the promise so long waited for would then be fulfilled in the coming of the Son of man from heaven. We say it was an unaccountable expectation. True, it professed to be founded upon Rev. xx. 2, where it was predicted that Satan should be loosed for a little at the end of a thousand years; but how the men of that age could have imagined the principle of evil to be already bound, it is difficult to conceive. To us, however, the interest of this expectation lies not in itself, but in what it indicates. It implies that into the heart of this hard, sensuous, worldly generation, there was entering a longing for light. It shows us that the human mind was again dimly awakening into the consciousness that this world is the evolution of a plan, that it moves not aimlessly through the circle of the suns, but is steadily and surely tending towards a definite consummation. It shows us that at last the Dark Ages were beginning to grow weary of their darkness, weary of present joys, weary even of past acquisitions; that men were thirsting for a new revelation, a revelation which would dispel what was dark in the old, and cast a flood of light over the pilgrimage of the soul. Nay, there was even something significant in the direction of mediæval thought towards the personal coming of the Master. It seemed as if the images, the relics, the forms and ceremonies, the cathedrals and altars, and the Virgin Mother herself, were for the moment all insufficient; as if the Church were waking up to behold the true object of its communion, and were stretching its hands through the darkness to lay hold of Him whom it had once recognised as its present Lord. To look forward is the first condition of progress, to look forward to a high ideal makes progress already half secured; therefore this hope of mediæval Christendom, notwithstanding the errors of its biblical criticism, was an indication that the night was far spent, and that the day was at hand.

If we turn now to the political aspect of the world, we shall see not less clearly the preparation for reviving life. We have pointed out how, in the prominence given to architecture, there was furnished a meeting-place for the Gothic and the Italian mind; we have said that in the idea of architectural beauty their marriage ceremony had begun. But the process was to be facilitated by a political event of great importance. Otho the Great of Germany, after a series of successful wars, became master of Italy, and was crowned, like Charlemagne, Emperor of the West. The conquest of Italy by Germany was more than a mere historical incident, more than a record of battles or a catalogue of triumphs; it was another step in the progress of that union of North and South, for which European culture waited so expectantly. Since the days when the first Western empire passed away, the mind of Italy had been approximating nearer and nearer to the standpoint of the German intellect. Through contact with the North, it had begun to develope that thirst for independence, and that impatience of restraint, which were already the indications of progressive life. It was in Italy that the decree of uniformity had been received with the greatest opposition; it was in Italy that, when the worship of images was becoming more and more the rule, the independent protest of Claudius of Turin refused to allow humanity to be quite borne down the stream. The conquest of Italy by Germany developed the tendency into a power; henceforth these nations moved much side by side. They stood together in that long and bitter struggle in which the Empire and the Papacy strove for the settlement of the question between Church and State. They stood together in the honour of being forerunners of the Lutheran Reformation; the one in the lives of the Waldenses, the other in the history of the Hussites. They stood together almost at the outset of the Lutheran Reformation itself; for if Germany had its Luther, Italy had preceded it by its Savonarola. It is true they parted there; Italy fell back into the past, refusing to travel any farther on the road of progress; yet the tendency to progress was rather eclipsed than extinguished. After sleeping for many ages, it has awakened once more in our own nineteenth century, and offered a new prospect of mental greatness to that land which has been favoured with so much physical beauty. We cannot refuse to attribute this Italian thirst for freedom, in some degree at least, to its contact with the German spirit; and we cannot fail to recognise the consummation of that contact in the day when the Emperor Otho became master of Italian soil.

Before this century closed, an additional bond was imparted to the union. Otho III. of Germany elevated his tutor Gerbert to the Papal chair, by the name of Sylvester II. In so doing, he gave to Italy more than a pontiff, he gave it a literature, he gave it an enthusiasm. Sylvester was the best man of the Dark Ages; his life, indeed, was the transition-point between the darkness and the dawn. His mind was imbued with the love of learning; his heart was impressed with the ideal of a cultured Christendom. He sought to inspire with this love the country over which he had been appointed spiritual guardian, to revive the thirst for knowledge which had gone to sleep, to resuscitate the life of civilisation which had long been dormant. He sought to kindle into flame the heart of Christendom, by presenting a new object of religious enthusiasm. It was by him that the first martial trumpet was sounded, the first call to identify the spirit of Christianity with the spirit of warlike heroism. He proposed a crusade against the Mohammedans. He felt that what his people wanted most of all was an object in life, a goal of aspiration, a point to strive after. He perceived that those days were dark, chiefly because they were lethargic, because they brought no aim, because they came and went without a purpose and without a plan. Here was a purpose, here was a plan, which would dispel the aimlessness, and awaken from the lethargy. Let the Church put on its armour, let the spirit of Christianity go forth to battle for the truth, to win back the land of its birth, to expel the intruders from its native soil. Such was the voice of Sylvester, and, in the circumstances of the age, it was a wise voice. But Sylvester was before his time; the age was not ripe for such a mandate, it wanted another century to prepare it for the thought. Was it the vision of the closing thousand years which damped its ardour for every other vision? Was it the expectation that the Son of man was about to descend from heaven that blinded it to the immediate wants and requirements of the sons of men? Doubtless this thought was not without its weight. The men of that day believed that they lived on the brink of an immediate second advent, and their ears were so filled with the promise, 'Surely I come quickly,' that they forgot that other utterance, 'Occupy till I come.' What matter who had the soil of Palestine, when the whole earth was about to be the judgment-seat of the visible Lord? what matter though they abstained from worldly labours, when the world, and the works of the world, were to be consumed with fire? It is, indeed, not surprising that, with expectations such as these, the human mind, in beholding the imminent future, should be paralysed to the practical present. Yet it is not alone to this belief that we must attribute the failure of Sylvester's project. There was wanted the transfusion of new blood into the European nations, for new blood is to a nation what change of scene is to an individual; it stimulates, it energises. Such a transfusion had already begun, but it required more time to circulate. France, the land of revolutions, had just shaken off its second dynasty. The line of Charlemagne had followed the fate of the line of Clovis, and the Carlovingian race of kings had been supplanted by the empire of Hugh Capet. But it was from the Normans that Europe was to receive its greatest force of vitality. Throughout this century they had been pouring over the nations, apparently with no other object than to arrest what little development each land might have attained. Yet this people had a higher destiny awaiting them, and already there were contained within them possibilities of more than destruction. They were a race pre-eminently plastic, both in the active and in the passive sense of that term; they had a power to mould, and they had a susceptibility of being moulded. Rude, uncultured, undisciplined in the laws of social convention, and seemingly at variance with the laws of social progress, there was yet in these men an element which made for refinement. We have called their age an age of stone, but all the iron that was in it was concentrated here. Sweeping over the seas on their missions of piracy, they seemed to catch up something of the ocean's life; its grandeur amid storm, its wild poetry amid the aspect of anarchy. Sweeping over the land to ravage and to desolate, they were themselves taken captive by every scene of beauty which the land could yield. They came to France, and they obtained there a province, which they called by their name; they came to England, and they left there a dynasty which still remains: in France they expanded in a few years from a band of undisciplined pirates into a people the most refined and cultured which that age could show; in England they found a nation whose first glory had departed, whose literature was depressed, whose very sense of freedom had been blunted, and in a few centuries they made it a home of poetry, a land of liberty, a sphere of social progress, and a centre of religious life.

CHAPTER XXV.

REVIVAL OF ASPIRATION.

THE world had expected the advent of the Son of man at the close of the thousand years. The thousand years had not long closed when the world received something which stood for a fulfilment of its expectation; not indeed a coming of the Master, but an increase of Christian light. The dawn of the better day manifested itself in the birth of one whose name was to be indissolubly associated with the palmiest season of mediæval history—we mean Hildebrand. There was a time when it was almost impossible to estimate his character, or to record his life with justice; a time when the minds of men lived and had their being in extremes, and when they weighed human conduct in the scales of a polemical bias. To such, Hildebrand was either the direct messenger of Heaven, or the immediate representative of the principle of evil. Even by the Catholics of his own day he was not fairly judged, and his partisans and enemies alike were warped by a one-sided view. We who live at a distance of eight centuries from the scene of conflict, have been able to look back upon the figure of this man with a calmer, a more unprejudiced eye; to assign him his true position, to rate him at his real value. Upon the whole, the result of modern scrutiny has leant rather to the side of his friends than of his enemies. The principles for which he struggled have, indeed, been generally recognised to be unfavourable to progress; but the principles of the Papacy have been separated from the character of this individual Pope. Surveying him from different moral standpoints, all have now beheld in him a certain moral grandeur; and the greatness which he displayed amidst admitted error, has been discerned alike by so good a Catholic as Fénélon, and by so earnest a Protestant as Dean Milman. That his character presents traces of inconsistency it is impossible to deny. In truth, there were in him from the beginning two diverse elements: the union of the North and South found expression in his very birth. He was born at Saona, in the southern border of Tuscany, and educated at the monastery of St. Mary's on the Aventine. By birth and by culture he was therefore an Italian. Yet his family name is purely German, and indicates a Teutonic descent. Germany and Italy thus conspired to constitute the man, and his life was the product of their union. That life was indeed to be in no sense national; it was to pass through many lands, and gather experiences from all.

It may not be wholly uninteresting to trace the gathering of these experiences. His life opened in the sunny and voluptuous South, in the period of its greatest voluptuousness. It is not unlikely that a nature so ardent as that of Hildebrand may have entered ardently into the pleasures of the world, for a mind which is susceptible of intense feeling is apt to be intense in every direction. Even the monastic life of Italy, into which he was early plunged, was by no means one of asceticism. The monasteries had shared in much of the prevalent corruption, and in the West especially they were by no means unexceptionable schools for youth. As the uncle of Hildebrand was Abbot of St. Mary's, it is possible that the young man may have received even greater indulgence than was accorded to the monks of that day; and if so, his early training must have been rather worldly than ecclesiastical. Be this as it may, however, there was coming a great change. In the course of a few years, we find Hildebrand quitting his native country, and abandoning the associations of his childhood; he passes over from Italy into France, and is transferred from the monastery of St. Mary's to the monastery of Cluny. The change was more than local; it involved the transition into a new atmosphere. If any spot could be found where the worldly spirit of the West approximated to the ascetic tendency of the East, it was the monastery of Cluny. Here there was preserved the austerity of a bygone day; here the ideal of Christian purity still burned in the hearts of men. And Hildebrand's was a combustible heart; it was ready to catch fire from every strong external impulse. If already it had been ignited by the love of pleasure, it had not yet been consumed by that love; it was still fresh and entire, ready to receive new impressions. The new impression imparted by the French monastery was the reverse of the old; it was the recoil from worldly love, the desire for a higher life. In the presence of this fresh experience, the nature of Hildebrand was stirred to its very depths, wakened from its apathetic sleep, and roused into the consciousness of a coming day. In the light of that dawning day, he saw himself, and he saw the age which had produced him; he weighed both in the balance, and found both wanting. He looked abroad upon the Church, and he found that its glory had departed, that its school-life had degenerated into a life of corruption, that its education had dwindled into a training for the lusts of the world. He looked abroad upon the Papacy, that power which had been constituted the Church's guardian, and he found that it had proved unfaithful to its trust, and had become the slave of the secular. Why was this? Hildebrand asked the question, and he answered it by another. Why had the Papacy failed to follow up the Isidorian decretals? These decretals had contemplated three objects, — Roman centralization, Roman independence, and Roman supremacy; wherefore had the first alone been achieved? Was it not clear that if the Papacy would be the pure representative of a pure Church, it must proceed to realise its second aim, to strike off the fetters of the State, to stand in the unclouded light of God? Did not its worldliness spring exclusively from its worldly contact? Let the Church go back to take up the thread which it had dropt in the age of Charlemagne; let the clergy go back to resume their ancient claim to be a caste unspotted from the world. Simony had been tolerated, let it be put down with a high hand; celibacy had been relaxed, let it be enforced with redoubled vigour; immoralities of life had been overlooked, let them be suppressed by all the mechanism of ecclesiastical law. Let the priests of the living God come forth from the haunts of men, let them separate themselves from the world as a world,—not alone from its vices, but even from its indifferent pursuits. Let them renew their aspirations after a heavenly life, and let them foster these aspirations by mortifying their bodily passions, by crucifying the outward man, by sacrificing the seen and temporal. Then would the Church rise pure and beautiful as the New Jerusalem coming down from God; then, in the highest sense, would the prophecy of the thousand years be fulfilled, and that kingdom of Christ, for which the world so long had waited, would spread its beneficent reign over the hearts and lives of men.

Such were the sentiments of Hildebrand as he meditated in the monastery of Cluny. They did not long remain sentiments; they soon became a power over his life. They craved for active expression, and they found their first expression in his own personal sanctity. That ideal which he planned for the Church, he planted first in his own breast; that purity which he desired for the clergy, he began by seeking for himself. And in proportion as the new life grew within him, it struggled the more to come out from him, to diffuse itself, to impart its power to the united Church. It was this desire for ecclesiastical regeneration, this enthusiasm for the Christianizing of humanity, which made the afterpart of his career so swift in its transitions, so eventful in its changes; he was impelled to act by the force that was in him. The incidents of his life crowd together. At twenty-nine he takes orders, and is immediately the first preacher of the day. His burning eloquence, his fervid zeal, his high intellectual gifts, his keen appreciation of the wants of humanity, his earnest denunciation of the corruptions and vices of the age, coming from one recognised to be aloof from them, all contribute to arrest the soul and to convict the conscience. He passes from France into Germany, and flashes like a meteor through the court of the third Henry. But he lingers not here; that court is to him the bondage-land of his beloved Rome, and stimulates anew his desire for its religious independence. To Rome he bends his steps; and the next stage finds him the chaplain of Gregory vi., inspired by the associations of the sacred city, and impregnating that city in turn with his own inspiration. Presently he is back at Cluny again, wearied, perhaps, with adulation, and longing for repose; but repose is not to be his portion in life or in death. His presence in Rome has been a power, and his absence has created a want; Rome cannot dispense with Hildebrand, and Hildebrand is recalled. He obeys the summons. For the last time, he bids farewell to that secluded retreat, which has been the home of his brightest days, and the centre of his fondest memories, and wends his way to the Italian capital, laden with the destinies of distant years; from that hour he is the man behind the scenes of Europe.

It was now that there occurred an event which, although rather an episode than an essential stage in the mission of Hildebrand, cannot be passed over without some reference,—we allude to the meeting of the Council of Tours. Since the days of Radbert, the doctrine of transubstantiation had been kept in abeyance. It had been steadily growing in the number of its disciples and in its power over the human heart, but it had never been formally declared to be the necessary belief of the Church. At every period of the Church's history, since Radbert had first propounded this doctrine, there had been good Catholics, in high ecclesiastical position, who had been unable to accept it; Hildebrand himself, the very representative of mediæval Catholicism, was amongst the number. But the time was come in which the Church desired to establish this faith upon a basis of ecclesiastical authority, to place it upon a rock against which the waves of public opinion should break in vain. It was not surprising that mediæval Christendom, which had banished the thought of an immediately present Christ from the world, should seek to restore that presence by creating a Christ within the sanctuary. It was to attain this object that the Council of Tours assembled. There, as at Nice long ago, there was seen the meeting of three ages. It appeared as if the world that was dead, and the world that was living, and the world that was about to live, had each sent a representative of itself;

for there stood in that assembly, prominent above all other figures, the man of the past, the man of the present, and the man of the future. The future was represented by Lanfranc; he belonged chiefly to a coming day. He was the man of system, the advocate for a developed creed. He came to support the scientific enunciation of the real presence in the sacrament, to contend for the establishment of transubstantiation as the final expression of ecclesiastical faith on this subject. On the opposite side to him stood Berengarius, master of the school of Tours. That school had been established by Alcuin, and was therefore a monument of the brightest days of Charlemagne; it carried back the thoughts of men to the memory of a glorious past. And Berengarius was worthy to be master of that school; he lived in its past, and felt its glory. He wanted to hold the real presence as the early Fathers had held it, as the first centuries had held it, as the Church before Radbert had held it,—to accept it as a feeling rather than define it as a dogma, to believe in it without explaining it. And between these two opponents stood Hildebrand, different from either, yet sharing somewhat with both. He, like Lanfranc, was pressing forward to the future; but it was a future of social reform rather than of theological precision. He, like Berengarius, preferred the general statement of the real presence to the definite theory proposed in transubstantiation; but, unlike Berengarius, he did not consider the point worth a controversy; he would take the mind of the Church upon it, and pass on to higher aims. These aims were centred in the regeneration of the age in which he lived. Not dogma but life, not belief but work, seemed to him the food which the men of his day most required, and therefore most of all he laboured for reform. The Council, however, was bent upon discussing theology; and Hildebrand was willing to accept its decision, whatever it might be. That decision was not long doubtful; transubstantiation was declared to be the doctrine of the Catholic Church; a new dogma was added to the creed, and a new power bestowed upon the hierarchy.

The conclusion of this matter left Hildebrand free to prosecute that course which seemed to him the more excellent way; and he was ere long to be placed in a position where he would have full scope for its prosecution. He was about to experience the most important transition of his life, to become the sovereign of the religious West. While Rome was reviving under the influence of the new enthusiasm, Pope Alexander II. died. All Italy, all Europe in general, united in regarding Hildebrand as the man best qualified to occupy the vacant throne. Germany, indeed, uttered a few mutterings of dissent, but Germany was influenced in this by interested motives. As feudal master of Italy, the Teutonic empire naturally looked with fear upon the growing power of the Papacy, and looked with special fear upon the wielding of that power by a man of such talents and such aspiration as Hildebrand. The opposition, however, was weak while it lasted, and short-lived in its duration; and within a brief space after the vacation of the Papal throne, Hildebrand, by the general acclamation of Europe, was saluted pontiff. He took the name of Gregory VII., but to preserve the association of old ideas, we shall crave leave still to speak of him by the former name. Indeed, in spite of the new elevation, there is an interest attaching to the ecclesiastic Hildebrand which does not pertain to the pontiff Gregory; one is almost tempted to think that the change of name was accompanied by some change of nature. From that hour when he entered upon the cares of the pontificate, we feel as if his brightest fortunes had sunk, and as if his purest days were past. A shadow seems to have fallen across his life, dimming our perception of what once was beautiful. Our impression is somewhat analogous to the feeling we have in contemplating the younger Pitt after 1792; we are conscious of an inconsistency, apparent or real. That Hildebrand was a self-denying churchman, we have not the slightest doubt; that he sincerely believed himself to be a self-denying pontiff, we are equally persuaded; but the manifestation of the latter does not equally appear. The life of Hildebrand was made enthusiastic by the desire to confer glory on the Church; the life of Gregory was embittered by a struggle which, to the eye of the world, seemed to have its source in his own personal ambition. For our part, we think the difference rather apparent than real. When Hildebrand became Pope, that which was formerly his duty was made his interest, and the path of personal ambition met and coincided with the path of religious aspiration. We do not believe that he really became a less unselfish man; but we do believe that he was less restful in his unselfishness. He lost much of the calm of early days, much of the equanimity which constitutes half the strength of every man; the cares of office, and the malignity of foes, fretted his spirit and broke his peace; henceforth his acts are more arbitrary, and his attitude less winning. He lost no time in initiating his schemes of church reform. Immediately after his accession, he issued his prohibition of simony, his exhortation to celibacy, and his denunciation of clerical immorality; but these were only preliminary steps. He regarded simony and marriage and clerical immorality as merely parts of a far wider system of evil; the contact of the secular with the sacred. The removal of that contact was the goal which had loomed before his imagination in the monastery of Cluny. It was the thought of this which had occupied his silent hours in the seclusion of youth. It was the desire of this which had kindled his heart into fire, and warmed his lips into burning eloquence, when he went forth to be the preacher of the age. It was the glory of this which had enabled him to become the greatest of political leaders—almost the prime minister of Europe. It was the prospect of realising this which, now when he had reached the plenitude of power, nerved his hands for action, and made his deeds uncompromising.

We are now approaching one of the most important historical epochs in the whole range of mediæval history—the earliest disruption between the Church and the State. Towards this epoch we have been led step by step through the course of past history, and have seen its approach accelerated in the progress of the life of Hildebrand. The subject has difficulties of its own; this disruption does not precisely resemble any later Erastian controversy, and therefore it may not be altogether inappropriate to offer one or two explanatory remarks upon the earliest form which this much agitated question assumed.

According to the feudal system, the lands of the vassal were the property of his master the baron, just as the lands of the baron were the property of his master the king. The benefices of the Church were endowed with lands by the State. In so far as the bishop and the abbot were holders of these temporal possessions, they were in the position of vassals; they had to swear fealty to him from whom they had obtained their donations. The State had no desire that the Church should forget this temporal vassalage; and to render the memory of it more indelible, the fact of feudal superiority had been proclaimed in a solemn ceremony at every ecclesiastical election. It was called the ceremony of investiture; because the custom was, that the presenter of the living should invest the presentee with a pastoral staff and ring. Now, strange to say, the earliest disruption controversy arose, not out of the fact, but out of the ceremony. Hildebrand had not the slightest objection that the Church should swear fealty to the State for the possession of these lands, but he had the highest objection to the special form in which its temporal dependence was proclaimed.

He declared, and declared truly, that the staff and the ring were emblems, not of temporal, but of spiritual power; the staff pointing to the right of priestly authority, and the ring to the marriage between the priest and his congregation. He argued, therefore, that if the State should confer the staff and the ring upon the presentee, this would be tantamount to the admission that the Church derived from the State its entire spiritual authority; and he claimed for the Church the future exemption from a ceremony so degrading to itself, and so derogatory to its mission. Let us examine for a moment this claim of Hildebrand. Stated abstractly and theoretically, it seems both just and reasonable. Every Church in the world—Catholic and Protestant, high, low, broad, and nonconformist—claims to be possessed of spiritual independence, and repudiates the notion that in matters pertaining to the soul it is answerable to any tribunal save that of Heaven. The Church of England to this hour, the Church of Scotland till recently, has received its ministers from the Crown; but neither the Church of England nor the Church of Scotland would submit to have its clergymen ordained by the lord of the manor, by the Home Secretary, by the sovereign, or by any Crown officer whatsoever. Yet it was undoubtedly some process analogous to this that the mediæval Church had been compelled to endure. The staff and the ring were, beyond all question, intended to be spiritual symbols, and the presentation of these symbols by a secular hand could suggest only one inference. Nevertheless, we are convinced that every Protestant Church in the world—established or dissenting, high, low, broad, or nonconformist—will without hesitation take its stand in this investiture controversy, not with Hildebrand, but with the State-power of Germany. We do not quarrel with the fact; it expresses precisely our own individual sentiment on the question. We read the grounds of the controversy, and say immediately, 'Hildebrand's principle is true,' and immediately afterwards we range our sympathies on the side of the anti-Papal party. Why is this? Is it that the Protestant world is inconsistent with its own principles when it is called to judge the actions of the Catholic world? We think not. Is it not rather because there is in the heart of Protestantism a conviction that the Papacy is not an ecclesiastical power, but itself a State-power; that the investiture struggle is not really a warfare between a natural and a spiritual force, but a strife between two forces equally natural, though not equally strong? We see at once that the staff and the ring symbolize a spiritual authority, but we are painfully conscious, at the same time, that the idea of spirituality stops short at the symbol, that the Papacy of this age is deluding itself into the belief that the exercise of a subtle temporal power is the putting forth of a spiritual influence. What guarantee had the State, that in relinquishing investiture by the staff and ring, it was not really abandoning its feudal tenure over the Church lands altogether? These badges were symbols of the spiritual, but to the Papacy every object, however secular, was within the range of spiritual jurisdiction; the Papacy contemplated the revival of a Jewish theocracy, in which no subordinate government would be recognised, and in which no secondary causes would be allowed to operate. In point of fact, twenty years had scarcely passed over until the Papal spirit fully revealed the scope of its action, and Urban II. followed up the work of Hildebrand, by forbidding the Church to swear fealty, even for temporal possessions. Therefore it is that in this controversy our sympathies are impelled towards the secular power. We concede the abstract justice of the principle advanced by the Papacy, we believe in the perfect sincerity of Hildebrand's individual convictions; but we feel that the language in which the principle is clothed has a different meaning to Protestant and to Papal ears, and we are conscious that the pretensions of Hildebrand involve far more than he himself supposed. Let us proceed now with the historical narrative.

The throne of Germany was now filled by Henry IV., a youth of three-and-twenty. He was precisely of that temperament which would resist any aggression or foreign interference. Bold, fierce, combative, quick in design, and resolute in action, his life had already been a protracted scene of wars and revolutions. He sat on an unstable throne, and was naturally jealous of every movement which might tend to increase its instability. The present course of Hildebrand was emphatically such a movement; and it was not long before these fiery spirits were brought into violent collision. Hildebrand issued his prohibition of investitures. Some refractory bishops disobeyed the mandate; Hildebrand banished them from their sees. They repaired to the court of Henry, where they were received with open arms, and encouraged in their opposition. Hildebrand summoned the emperor to Rome; Henry retorted by assembling a German council, and pronouncing against the pontiff a sentence of deposition. Hildebrand returned the fire by fulminating against Henry the thunderbolt of excommunication. That thunderbolt did more execution than Hildebrand either intended or desired; it kindled a fire in the future which consumed all outward authority whatsoever. By the law of Germany, the effect of excommunication was to loosen feudal ties, to relieve the subject from allegiance to the sovereign. Italy belonged to Germany; here the feudal chain had long been shaking, and this act almost shattered it. The unity of its State-power melted like snow, and the authority of the great lords was more and more loosened every day. And as the old system faded, a new order of life began to appear. Those Italian cities which hitherto had no political existence, and lived only to represent the southern love of the beautiful, burst forth like islands emerging from the sea of history. Within a very few years from this date, they claimed an independent government of their own, obeyed their own laws, framed their own constitutions. Within a few years more they began to claim an empire over higher laws than those of government—

the laws of human thought. They stood out in the spiritual universe like separate and independent suns, each the centre of its own planetary system, each the orb round which its own worlds revolved. They gathered within their radius all possibilities of civilisation: commerce, and the luxury which necessitates commerce; social refinement, and the appliances which conduce to refinement; the beauties of nature and the beauties of art, the pursuit of science, the study of philosophy, the symmetry of sculpture, the love of poetry, last, most conspicuously of all, the triumphs of painting. Yet it is not in any of these achievements that the free cities of Italy contributed most to the development of the Christian spirit; it is in a work whose progress was unseen, and whose glory appeared only in its consummation. In those wars through which lay their early years, they felt themselves to be individually weak, for their populations were small, and their armies inconsiderable. To supply the want, they put arms into the hands of the serf, and told him that his purchase-money would be his freedom. The effect was a splendid moral revolution; in the course of a hundred years there was not a slave in Italy. The thunderbolt of Hildebrand was a stroke in the interest of ecclesiastical despotism: it missed the object at which it aimed, and struck down despotism itself; its fire woke into vitality the seeds of human freedom, and kindled into flame the enthusiasm for the rights of man.

Meantime, the immediate effect of this excommunication was all that Hildebrand could have desired.

The proud emperor saw himself at once surrounded by enemies in the heart of his dominions, and his pride gave way. He yielded, and he yielded in a manner which has done more to impress mankind with the power of the Papacy than all its decretals and all its fulminations. In the depth of winter, in the freezing January cold, there waited at the gates of the Castle of Canosea one in the attitude of a beggar; his head uncovered to the blast, his feet bared to the cruel snow, his form meanly clad in the haircloth shirt of the penitent. Three days, three nights, he waited, a shivering suppliant, for mercy to him who dwelt within; the suppliant was the Emperor of Germany, the man to whom he prayed was Hildebrand. Never before had such a spectacle been witnessed by the world; never again has a scene so dramatic been enacted in history. The Church and the State had stood side by side at Charlemagne's coronation; the Church the willing servant, the State the complacent master. Now, after long years, they stood side by side once more, but what a change was here!—the servant had become the master, and the master had sunk into the servant. The crown which the pontiff had placed upon the head of Charlemagne had faded from the brows of Henry; he came to confess himself uncrowned, to cast his sceptre at the feet of him who represented the King of kings. That was the proudest moment of Hildebrand's life. For one instant he stood upon Mount Nebo, and beheld the promised land — the land of his dreams, the land of his aspirations. The wilderness was nearly past, the battle was almost won; surely the spiritual Canaan was about to rise, and majestic Rome to be again the mistress of the world.

It was the last vision of the promised land Hildebrand ever saw; from that hour he began to descend Mount Nebo. The suppliant emperor obtained the answer to his prayers, and went back to his dominions with the ban of excommunication removed. He valued its removal only for the moral effect it would produce upon his subjects; his humiliation had been entirely a homage paid to self-interest. Nor did he miscalculate the power of this religious influence; he became again the leader of a strong army. The Saxon princes had cast off their oath of allegiance, and the empire was divided against itself. The war which followed was long and bloody; sometimes inclining to one side, sometimes to the other. At last the emperor prevailed; the sun of fortune rose upon him, and he stood a conqueror upon the soil of a consolidated Germany. Now was his time for vengeance. He smarted with the memory of his humiliation,—a humiliation paid to policy rather than to principle,—and he longed to wipe it out by an act of signal retribution. The scene which followed was like a repetition of the fifth century. The Teutonic descendants of the old barbarians swept once more from north to south, and gathered again on the plains of Italy. Once more the city of the Cæsars was invested by a besieging army; and the Papal, like the temporal empire, trembled in the balance. And once more the North prevailed.

For three years the city of the Cæsars was encompassed. The holy Roman empire defended itself with a bravery which, in the eye of history, puts the old secular empire to shame; and the Papacy showed that, in addition to its spiritual weapons, it was able to wield the sword. But Papal Rome was no physical match for imperial Germany; and the unequal contest, so long and so bravely protracted, was closed at last in defeat and humiliation; the city opened its gates, and the imperial legions entered. There was one man unyielding even in defeat, and that was Hildebrand. Disappointed in his life-dream, robbed of his glorious vision, despoiled of his temporal dominion, in danger even of his personal safety, he remained uncompromising still. One solitary stronghold was yet untouched,—it was the Castle of St. Angelo; thither Hildebrand retired, and thither the legions followed him. Immured in that strong fortress, the pontiff bade defiance to his foes, and maintained that indomitable strength of will which has given him his place in history. But the odds were too unequal; outside the gates stood a besieging army, and inside was the pressure of famine. The stubborn will was nearly bent at last, and the proud pontiff prepared to surrender. At the eleventh hour relief came. Robert Guiscard, the Norman duke of Apulia, advanced to the rescue. The besiegers, suddenly attacked, were taken by surprise, and fell back in confusion. Before the emperor could resume operations, he was arrested by disquieting rumours from Germany; he felt that his own interests imperatively demanded his return, and he gave the order for retreat. The host of the Teuton, like a receding wave, rolled back from the soil of Italy, and Hildebrand was free. But he had lost his confidence in the Church's destiny. He saw that Rome was only liberated for the hour, and that to remain within its walls was no longer possible. All Europe was against him, — France and Norman England, Germany and Northern Italy. He had no longer any trust in the infallibility of his capital; he abandoned it and fled. For a time he found no resting-place, no spot where he could find himself secure. At last he came to Salerno. Here, after all his toils, a long rest awaited him—the rest of death. His life had been a life of anxiety, a life of privation, a life of corroding cares, and now that the reaction had come, his past labours told upon his frame. He was exhausted in body, he was depressed in soul; and body and soul reacted upon each other. He felt that the end was approaching, and he prepared himself to die. His last words are strikingly suggestive,—' I have loved righteousness and hated iniquity, therefore I die an exile.' What a satire on the trial by hot water! A century ago, a man's favour in the sight of Heaven would have been estimated by the absence of the marks of fire; here is a man pointing to the traces of the suffering that has scorched him as the proof that he has fought a good fight and won the prize. Through that closing utterance there breathes an air of pure sincerity; the consciousness of a heart which, up to the measure of its light, had walked in its integrity. For ourselves, we like Hildebrand better in his declining fortunes than in the hour of his prosperity; find him more worthy of reverence at the foot of the mountain than when standing on the summit of Nebo. His life had, to his own generation, been a light, but not a uniformly progressive light. It was beautiful in its dawn, as it rose amid the shades of Cluny; it was more beautiful in its ascent, as it struggled to disperse the clouds of surrounding ignorance; it paled on reaching its meridian, and threatened to disappear amid the shadows of the world; it regained again at evening the brightness it had lost at noon-day. Looking at this life of Hildebrand from the standpoint of far distant years, surveying him from an eminence removed from all prejudice, and exalted over all polemical bias, the verdict of our age must undoubtedly be: that while his errors were bequeathed to him by inheritance, his virtues were all his own. The mistakes of his life were the result of an erroneous system, which he did not originate, and which he had no power to modify; the sincerity, the love of virtue, the zeal for human welfare, the desire for a pure church, and the willingness to spend and be spent in seeing that desire fulfilled, were the product of a nature wider than the circumstances of his age and higher than the aims of hierarchical ambition: the man was greater than the pontiff, let him rest in peace.

The death of Hildebrand did not break the spirit of the Papacy, did not for a moment divert it from its scheme of empire. It was now that, at the low ebb of its fortunes, there entered into its imagination a design which altered the destinies of Europe. It was really the revival of that project which had been contemplated by Sylvester II., but it was the revival of the project with a new motive. Sylvester had proclaimed a crusade, with no other object than to kindle religious zeal; to the Papacy of this century, the crusade had a political importance. Why had Papal Rome been worsted in the war of investitures? why had the German legions triumphed over the soldiers of the cross? Was it not because Christianity had neglected to utilise the pagan element of war, had isolated itself too much from the sources of worldly strength? Why should not that enthusiasm which had been communicated to the monk in the cloister be imparted also to the armies of Europe? Why should not the patriotism, the loyalty, the allegiance of the earthly soldier, be subordinated to the love of a better country, the devotion to a higher king, the fidelity to a nobler cause? If the military strength of the age could be enlisted on the side of religion, would not this secure for ever the triumph of Papal dominion? and how could that strength be better enlisted than by presenting such an object as Sylvester had proposed? Here was a field for the exercise of religious enthusiasm, on which the soldier of the cross could march side by side with the soldier of the crown, where the kingdoms of this world might circle round the banner of the kingdom of Christ. Jerusalem, the city of so many hallowed associations, the very home of Christianity itself, was trodden down by the feet of the Mohammedan, and its sacred relics polluted by the touch of the infidel. Let Rome lead out the armies of Europe into Asia; let it point the imperial soldiers to a goal of aspiration higher than the conquest of lands, richer than the spoils of war; let it show them the hope of becoming the saviours of the Saviour's home, the lofty ambition of being deliverers of the hallowed soil. Then would Rome rise supreme in power; it would command the military strength of the world, it would sway the armies of the West, it would mould the destinies of kings.

Such was the new scheme of Papal aggrandisement. It is curious to observe its result in history. It produced two effects, which must be carefully kept apart: an immediate historical one, and a silent moral one. Here, as in the case of Hildebrand's thunderbolt, the Papacy received, by its own action, a present gain and an ultimate loss. Its gain appeared in the speedy revival of its outward fortunes. Thirty-seven years after the death of Hildebrand, the war of investitures terminated; it terminated in favour of the Papacy. The staff and the ring were relinquished by the State, and Rome stood forth as an independent power; an empire within the empire. Two steps of the Isidorian decretals had been achieved, and there was but one remaining: the subordination of the State into a province of the Church; this also the Papacy was soon to gain. Thus far the crusades proved a triumphant stroke of policy; but all this was only on the surface. Through these years of triumph there was going on an underground process of reverse; unseen by the world, unknown to the Papal power, but potent in its very secrecy. The crusades were the generators of a new life; they initiated the spirit of romance, and the spirit of romance is ever antagonistic to outward authority. Hitherto the school-life of Christianity had moved in strict union with the will of the schoolmaster. Since the opening of mediævalism, the interests of the Papacy had been identified with the interests of the Church. The spirit of mediæval Christianity had recognised in the Roman pontiff its true representative, had thrown itself into sympathy with his schemes of ambition, had persuaded itself that his elevation was its glory. But that was because the spirit of Christianity had not yet become conscious of its own inward resources. Its school-life had up to this time been the prose of existence; it was about to learn its poetry, and the poetic sense of future possibilities was to make it discontented with the prosaic light of common day. It was to be carried into a sphere wider than it had ever occupied before; was to move amid the roar of battle, and dwell amid scenes of military glory. In the army of Constantine, it had shared the triumph with the forces of paganism; it was now to be the one directing force on every battle-field, the one impelling power in every deed of heroism. The wider sphere was to create wider aspiration, to extend the horizon of its possibilities, to bring it into contact with influences which once it had despised; with love, with chivalry, with romance, with the arts of social refinement, with the delights of literary culture, with all the good, and somewhat of the evil, that pertains to the seen and temporal.

The march into Palestine was the march into its romantic age; and its romantic age was to open the first breach in the friendship of the pupil and the teacher. That war which the Papacy had carried on wholly with the powers without, was to begin to be waged with those of its own household; and the opposition which the sacred empire had received only from the arms of kings, was to be kindled within the heart of the spirit of Christianity.

CHAPTER XXVI.

FIRST GLIMMERINGS OF THE ROMANTIC AGE.

THERE are three distinct results which the history of mediæval Europe can trace to the influence of the crusades. The first is the confirmation of chivalry as an institution, the second is the birth of religious scepticism, and the third is the diffusion of secular education. We say these are distinct results, because, although they ultimately blended in producing one ecclesiastical reaction, they originated at the outset in different impulses. We begin with the confirmation of chivalry. An age of chivalry must be an age of enthusiasm, for enthusiasm is its very fountain. Perhaps there never was a period when the spirit of Christianity had been stimulated into such heights of fervour as that on which we are now entering. It is doubtful if even in its opening days, when it was confronted by the sights and sounds of a new world, it experienced such a thrill of rapture as at the dawn of the crusading era. Its gaze was then the gaze of infancy; and when all was equally new, nothing could appear specially wonderful. Now the infancy and the childhood had alike passed away, and with them the old forms had vanished, leaving the scenes in which they dwelt in the possession of the stranger. To the heart of Christianity, these scenes had become dearer in retrospect than they were in actual vision, and shone more fairly through the mists of time than they had done in the golden present. Christendom longed to repossess them, to retrace its steps into the vanished past, and rescue the objects of that past from the hands that were destroying them; and it welcomed with acclamation the blast of that warlike trumpet which summoned the armies of Europe to reconquer Israel for God. The blast of that trumpet seemed to call the world into unity. It was not from one lone corner that its notes were responded to, it was not from one rank or station that its summons was obeyed. Earth poured forth at its call the representatives of all humanity. The noble came with his power and opulence, the peasant came with nothing but his unlettered zeal, the artisan came with his hands rough with daily toil, the priest came with his beads and his rosaries; the poor, the old, the sick, the infirm, the outcasts whom society had spurned, manhood with its strength, and womanhood with its fragile form, crowded the ranks of that enthusiastic band. Here at last was a grand sphere for the operation of the Christian spirit,—a sphere for a work better than crusading. In this multitudinous host there were the weak as well as the strong; must it not become the duty of the strong to protect and succour the weak? It was in answer to this question that the orders of chivalry arose; first the

Knights of St. John, a little later the Knights Templars, and last, the Teutonic Knights of St. Mary. They arose with a twofold mission: they were to harass the Mohammedans, and they were to succour the pilgrims,—the poor, the sick, the helpless. In that mission were blended the elements alike of the pagan and of the Christian world; the warlike strength of the one, and the self-sacrificing gentleness of the other. The lion and the lamb slept side by side in their bosoms. All the fire of the old warrior was there; the physical heroism of that pagan world, whose glory was to despise death and laugh at pain, the valour that never shrank from the sword of a foe, and ever courted the hour of danger. But more than the fire of the warrior was there; there was the fire of the Christian too,—the heroism which found its glory, not in self-exaltation, but in self-forgetfulness, which sought to repress for a time its rough material strength, that with gentle hand it might minister to the sorrows and the wants of those around it. Chivalry was the union of war and peace, the meeting of strength and softness, the conjunction of egotism and self-sacrifice, the touching of paganism and Christianity. United in themselves they were not, and never could be; but they found for the moment a meeting-place within one individual life, and the very closeness of their proximity deepened the contrast between them, and brought out into stronger prominence the features peculiar to each. Undoubtedly, in the efforts of these contrary tendencies to find a point of union, there might be seen the unconscious straining after the appropriation of one great truth, the power which resided in the Christian spirit to lift up the secular into itself, and tinge all objects with its own divinity.

But let us advance a step farther. We have seen that chivalry had for one of its objects the protection of the feeble. The idea of human feebleness soon came to personify itself in the gentler and more fragile sex, and the province of the knight came to be indissolubly associated with the protection of woman. With the growth of this thought grew the influence of woman herself. Hitherto she had been esteemed, but esteemed chiefly as an organ of the religious life, as a representative of ecclesiastical purity, as a missionary spirit in the vineyard of the Master. But now the range of her influence was to be extended, and she was to be allowed to exert her power over man in other spheres than that of the religious life. The secular world was to be thrown open to her, and she was to carry into that world many of those graces which had hitherto belonged exclusively to the spiritual region, — was to refine, to chasten, to touch it with her own softness. It is not difficult to trace the reason of her influence. The transition in the heart of the knight from the sense of protectiveness into the feeling of reverence was swift and easy. He found that the object of his protection was a source of strength, —inspired his spirit in the hour of danger, and nerved his arm in the moment of conflict. Accordingly, he resolved to make the championship of woman his perpetual goal, to keep the ideal of female perfection ever before the eye of his mind, and to make the motive of all his actions the winning of her favour and approbation. When he went forth to single combat, he was nerved for the strife by the knowledge that his victory would bring joy to the object of his devotion. When he joined the ranks of the tournament, he contended under the patronage, so to speak, of some fair sovereign of his heart, and his triumph was only dear to him from the knowledge that from her hands he would receive the prize. If the influence of woman contributed thus far to foster the love of war, it contributed at the same time to soften the horrors of war itself. It was impossible that such an influence should exist without diffusing through the martial atmosphere of that age the current of a milder air. It was inevitable that in the heart of knighthood it should implant the seeds of a life more gentle and serene; should uproot many of the rugged tares, and prepare the soil to receive the warmth and the sunshine. Chivalry was to the eleventh and twelfth centuries what philanthropy is to the nineteenth. Men were not ripe for obtaining an interest in universal humanity,—the thought was too abstract to be grasped by the school-life of the Christian spirit,—but they were ripe for fixing their eyes upon the softer side of human nature; and by looking upon it, they were assimilated to it; its gentleness made them great.

But it was not only in martial exercises that the age of chivalry found its field of enterprise; to this age we owe the birth of continental poetry. Chivalry had not only its tournaments, but its troubadours; that long line of amateur bards who brightened the courts of France, Spain, and Upper Italy, from its rising amid the crusades, with the muse of William of Poitiers, till its close in poverty and neglect, with the broken harp of Guiraut Riquier. The troubadour did 'all for love, and nothing for reward.' He was himself a knight, and the object of his inspiration was the same that inspired the knightly heart. It was no uncommon occurrence to find the tournament transferred from the physical into the intellectual sphere. At the great court festivals there were frequently held what might be called mental combats. The troubadours would meet together to deliver in verse their sentiments on a debated subject, and the finest poem obtained the prize from the hand of her who had acted as arbiter of their merits. It was impossible that the consciousness of female arbitration should do otherwise than contribute to refine literature itself; to expunge from it what was base and coarse and mean, and to raise it into an atmosphere of sweetness and of beauty. The dawn of chivalry is the birthday of a nobler intellectual life, of an aspiration more elevated, of an imagination more pure. We have scarcely touched the threshold of this romantic age when we are made aware that we are on the borders of a mighty renaissance,—a renaissance the longest in duration, the widest in extent, the noblest in influence, which had ever stirred the hearts of men,—a renaissance which, after dying in

France, was caught up by the life of Italy; which, after waning in Italy, was revivified by Elizabethan England; and which, after losing its power over England itself, was resuscitated into transcendent glory in the literary outburst of Germany, which marked the opening of the nineteenth century. It is thus to chivalry that modern life owes its intellectual fervour; the poet of our day has an apostolic succession from the mediæval troubadour. But modern life owes to chivalry something more than its intellectual fervour,—it owes its very existence. The rules of etiquette, the customs of social urbanity, the delicacy of feeling which we stamp by the name of good taste, the politeness which we attribute to high-breeding, but which has really its seat in the pure heart,—what are these but the survival of those knightly accomplishments which cause the middle ages to glitter with stars? They have been transferred from the tournament to the drawing-room; but under different garbs, their nature is the same. Nor can it be said that this region of chivalry lies outside the development of the spirit of Christianity; it is itself an integral part of that development. If on one side it touches the world in which we dwell, on another it is contiguous to the earliest days of Christian life. Its impulse over mediævalism sprang directly from the adoration of the Virgin Mother—the love of ideal womanhood; but indirectly its source was an object older and nobler still, that human side of the Master's portraiture, of which the worship of the Virgin Mother was but a broken and distorted image.

The second of those effects which the crusades produced upon the history of Europe was the birth of religious scepticism. The scepticism sprang from the sense of failure, and the failure consisted in romance losing its first object. What rendered the scepticism more complete, was the fact that the disappointment created by the crusading movement did not originate in any want of outward success. The opening of that movement was a triumphal march from victory to victory. The mighty host which Europe poured forth into Asia seemed at first to be impelled by a strength which nothing could resist. One by one the strongholds of the Mohammedan fell down before them; Nice was taken, Antioch was stormed, the armies of the Sultan Soliman were twice encountered and overthrown, and at last, after a resistance of but five weeks, the sacred city of Jerusalem opened its gates to the conquerors. Then there was witnessed a scene such as Europe had never beheld before, and which it is to be hoped Europe will never behold again. The soldiers of the Cross showed no mercy to the followers of the Crescent. Entering the sacred city sword in hand, they massacred without distinction man, woman, and child; the worst passions of their nature were awakened by that hour of religious enthusiasm. Immediately afterwards the scene changed, in a manner that would have been ludicrous if it had not been revolting. These men, reeking with the blood of their fellow-creatures, threw themselves prostrate upon the supposed site of the holy sepulchre, and upon the spots pointed out as the scenes of gospel history; they stretched themselves upon the ground in abject humiliation, and poured forth their lamentations and their tears. There was no hypocrisy in this; they were perfectly sincere in both actions,—sincere in the massacre, sincere in the reverence for the home of the visible Christ. It never would have occurred to these men that there was any incongruity between the one and the other. There were struggling within them two different, two opposite lives,—the life of paganism and the life of Christianity, the force of self-assertion and the force of self-abnegation,—and by each in turn they were swayed and dominated. Upon the whole, however, the paganism prevailed; even the Christian reverence had a touch of the pagan element in it. What they revered was not the Christian spirit, but the outward locality where that spirit had first been manifested. The crusades, like the worship of the Virgin Mother, were attempts to supply the place of a direct communion; and, like the worship of the Virgin Mother, they failed to effect their aim. The armies of Europe obtained everything they desired, except satisfaction. They conquered the city, they rescued the sepulchre, they gazed unimpeded upon the scenes of sacred history, they placed over Jerusalem a Christian king, and established a monarchy which lasted for many years; and they found that the result of all their labours was 'vanity and vexation of spirit.' The enthusiasm which had centred around Palestine while yet it lay in the far distance faded from the heart of Europe when Europe drew near; while yet untouched it was a golden treasure, but the instant the hand was laid upon it it became dust and ashes. The scenes of sacred history lost in immediate vision that glow which they had possessed to the eye of poetic imagination; and the romance which had encircled the memories of the past received a terrible shock, and was driven from its home. And the result of this feeling of disappointment was the birth of religious scepticism. The failure of the sacred localities to ennoble the heart of man was transferred vicariously to the historic incidents which had been associated with those localities; and the crusaders, in breaking with the scenes of the past, were bitterly tempted to break with the past itself. This religious scepticism did not indeed burst upon the world full-blown; it was a growth, and this was but its beginning. Yet the whole plant is potentially in the seed, and the revolutionary spirit of an after-age revealed itself in this period even in the germ. In contemplating the religious features of this age, there rise up before us, as there did at the Council of Tours, three distinct figures, each the representative of a separate phase of belief. In the heart of the orthodox world stands Bernard of Clairvaux, a true son of the Papacy, a sincere believer in ecclesiastical authority. He is opposed to all inquiry; he would have the individual submit himself implicitly to the will of the universal Church as expressed in its great representative, would silence all reason in the presence of apostolic tradition. One step nearer the borders of the liberal world stands Anselm, Archbishop of Canterbury. He, too, like Bernard, bows submissive to the authority of the Church, but he wants a place for reason also; he will allow the human mind to sit upon a throne, even though it be an inferior throne. The mind must first yield itself to the ecclesiastical will; but shall it not find its life by losing it? It must believe before it sees; but shall not sight follow belief? Anselm's place for reason is to be the handmaid of faith, to prove what faith asserts, to corroborate in human nature what it proclaims through the divine oracles; we are here a little farther out of the range of Papal dominion. One step more, and we are out of it altogether. At the extreme left of Bernard rises a figure, as yet solitary and unbefriended, but strongly prophetic of an approaching change; it is the monk Peter Abelard. He is the child of the romantic age, and the spirit of its romance struggles in him with the monastic spirit; the love of Heloise is strong, but the mandate of the Church is stronger. He stands outwardly submissive, but inwardly defiant, chafing against the restraints of hierarchical domination; separating himself from the object of his affection, yet denouncing the power which had compelled him so to do. He proclaims the paramount sovereignty of reason, he asserts the right of the human understanding to be the first judge of truth and error; and he vociferates down the stream of all the ages that intellectual conviction is superior to ecclesiastical tradition, and that the inward perception of truth is a better evidence than the authority of that Church which declares it.

Now, what Abelard was individually, the school-life of this period was collectively; a spirit of incipient revolution. The life of Christendom at large was actuated by the same inward conflict which stirred the heart of the individual man—the conflict between romance and tradition. It had appeared at first as if the spirit of Christianity might have found food for its romantic age in the reconquest of the past; it had appeared as if its poetic imagination would have been satisfied with garnishing the tombs of the prophets, and adorning the sepulchre of the Master. That hope had been bitterly disappointed; the garnished tombs had brought no enthusiasm, the consecration of the sepulchre had carried no charm. From such a conflict between imagination and reality there could result but one issue. The spirit of Christianity was full of the first ardour of romantic days; the scenes of the past were inadequate to meet that ardour; was it not inevitable that Christianity should seek to be severed from the past? must it not find new spheres of enterprise and higher heights of contemplation? It was now that for the first time the school-life experienced a sense of estrangement from the schoolmaster; an estrangement expressed originally only by the voice of Abelard, yet silently felt by many, and ultimately growing into a chorus of multitudinous voices. The Papacy, outwardly strengthening, as it was, day by day, was, unknown to itself, being sapped in its very foundations; and the silent influence of a public opinion, as yet unuttered, was preparing a force of opposition superior to that of all the crusading armies.

We come now to the third of those effects which the crusades produced upon the history of Europe—the diffusion of secular education. It is from an early period of the crusading era that we date the rise of universities. The universities were essentially secular institutions; they ultimately included a theological faculty, but their theology itself was the secular side of their religion, and more allied to logic than to divinity. For a long time, however, the universities embraced no theological teaching. Paris, Oxford, and Cambridge were originally occupied entirely with the arts; Bologna was engrossed with the pursuit of law; Montpellier and Orleans were even forbidden to teach theology. Up to this period a school had been attached to every cathedral and monastery. These schools had, indeed, professed to be diffusers of secular education, but they had manifestly failed in their object; the shadow of the cathedral and of the monastery was clearly unfavourable to the unfettered progress of the human mind. It would be too much to say that the universities were an anti-Papal movement. They were originated with no such deliberate motive; indeed, deliberation of any kind did not mark their rise. They were not created; they grew spontaneously from the will of the people. A company of great teachers would take up their abode in a city, and presently each would become the centre of a circle, the sun round which revolved those spirits under the power of his attraction; by-and-by these separate systems would unite into one corporation, and the schools which at first were rivals would form a great university. But though it would be too much to say that institutions so spontaneously formed had an anti-Papal aim, it is unquestionable that they sprang up at a time when the common heart of Christendom had begun to beat with the pulse of freedom. Arising at such a period, it was impossible that they should not be impregnated with the breath of the new atmosphere, and even, unconsciously to themselves, affected by the thirst for progress. Hitherto the education of the school-life had been confined to what were called the seven liberal arts; but from these there had been excluded two studies, which of all others were to prove the most powerful sources of mediæval advancement; we mean the study of law and the study of languages. Both of these the universities immediately supplied; and both of them in the sequel were unfavourable to Papal dominion. The absolute monarchy of the pontiff was greatly promoted in Europe by the universality of the Latin tongue; but as that universality was broken, the sense of individual freedom revived more and more among the nations. The absolute power of the pontiff owed part of its influence in Europe to the European ignorance of civil and ecclesiastical law; but when men began to study law, they began to shrink instinctively from the exercise of arbitrary power: the progress of legal knowledge, and the progressive knowledge of national language, were the two great intellectual agents which produced the fall of feudalism; and the fall of feudalism itself was essentially and inextricably connected with the decline of all ecclesiastical authority which was not based upon the principles of human nature. Feudalism, as we have seen, was, relatively speaking, a liberal movement, but it had one great defect, and that defect it shared with the hierarchy: it had no place for the common people. It recognised the rights of the vassal as a vassal, but not as a man. No grade of society inferior to knighthood had a representative voice in the deliberations of its country; a House of Commons was as yet unknown. It was clear that before the vassals could receive the privilege of representation they must be brought to desire that privilege; and it was equally clear that they could only come to desire it by having their understanding enlarged. Accordingly, we find that the tendency towards the existence of a House of Commons is almost coeval with the rise of the universities, and grows stronger in proportion as education is diffused. It is to the honour of France that it took the lead in this matter; in 1126, that is to say, less than thirty years after the close of the first crusade, the first burgh was represented in the French Parliament. It is curious to read the comment of a contemporary historian on this great innovation. 'They are bringing a herd of slaves to vote amongst us;' such was the genuine feeling of contempt with which the lords of that day regarded the commoners. It will not therefore surprise us that the progress of 'the herd of slaves' was slow. We hear of no further representation for upwards of eighty years, and then again it was France that led the van; in 1207, Falaise and Rouen obtained a voice in Parliament. We pass over a period of fifty-eight years more, and then England begins to unite the elements of the British constitution; in the Revolution of 1265 it received its first House of Commons. From that hour British feudalism declined, and the people became more and more a power. The movement towards liberty was consentaneous throughout Europe; at the close of the thirteenth century, Germany had not a slave; at the opening of the fourteenth, a royal edict proclaimed the emancipation of the serfs in France. But let us not forget, that by this time the universities had become predominant, and the masses had been elevated by the intelligence they diffused. It is to these institutions that we owe the progress of public liberty; it is to these that we ascribe the decline of all despotism, whether feudal or hierarchical. They enlarged the human soul, and taught man his own value. They showed him that beneath the distinctions of caste, beneath the gradations of king, baron, vassal, and serf, there was a humanity common to all,—a humanity essentially noble, and giving to every man inalienable rights. They told him that these rights belonged to him, because he was a human being; that no social grade could obliterate them, that no depressing circumstances could crush them; and they inspired him to assert, in the face of all the world, his claim to those privileges which he inherited from humanity.

We have associated the rise of the universities with the era of the crusades. If we inquire how a movement so warlike should have created the demand for institutions suggestive of peace and culture, we shall not need to look far for an answer. Whence proceeded this tendency towards the development of a secular education? It came not from the pomp and pageantry of a crusading Europe, it came not from the romantic enthusiasm of an age eager to revive the past, it came not from the triumphant march of an army whose every enterprise was crowned with unqualified success, it came not from the strength of the Christian prejudice against Mohammedanism; it came, strange to say, from Mohammedanism itself. Europe had entered Asia sword in hand, and had returned a physical conqueror; it had returned at the same time an intellectual captive; its old forms of thought had been shaken, its mind had been captivated by the mental force of the Musulman. This was now the second time that Europe had bowed submissive to the intellectual power of Asia. Four hundred years ago the Mohammedan had planted his foot upon European soil, and planted along with it the seeds of a life that well-nigh made all things new; the images were shaken in the temples, and the idols of superstition were broken in the hearts of men. That danger had passed away, and now the West had taken up the sword to retaliate its invasion by the East. It had conquered, and it had been conquered; it had subdued the bodies of its enemies, and its enemies had subdued its spirit; it caught fire from the life of that secular culture which was circling round it, and it carried the seeds of that life into the heart of its empires. Does it seem a startling declaration, that the Cross should have been intellectually vanquished by the Crescent? It will cease to be so, if we reflect how little the symbol of the cross was a real expression of the Christian character of that day. We have said that the crusades exhibited the struggle between Christianity and paganism, and we have said that the paganism was stronger than the Christianity. In so far as Christianity was possessed of a pagan element, it was confronted in Mohammedanism by a power superior to itself. Mohammedanism was a survival of the breath of Judaism, and the breath of Judaism was the destruction of idolatry. Mohammedanism was strong, because its faith was the faith of Israel,—that is, because it felt the overruling, all-controlling presence of One, who in the heavens sat alone, His majesty unshared, His glory unrivalled; because, in comparison with this power, it held all the kingdoms of the earth, and all the riches of the universe, to be dust and ashes; and because it recognised submission to His will as the only destiny worthy of a spiritual being. Mohammedanism, like Judaism, claimed all for God. It allowed no separation between the secular and the sacred; for the earth was the Lord's, and the fulness thereof, and His sovereignty over all made all things sacred. It had no fear of knowledge, of science, of philosophy; these were the avenues to self-humiliation, and self-humiliation was its goal. Therefore its studies were deep and wide, and every object of its study had a religious significance. Its astrologies, its alchemies, its efforts to penetrate, into the arcana of the universe, its search for hidden and mysterious properties in the forms of material nature, —what were these but the attempts to discover that bridge which links the Creator with His works, and binds earth 'with golden chains about the feet of God'?

We have now traced those three effects which the crusades produced upon the life of Europe,—the institution of chivalry, the birth of religious scepticism, and the diffusion of secular education. There was at this period one spot in which all these three were already concentrated, as if the world were in miniature prefiguring its future history. There was a region in the south-east of France, laved on its southern shore by the waters of the Mediterranean; a land of cornfields, a land of vineyards, a land of luscious fruits, where the sun was ever bright, and the heart was ever gay. Physically and intellectually, it might be called the garden of Europe, but intellectually it was the garden beside the sepulchre; it stood amid the gloom of the contemporary world, conspicuous in its solitary brightness, unapproached and unrivalled. If we could imagine modern London or Paris to be transplanted in their present condition into the wilds of Africa, we should have no exaggerated image of that mighty contrast which the provinces of Languedoc and Provence presented to the world of their day. In every sense they stood alone. Comprehending a future part of the French monarchy, they were then distinct from that monarchy, a nation by themselves, speaking their own language, enjoying their own customs, framing their own laws. And their character partook of the nature of their surroundings. The rich luxuriance of their soil woke up their hearts into poetry and romance; the free breath of the ocean which washed their shores inspired them with the thirst for religious freedom; the proximity of Mohammedan Spain fired them with the love of secular knowledge. All those influences, which in other lands were scattered and isolated, were united and concentrated here,—the chivalry, the scepticism, the learning. Chivalry found in Provence its brightest home, and exerted there its utmost powers of refinement. Scepticism found there its first audible voice, and displayed there its unconcealed sneer. The knights of South France laughed at the Papacy, laughed at the hierarchy, laughed at the image-worship and the men who practised it; it had become a proverbial commonplace to say that a man was as vile as a priest; and when such sentiments as these can come forth proverbially, they must already have had a long history within the silence of the heart. Finally, culture was there. It was not alone in the lyric composition, in the pointed epigram, or in the stinging satire, that this culture was displayed; in these it had indeed most powerful instruments. But its highest power consisted in the fact that it threw open the mind to every elevating influence, and disposed it to receive all truth, from whatever region it might come, presenting thus to the hierarchy a purely antagonistic force,—antagonistic now, and promising to be dangerous soon.

It would be unfair to conclude this subject without alluding to one circumstance which has shed a ray of real glory over the memory of the crusading era. That era did not pass away without contributing somewhat to the history of Christian charity. It was then that for the first time Europe began to abound with hospitals for the leper. This impulse of benevolence proceeded undoubtedly from that same heart of chivalry which had found the glory of its life in sympathizing with the poor and needy. There is to our mind something strikingly grand in the meeting of extremes suggested by this charity,—the knight and the leper, the poles of human existence, the courted and the despised of society; it is grand, but its sublimity is greater than its grandeur, for it shows us that even in an age conspicuous for its social distinctions, the spirit of Christian brotherhood was stronger than them all. And was there not here too an additional contribution to the progress of liberal thought? The provision for the leper struck directly at two strongholds of the hierarchy: its Judaism and its paganism. It assailed its Judaism when it took in those outcasts whom the Israelite had driven from his gates; and it assailed its paganism with a powerful hand, when it showed Christianity to be the helper of the helpless, the friend of the friendless, the home of the houseless, and the refuge of those whom the world had cast away.

While this movement was going on on the outskirts of the Christian Church, there was growing up within the innermost heart of that Church a tendency towards liberalism, not indeed as yet so pronounced, but prophetic of equal power in the future. Humanity being one united life, moves ever consentaneously; and the great revolutions of one country are paralleled by analogous convulsions in another. While, therefore, the soldiers of the cross were catching fire from the life of chivalry, while Provence and Languedoc were waking into religious opposition, while Mohammedanism was for the second time impregnating the world with the germs of secular culture, the inner court of the tabernacle itself was, under the very eye of the hierarchy, admitting into its sacred precincts the elements of discord and disunion. To the consideration of this liberal movement within the heart of the ecclesiastical world, we propose in the following chapter to direct our attention.

CHAPTER XXVII.

EXPANDING OF CHRISTIAN INTELLIGENCE.

WE have seen the school-life entering upon a stage of advancement, promoted from the academy into the university. We are therefore prepared to find that the transition shall be marked by an increase of its speculative power, and a wider grasp of the subjects of its contemplation. It must be confessed that our first impression is bitterly disappointing. Instead of entering with the dawn of university life into a region of pure thought and earnest spiritual meditation, we seem to be ushered into a world of fantastic forms, and into the contemplation of subjects less allied to philosophy than to fairyland. We find, undoubtedly, an increase of reasoning power, a love of argument, a growing passion for debate; but the objects on which this strength of reason is expended are not like anything in heaven above, or on the earth beneath, or in the waters under the earth. One feels naturally startled to behold a company of the most learned men of their day meeting together in the presence of a crowded assembly, gravely and deliberately to discuss the question whether a hundred thousand angels could dance at one moment upon the point of a needle, whether two celestial intelligences could at one time occupy the same amount of space, or whether a celestial being could be present on one spot of earth at the same moment when he was present in another corner of the world.

As we have said, the first impression awakened by such a spectacle as this is a sense of declining energy in the intellectual life in Christendom. Yet, if we are not mistaken, our first impression is erroneous, and exists only to be corrected by subsequent and deeper reflection. It seems to us, that if we look at these subtleties of the schoolmen rather from the standpoint of their own circumstances than from the height of modern elevation, we shall come to regard more leniently those strange and phantastic speculations, over which M. Taine, the French writers generally, and the English writers frequently, have loved to make merry. What, then, were the circumstances of those mediæval schoolmen? They had received, as it were, a new gift of tongues; had felt within them the dawning empire of reason. The power of the new life impelled them to speak; they could no more refrain from utterance than the apostles could have refrained when the pentecostal gift descended upon them. But here lay the difference: the early Christians were allowed to give utterance to that which they believed to be true, the mediæval schoolmen were accorded no such liberty. They had awakened to the power of reason; but they were forbidden to use that power in any other way than the Church directed. They were authorised to prove that which the Church had already declared to be true, but not to discuss it, not to doubt it, not even to investigate it; they had a lesson to learn, but the lesson was printed in a book, and had to be committed to memory apart altogether from their personal experience of its truth. This was a miserably narrow sphere for minds just opening out into the freshness of intellectual power; it was telling the artist of original genius to confine himself to the transcription of copies, or commanding him who had been born a poet to limit his imagination to the translation of the works of others. The school-life of Christianity wanted to exercise its reason; not merely to prove what the hierarchy had affirmed, but to inquire, without bias, whether its affirmations were just. This power was denied to it, and it turned aside with disgust from those theological themes whose foundations it was forbidden to examine; the gates of the temple were shut against it, and it went forth in search of other gates. It wanted a field which did not belong to the Church,—a field which it might traverse without the blame of trespassing; and such a privilege it was not easy to find. There was scarcely a sphere of human thought over which the Church had not stretched its dominion, scarcely a region of human speculation to whose entrance it had not closed the doors. It had claimed the whole earth as its empire: the kingdoms of the world, and the glory of them; the sacraments of religion, and the power of them; the statements of Scripture, and the explanations of them. It had claimed the half of heaven as its province, had ascended up within the veil, had arranged the orders of the celestial hierarchy, had given names to angel and archangel, had asserted its intercourse with those things which 'it hath not entered into the heart of man to conceive.' It had claimed another region still; a region intermediate between heaven and earth, and forming the boundary line between heaven and hell, where the souls of the departed still formed, as it were, a province of its dominion, and waited for its intercession to usher them into the realms of light. Such was that vast empire over which the Catholic Church professed to hold sway, and to the knowledge of whose mysteries it aspired to have the key; an empire nearly co-extensive with the universe, and more than co-extensive with the realm of possible human knowledge. In a world whose every corner was thus monopolised, where was the young reason of the school-life to find a vacant field, over whose untrodden path it might sport without trespass and run without interruption? In the actual world there was none; the entrances to speculation were all blockaded. The school-life, therefore, must invent an artificial world; a world of imagination, a world of phantastic shapes and of unknown forms. It started unearthly subjects of controversy, too unearthly to be dangerous, too far above experience to be within the reach of the hierarchy; questions which involved the abstract nature of being, the elements of matter, the essence of spirit, and all those themes of contemplation which Mr. Carlyle has pronounced 'unutterable.' We do not for a moment imagine that the decision of the subtle points on which the schoolmen disputed was to them a matter of the slightest importance. Theirs was a debating society, whose value lay in the fact that it afforded opportunity for debate. We do not suppose that it is at any time the province of the school-life to form definite opinions on the truth of controverted subjects; such opinions will assuredly be corrected by the judgment of a maturer age. But the province of the school-life is to prepare the powers of the mind for the formation of future opinions; to exercise the reason, to calm the judgment, to regulate the imagination, to balance the will. Hence to the schoolboy the importance of a debating society is the debate itself; it is of little consequence which side of the question he takes; it is of immense consequence that whatever side he takes should engross for the time all his reasoning powers. And so was it with the school-life of Christianity. It was not in search of absolute truth; it was quite content to leave the possession of that in the hands of the hierarchy. What it wanted was a field for the exercise of its powers, an opportunity of speaking, even though it should speak nonsense; the free play of its imagination, in a region where no voice would be heard to say, 'Thus far shalt thou go, and no farther.' And in this instinct of the awakening Christian reason, there was, undoubtedly, the tendency towards a freer and more Protestant position. Scholasticism has been commonly regarded as the hotbed of Catholicism. The school-life of the Church was indeed bound by the rules of the schoolmaster, and to this extent it might be called the servant of the hierarchy. Yet it requires no profound investigation to see that it was at best a half-hearted service, that the pupil was restive under the yoke, and ready to break away the moment the master's eye was averted. The absurdities of scholasticism are alone sufficient to reveal its incipient revolutionary tendency; its eccentricities are the outbursts of a mind weary of convention and tired of propriety; and its subtleties and obscurities are forms of that growing dissatisfaction with which the spirit of Christianity was beginning to regard the objects of sensuous worship.

Amidst these many phantastic themes, however, there was one subject of discussion which deserves to be singled out for its comparative earnestness; a subject which was not wholly unearthly, not altogether unpractical, and not purely unscientific. The schoolmen inquired, with accents of perfect sincerity, what was the meaning of this mysterious world. Into the ranks of debate there started up two opposing schools, whose names have survived all the subtleties of their systems; the nominalists and the realists. With the philosophy and the theology of their discussion we have here nothing to do,—these belong to another province, and fall to be treated by other hands; all that concerns us is the moral bearing of the question, its relation to human nature, and its relation to the spirit of Christianity. Viewed in this light, however, it is not without interest, and should not be passed over without a few words of comment. The nominalist and the realist looked upon the order of creation with totally different eyes. The nominalist said, This world only exists for the sake of the individual; the realist said, This world mainly exists for the sake of the race. The nominalist asked, What do I mean by humanity? is it anything more than a general name, by which I try to embrace in a single thought all the human beings who have lived, are living, or will live upon this earth? The realist retorted the question; he asked, What are these human beings of whom you speak but the outward manifestations of a great life which lies behind them, a life which existed before any one of them, and of whose breath they are but the exhalations? The nominalist looked upon the course of history as a panorama of isolated and disconnected forms, following each other in swift succession, yet exhibiting no sequence in their following. The realist contemplated history as the flow of a continuous existence, rising from the tiny stream, swelling into the rapid river, and merging at last into the great ocean; an existence which faded not with the disappearance of the scenes through which it passed, and which remained immutable amid the changes of its individual manifestations. The nominalist was not very far removed from the standpoint of modern Positivism; the realist was scarcely a step from the threshold of spiritual Pantheism. Each accused the other of heresy, each was in turn the conqueror over his adversary. The truth manifestly lay in their reconciliation. The one-sided contemplation of either view was an ignoring of the facts of the universe. To give exclusive prominence to the rights of the individual was to disregard the truth, that we are members of a brotherhood; to fix undivided attention upon the progress of the race was to ignore the fact, that the lives of individual men compose the history of humanity. There was one principle, and one alone, which could reconcile these conflicting views, and that was the spirit of the Christian religion; the great reconciler of all divergences. The thought of Christian brotherhood was the true meeting-place for the nominalist and the realist, the point where they could shake hands and part in peace. There the individual was not forgotten; he received his full share of life, but he received that life only by yielding it up to the universal good. Nominalism and realism were reconciled in the Protestant Reformation. Protestantism is that middle term which unites the extremes of the individual and the community. Catholicism emphasized the general life of the Church, and commanded the individual life to yield up its personal convictions to the authority of the universal whole. The Anabaptist movement, in its extreme revolt from Catholicism, left too much out of view the sentiments of the Christian brotherhood, and enjoined each individual man to trust exclusively to the divine light within him. Protestantism came between them as a mediator, and laid its hands upon them both. It showed that every man ought to be the member of an invisible Church, the general assembly of the first-born in heaven; and that only in the sense of this brotherhood do the separate lives of men rise into real grandeur. It showed, on the other hand, that the invisible Church must provide for all its members, must suffer not even the smallest or most insignificant to be maimed or destroyed, must seek to impart to each the happiness it designs for all. Thus the particular and the universal met side by side, the individual and the race recognised their mutual relations, and the separate existence of every man found that it derived its perfect riches from the remembrance of the truth, that it was keeper of the life of its brother.

We have alluded, however, to this controversy of nominalism and realism, not for the purpose of showing the relation of the Protestant to the Catholic system. We have done so with the view of exhibiting the growth of Protestant feeling itself. The very fact that such a subject of controversy should have suggested itself to the school-life, is a proof that the school-life was already beginning to transcend the limits of scholasticism, and was seeking a sphere of independent enterprise. We must now divert our eye for a time from the heights into the valleys, from the sons of learning to the sons of manual toil. It will be remembered that the mass of the people still remained ignorant. The system of the hierarchy was not one which necessitated the education of the masses; nay, the position of the hierarchy must have been felt to be more secure while these remained uneducated. The aim of the priesthood had been to communicate so much knowledge as would make the people familiar with the facts of Christianity, without awakening their minds to the principle of Christian liberty. To effect this object, it had made use of the image in preference to the written word, for the written word had a life in it which was apt to be contagious. It is not difficult to see, however, that in spite of these disadvantages the masses had been surely, though slowly, growing in intelligence. We find from time to time a refinement of image-representation, and is not this alone a proof that the spirit was outgrowing the form? First we see the reverence for real or supposed relics, afterwards the simple pictures or engravings as they appear in the Catacombs, and then the massive statues, increasing in symmetry and beauty with the development of Christian sculpture. But now there had come a time in which even these symmetrical forms were no longer large enough to hold the conceptions of the awakening spirit,—a time in which the Church had become dissatisfied with what once appeased its hunger, and had come to esteem as swine-husks what once it had deemed the true bread from heaven. The statues could represent form, but they could not indicate action; they might recall what the saints of old were, but they were unable to record what they had done. And the Church wanted such a record; it was weary of dead formalism, weary of empty pageants, weary of lifeless and burdensome rites, which brought a heavy yoke without communicating the strength to bear it. It longed for a personal intercourse with the men of sacred history; it thirsted for a living communion with the scenes of the golden past. The outward image had failed to give it; the sight of the holy sepulchre had failed to give it; the hallowed associations of Jerusalem itself had failed to give it; the bowing of the head, the bending of the knee, the contortions of the body, the lacerations of the outer man, the prostration of the frame before the statue of every saint in the calendar, including that of the Virgin Mother herself, had proved powerless to reproduce the vital freshness of early days. The Church desired to see the past reacted; to behold not alone its personages, but its personages engaged in their peculiar work, to have the deeds, as well as the forms, of saint and martyr presented to its present gaze; it cried out for an active representation to supersede the apathy of the moveless, lifeless image. And the answer to that cry was an event of great importance,—nothing less than the rise of the theatre in Christian Europe.

To the popular reader it may seem a strange, even a startling, statement, that the theatre was the immediate offspring of a theological necessity. We are no longer in the habit of associating the Church with the pursuits of the stage; there is in many minds a tendency to place them in antagonism. And yet the modern drama owed its rise entirely to the spirit of Christianity, was as much a result of the development of that spirit as the foundation of hospitals or the institution of houses of refuge. Not only was the theatre originally in alliance with the Church, the theatre was itself the Church; it had the same relation to early Catholic worship which the Sabbath-school bears to the modern pulpit,—was designed to prepare the masses for the services of the sanctuary. The places of meeting were the churches, the actors were the clergy and the choristers; the dramatic personages were the heroes of the Old Testament, the apostles of the New, and the saints of the monastic age. The subjects of the dramas were sometimes called 'miracle plays,' and sometimes designated 'mysteries,' according as they dealt prominently with history or with doctrine. They ranged over every topic, from the dogma to the parable, from the secrets of heaven to the facts of earth, from the nature of God to the life of man. Ultimately they came to include Scripture morality itself; they personified the different virtues and vices, gave them a voice, and made them alive. It is incalculable how much good was effected by such devices as these. The theatres were the Sabbath-schools of mediævalism. They filled up that which was behind in the representation of the image; they supplied in great measure that want which the people had suffered by inability to read the sacred writings for themselves. They imprinted on the memory, in a popular form, those scenes and incidents which might otherwise have remained for ever curtained from the gaze of the vulgar. They caused the characters of sacred story to become instinct with life and power, to take hold of the imagination by the touch of human sympathy, to live and move and have their being in the heart of the present world. What wonder that instantaneously they should have enlisted the popular mind! what wonder that the minds they had enlisted should have been elevated to a higher platform! Their progress in the favour of the multitude was indeed rapid and unequivocal. They began on the shores of England, and spread thence, in swift succession, through France, Spain, Italy, and Germany. They united two tendencies in the spirit of that age which had threatened at one time to fall into collision: they joined together the romance of chivalry and the earnestness of religious feeling. They laid hold of the romance, for they opened the minds of the people to the influence of creative imagination, and, even in the most primitive form of the drama, planted them on the threshold of the proudest shrine of poetry. They laid hold of religious feeling, for they revived that sacred history which professes to be an epitome of all God's ways to man, and, as it were, visibly embodied those precepts which claim to point the soul into the path of peace. They were therefore related to two worlds: the world of the renaissance and the world of the Reformation, to the culture of the intellect and to the vision of the heart, to the stores of earthly experience and to the aspirings after that light which transcends earthly experience. They gave to the Catholic world the nearest approach to an open Bible it had yet received, and they formed the highest manifestation which had hitherto been reached by the representation of truth in material forms. One higher manifestation still remained, and that the grandest which the Catholic world was ever to attain: the triumph of the canvas, a triumph which was to give at last a prominent place to that long-neglected element in mediæval worship—the earthly side of the Christian portraiture, the human Christ, the Child Jesus. The exhibition of this triumph lay as yet in the future, and we shall defer its consideration until we have neared the conclusion of this volume; because, if we are not greatly mistaken, it is the true intellectual transition to the Lutheran Reformation. Meantime, is it not evident that we are already on the road to such a transition, that the coming event is casting its shadow before? We have reached a stage of the school-life in which the forms have become inadequate to hold the spirit. The Christian consciousness is beginning to awaken to a sense of its own responsibility, and, for the first time, is realizing the depth of its own being. It has begun in the field of reason that great intellectual struggle, which can never pause until truth has become the soul's possession. It has entered on a course of speculation, wayward indeed, and futile, yet prophetic of heights and possibilities to be attained hereafter. It has found a point of union between the life of religion and the life of the world; and has united itself to the culture, the civilisation, the poetry of all the ages. Already it has become restive under the yoke of authority, and is in search of a firmer basis on which to rear its temple of truth. The spirit of Christianity is about to become the spirit of history,— the moving cause of all causes, the first breath of every change. The Christian Church, indeed, has still to struggle; trials and persecutions lie yet before it, and its path is strewn with many thorns, but it has received a life which must ultimately surmount the trials, and bear its pilgrim footsteps onwards to the happy land of Beulah.

It is not without pain that we are forced to turn from such a prospect to view the outward fortunes of that power which was already beginning to reveal its inherent antagonism to progress. All this time the strength of the Papacy had been steadily increasing. Let it be remembered that the progressive movement we have been describing was an underground process; it was working beneath the surface, and on the surface its effects were not seen. The crusades had essentially a Protestant impulse; but it was an impulse beginning from within, and working its way slowly into the light of common day. The immediate effect of the crusades was, as we have seen, to kindle enthusiasm for the welfare of the Papacy. This had been the design of their institution, and at first they did not fail in their design. The Papacy had devised the movement, and the Papacy reaped the prestige of its opening success. It had equipped the armies of Europe, and the armies of Europe had henceforth felt themselves to be bound to its sovereignty by all the ties of loyalty. But it was not alone by enlisting the military strength of the world that the Papacy had accomplished its scheme of temporal dominion. In addition to this force, it had laid hold of a power not less influential, and much more widely diffusive than could be attained by any European army, for it had conciliated the favour of the greatest of maritime states—the ancient, the venerable republic of Venice.

When the armies had gone forth by land to the conquest of Palestine, the fleets of Venice had gone forth by sea to accompany and aid them. We do not for a moment suppose that the fleets of Venice were actuated by the same motives as the European armies; the soldiers were animated by religious zeal, the Venetian sailors contemplated chiefly the increase of their commerce. Yet the fact, that to them the Papal power of Rome had made itself useful, was alone sufficient to constitute a bond of sympathy and alliance; Venice recognised in the Papacy the power which could minister to its selfish policy, and recognising that power, it naturally truckled to it. Nor is it easy to estimate the importance of such an ally to the Roman pontiff; a union with Venice was worth the submission of many kingdoms. The power of that republic was now at its zenith. What Scandinavia formerly was to the ninth century, what Spain afterwards was to the sixteenth, that was Venice to the twelfth century—the mistress of the sea. Spreading her white wings over the blue waves of the Adriatic, she occupied alone the sovereignty of the maritime world; conspicuous by her solitary majesty, and resplendent by her undisputed sway. Her relation to classic times, her long ancestry, extending back through generations, her catalogue of great achievements in the annals of the past, her enterprising spirit in every vicissitude of the present; above all, her heroism on that element which has always been regarded as demanding qualities peculiarly heroic, and which was even more terrible in days when navigation was in infancy, all contributed to render her an object of admiration to her friends, and of terror to her foes. Nor was it only in exploits of war that she was strong; she was even more powerful in the influences of peace. She was to the Europe of that day what the electric telegraph is to ours, she carried the tidings and the thoughts of one land into another. There was not an arm of the sea which her ships did not penetrate; there was scarcely a nation of the earth which her merchants did not visit. She went to Britain, and brought back what Britain had to give; she carried the iron from Stafford, the tin from Devon and Cornwall, and the wool from Sussex. She touched at the ports of every country on the European continent, and brought its produce home to enrich her dwellings, and add to her comforts. She went to Constantinople, and re-established that intercourse between the East and West which, but for the influences of Mohammedanism, would long since have entirely ceased, and which even with these influences had greatly languished. She travelled beyond Europe itself; she advanced to Syria, she passed through Egypt, she penetrated even to the coasts of Hindostan. She formed thus almost a girdle round the world, and helped the world to realize its natural unity. Nations that lived remote were brought comparatively near; lands separated by oceans were united by commercial enterprise. And when Venice returned from her travels, she brought with her more than merchandise; she brought that knowledge of foreign customs, and that acquaintance with different manners, which, alike in the individual and in the nation, must widen the understanding and expand the sympathy. She told the world what she had seen, and she woke within the world the desire to see it. She generated that love of travel, and that thirst for discovery, which bore its fruit in due season,—which stimulated the Spanish sailors, and emboldened the mariners of Elizabethan England. Such a power might have been already the handmaid of the renaissance, instead of the servant of the hierarchy; and the time came when she asserted her right to be so. But that time was not yet. The spirit of the renaissance had not yet passed from France into Italy, and Venice felt not the glory of being its possible possessor. On the other hand, she did feel very powerfully the advantages of her position as an ally of the Papacy. She felt that the wars of the crusades, which brought pecuniary loss to so many, brought profit and opulence to her; extended her sphere of commerce, and increased the necessities of East and West for the reception of her merchandise. That intercourse with Mohammedanism, which to the rest of the world was hostile, was to Venice essentially a friendly intercourse. She found in the Crescent a spirit kindred to her own, and she desired the continuance of that contact, which must cease with the close of war. She supported the crusaders, because they were the instruments of the war; she gloried in the war, because it was the only means of intercourse with the most mercantile nations of the earth; and she clung to the alliance of the Papacy, because she felt that there alone could she unite the spirit of Christianity with that military ardour which had constituted the glory of paganism.

And by this selfish policy the Papacy was a gainer. It was supported by two elements, by the land and by the sea; it was opposed by only one element, the dissatisfaction of the Christian heart, and even that had not yet been expressed in words. Accordingly, during the entire course of the twelfth century, the outward fortunes of Papal Rome exhibit an ascent from peak to peak of power. No difficulties could daunt its efforts; no reverses could shake its resolution; no opposition could, even for a moment, divert it from its towering purpose. It was in vain that Henry II. of England drew up the Constitutions of Clarendon, to restrain the influence of the hierarchy from becoming a separate government within his own kingdom. It was in vain that Becket of Canterbury fell before the altar of his cathedral, a victim to the anger which his ambitious claims had provoked. It was in vain that Frederic Barbarossa, the brave and enthusiastic Emperor of Germany, struggled through peace and war to preserve the liberties of his country. Before the power of the Papacy, all these barriers were swept away. That power asserted openly those pretensions, which in its system hitherto had been rather implied than expressed. The pontiff had long since been recognised as the Church's schoolmaster; he now aspired to change the guardianship into a permanent and arbitrary dominion. He had long since been recognised as the equal of the State, and the conclusion of the investiture struggle legalised that position of equality. He now aspired to transform equality into sovereignty, and to complete the last step of the Isidorian decretals, by making the State itself his vassal. He claimed from the Church a power almost equivalent to self-election, that he should no longer be chosen by general suffrage, but appointed solely by the votes of the cardinals. He claimed from the ecclesiastical councils that power which had been vested in them alone, the right to canonise; he claimed from the State that power which hitherto had been exclusively its own, the privilege of creating kings. Not without opposition, not without temporary reverses, were pretensions so lofty thrust upon the view of Christendom. Twice in this century was the pontiff driven from his capital, and forced, like Hildebrand, to purchase safety by exile. But the reverses were only the momentary receding of the wave; Rome had at this juncture the strength of Europe on its side. The armies of the Cross fought for it by land, the fleets of Venice contended for it by sea, and the Venetian victory decided its triumph. In less than a hundred years from the flight of Hildebrand, the pontiff stood upon the summit of the mountain, and looked down upon the kingdoms of the world as the provinces of his empire and the tributaries to his mighty power.

CHAPTER XXVIII.

SECOND REVOLT OF THE SCHOOL-LIFE.

AT the moment when the Papacy stood upon the mountain's brow, the mutterings reached their climax in the plain below. The Christian intelligence and the Christian heart were filled to overflowing with the spirit of revolution, and were no longer able to restrain themselves; they burst forth into torrents of indignation. We are altogether unable to place our hand upon the last straw which broke the back of the camel; we cannot tell what definite act brought into outward antagonism to the Papacy that life of the Christian Church which had long been secretly divorced from it. A process of separation is generally slow, but when it has arrived at its last stage it is always sudden. In this instance it emphatically proved so. As we stand and survey the scene, the transition from the long-hidden discontent to the openly-expressed aversion is swift and startling. We are prepared for it by no petty deeds of opposition. We stand for a moment in a misty atmosphere, and hearing no voices, we say all is peace; suddenly the mist clears away, and without warning, without preparation, we find ourselves in the centre of a vast battle-field, where three hosts are encamped to fight for the verdict of posterity. One of them is stationed around the capital of the West; it is the sons of the hierarchy, prepared to draw the sword for Papal dominion. Another lies in the valleys of Piedmont and Dauphiné, with the great Alps overhanging them, and the great hierarchy towering above them, a humble, unpretentious band, but strong in the very depth of their primitive simplicity; these are they who have been since known as the Waldenses. There is another band still arrayed, along the south-east of France, the descendants of that mighty intellectual revival whose birthplace had been the plains of Provence and Languedoc, the men of speculation, the men of thoughtful research, the men disposed to fight by theory rather than by action; these are they known as the Albigenses. Let us clearly distinguish between the second and the third company. They have this in common, that they are both modes of the revolutionary school-life, but they are altogether different modes of that life. The Waldenses are simple, the Albigenses are cultured; the Waldenses are morally earnest, the Albigenses are romantically enthusiastic; the Waldenses are seeking purity of life, the Albigenses are in search of a purer doctrine; the Waldenses are men of practice, the Albigenses are men of knowledge. They are united on one point, and on one alone: opposition to the power of the hierarchy. The miracle-plays and mysteries had contributed, as we have seen, to unite the earnestness of religion with the romance of chivalry; and the tendency to this blending has found its historical consummation in the union of those bodies of men, so dissimilar in character, and so unlike in temperament.

We propose to consider for a few moments each of these manifestations separately, and we begin with that party whose name is most familiar to the popular reader: the sect of the Waldenses. The opinions regarding their origin are many and conflicting; and were we writing a history of the Church, it would be necessary to examine the claims of each and to adjust the pretensions of all. As we are not writing a history of the Church, but attempting merely to trace the course of Christian development, we intend, instead of examining these conflicting theories, to offer a brief historical statement, which, if accepted, would form a harmonious link between them. We do so only tentatively, very much in the manner of the critics who have arranged the probable dates of Shakespeare's plays; in a matter where so much is obscure, it would be foolish and unscientific to attempt more than a plausible solution. There is, indeed, one theory regarding the Waldenses for which we can find no meeting-place; it is that of their own modern Church, which dates their origin from the very dawn of Christianity, and claims for their ancient bishops a direct succession from the apostles themselves. That there has existed in all ages a stream of pure Protestantism, whose continuity has never been broken, and whose waters have never been corrupted,—a stream which has been hourly fed by the fountain of life, and prevented from diverging by the embankment of divine grace,—

is a doctrine which has been dear to the heart of many evangelical Protestants. It is a doctrine, however, which, with one exception, all Protestant historians of the slightest eminence, be they evangelical, moderate, or negative, have rejected as contrary to fact. The exception to which we allude is that of one whose work was in his day considered a standard, and which in any day cannot be mentioned without respect. Dean Milner wrote what professed to be a history of the Christian Church; it was in truth a very admirable history of a very small part of it. To Milner the Christian Church was equivalent to the Church of developed Protestantism. Coming to his task with such a view, he was compelled to adopt one or other of two alternatives: he must either hold that the Christian life had during the long centuries of mediævalism slept the sleep of death; or he must find in the course of these centuries an undying remnant of God's people, stretching as a line of light through a dark world, and preserving, amidst persecution and tribulation, the pure doctrines afterwards promulgated by Luther. Milner adopted the latter alternative, and accordingly, in every reaction against the hierarchy, he is prepared to hear the ripple of this continuous, this spotless Protestant stream; the Waldenses are to him sojourners amongst this band of testifying pilgrims. We need not say that all historical criticism is at variance with such a view. It is opposed to facts, and it is opposed to human philosophy. No man ever produced the evidence for the existence of a Church miraculously, or even artificially, preserved from error; and if such evidence were produced, it would lower rather than heighten our conception of the modes of divine agency. No omnipotent mandate has ever said to the moral world, 'Let there be light'; if it did, that world would immediately cease to be moral, for the condition of all spiritual strength is conflict, and it is the fruit of conflict which makes the difference between the spontaneous beauty of innocence and the conscious charm of virtue. Christianity is a life; and it is the nature of life to grow, to expand from the little into the great, to develope from the child into the man. The history of Christianity is the history of a life developing; not the immediate creation of an Adam in the garden, but the slow and steady advance from infancy into maturity of an existence which has dawned in the midst of corruption, and will require through all its journey to contend with that corruption; sometimes manifestly progressing, sometimes apparently receding, conquering the spheres of its being one by one, and bringing forth its fruit only in due season. This being our view of the scope and purpose of the Christian life, we are naturally not eager to prove that Martin Luther was an anachronism, or to discover indications that his Protestantism was already fully developed in the middle of the twelfth century. We believe the history of the Catholic Church to be itself a growth of the Protestant principle, a gradual shading of the old into the new; we believe the scholasticism of that Church to have been the educational process of the Christian spirit, whereby it was trained for a sense of personal responsibility; and we believe the revolts against that scholasticism to have been the premonitory symptoms that such an age was coming, the indications that the school-life was becoming too old for school. The revolt of the Waldenses was one of these movements, and it is in this light that we intend to view them. We shall not claim for them what they did not claim for themselves, an apostolic succession of Protestant bishops; we shall not thrust upon them what they did not possess, a full acquaintance with the doctrines of Lutheranism; but we shall ask for them that place in history which they themselves aspired to fill, the right to be regarded as the pioneers of religious progress and the harbingers of a clearer day.

We now proceed to state, as briefly as possible, what seem to us to be the leading facts of the case. In the valleys of Piedmont and Dauphiné, forming a boundary-line between France and Italy, there dwelt for many centuries—we know not for how many—a very primitive and simple-hearted people. There was a singular analogy between their geographical and their social position: they lay at the foot of the Alps, and they lay at the foot of the ladder of society; in both senses they were the people of the valleys. They were humble, obscure, unknown to the great ones of the earth; they earned their livelihood by the sweat of the brow; they wore the wooden shoes of the peasantry; they knew nothing of luxury or refinement. Their poverty kept them beyond the pale of growing civilisation; but it kept them, at the same time, outside the range of growing corruption. The manners of early days linger longest in the villages; the poor are always the most conservative of old impressions, chiefly for this reason, that they are brought little into contact with the new. So was it with these dwellers in the valleys. They formed a real portion of the Catholic Church, and were under the government of Catholic bishops; but they were originally unable, and ultimately undesirous, to keep pace with the innovations of that Church. They had no rich patrons to endow monasteries with lands; no wealthy citizens to build them gorgeous cathedrals; no personal affluence to furnish them with the means of enriching and complicating their ritual. And so they remained in the valleys, in the rear of what was then called progress, until the growing power of the Papacy began, in its efforts after unity, to stretch alike over valley and mountain. In the eighth century there came a decree for uniformity of worship, and we remember how many parts of Italy resisted that decree. We have every reason to believe that some of the dissentient voices issued from the valleys; the dwellers in these regions had been made primitive by their poverty, and it is the characteristic of primitive minds to love spontaneity of action. Uniformity of worship would have been to them an abandonment of individual freedom, which they could not have accepted without murmurings of discontent. We pass over another hundred years, and we find that the rites of the Catholic Church have multiplied to an extravagant degree: formalism everywhere is struggling to press out spontaneous life, and the life of Christianity is making but feeble efforts to retard its progress. But there is one figure standing out conspicuously from all beside, holding up a threatening hand to the advancing phalanx of ritualism, and refusing to admit its force within his gates: it is Claudius, Bishop of Turin, a man whose name has come down to us as one of the lights in the Dark Ages. But Turin is in the vicinity of these valleys, and the valleys in all probability formed part of his diocese; if so, then their inhabitants must have even then exhibited a Protestant attitude, and anticipated by three centuries the work they were destined to do. From this time there is a long and unbroken silence over these glens, and we listen in vain for any indications of that life which had been so busy and so prophetic of greater work to come. It is probable that during the deep darkness of the tenth century,—a darkness which, as we have seen, proceeded chiefly from lethargic indifference,—the inhabitants of these lowly spheres were allowed to preserve in peace the comparative simplicity of their worship; while the fierce hierarchical struggles which marked the age of Hildebrand must have given the Church no leisure to cast its eyes on so unpretentious a region. Suddenly the blast of the trumpet of chivalry woke the world into a new life; the mountains came near to the plains, and the poor were exalted. The aristocracy began to retreat from the march of Papal dominion, and gradually fell back upon a position analogous to that of the peasantry. They, like the lower orders, were in search of spontaneity; not, indeed, a spontaneous worship, but a spontaneous literature. Imprisoned culture let loose bears a strong resemblance to primitive simplicity uncultured: both are a revolt against form, an opposition to convention, a repugnance to the restraint of outward authority. The chivalry of the Templars, the romance of the crusaders, the literary enthusiasm of Provence and its troubadours, all contributed to withdraw the heart of the higher circles from those rites and ceremonies of the Church, from which the lower orders of society had long since recoiled. And as the extremes of life met together, the different parts of the world itself drew nearer. The increasing enterprise of the fleets of Venice lessened the distance between land and land, and made the very sea a bridge to connect one country with another. Spots that had lately been desolate became vocal with life; districts which had been almost unknown burst forth into prominence; races, whom the quick march of the ages had left behind in the fields of the past, were invaded by the wheels of commerce and shaken from repose. Amongst those primitive bands dragged from their obscurity by the force of the great renaissance were the dwellers in the Alpine valleys. There came into the midst of them a wandering merchant of Lyons, named Peter Waldo. He was evidently a man of learning, a man of natural parts, and a man of moral earnestness. The spirit of the times had taken hold of him, and made him its own. He had been seized with the enthusiasm which had permeated the south-east of France: the enthusiasm for religious liberty, for emancipation from the hierarchy, for the privilege of private judgment, for the protection and consideration of the poor, for the universal rights of man. He had caught the intellectual and the moral fervour which had issued from the minstrelsy of Provence and Languedoc; he had come to feel in himself that life could be rendered beautiful, and he desired to have that feeling transfused through the brotherhood of humanity. He came into the glens of Piedmont, and he found there a spectacle which refreshed him: a race of men who, through another avenue, had approached the same temple of liberty; a race who, through the very absence of culture, had preserved that spontaneous freshness which had been created in himself by the outburst of a literary revival. The spectacle fired his enthusiasm anew. Here, indeed, was treasure hid in earthen vessels. Here was a company of reformers, who by the sheer force of nature had, through poverty and neglect and obscurity, kept alive that fresh life which France was only now receiving through the appliances of art. Was it not fitting that these men, who had done so much by unassisted nature, should obtain as their reward the assistance of art as well? France had its literature. Ought not the valleys of Italy to be furnished with a literature too,—a literature which should wake within them the echoes that still were dormant, and intensify the power of the voices that now were speaking? And where could there be found a literature so well adapted for such a race as the sacred volume itself, the book which speaks to all men, rich and poor, lord and peasant? Here the dweller in the valley would find a source of exaltation, —he would realize the greatness of that humanity that slept within him, the vastness of those possibilities which lay before him; and the words of the Christian record would come to him, as they came of old to the humble fishermen of Galilee, as a call to action and a promise of victory.

It was, we believe, such reflections as these that led Waldo to translate the four gospels from Latin into French, and to act himself as their expounder to the people. Probably most of his audience were themselves unable to read, and he felt that they could gather no adequate idea of the Scriptures from listening to the short and detached passages quoted by the priest in the sanctuary. He therefore not only translated the gospels, but he claimed the right of the laity to be their interpreters to the mass of the uneducated. The effect produced by his teaching was electrical; it was as if he had opened a door in the soul's prison-house and set it free. The valleys were stirred to their depths, and their primitive innocence began to shade into the possibilities of conscious virtue. When Waldo returned to Lyons he went not alone, he was followed by a crowd of those dwellers in the valleys. When he reached his native city, he seems to have constituted them into a distinct religious community,—a community whose priest was a layman, and whose teaching was derived from the exposition of the written word. There were many in the surrounding districts who sneered at the motley band; they called them the poor men of Lyons, the men of low degree, the men with the wooden shoes. But the hierarchy did not sneer; it deemed the matter so serious as to be worthy of a Council, a fact which alone shows significantly the growing influence of the people. The Council of course condemned the opinions of Waldo, but its condemnation could not quench them. He withdrew his followers once more within their native glens, and sheltered by the friendly obscurity of those sequestered shades, he began more widely to organize them. It is now that for the first time the inhabitants of the valleys come before us under a distinct name. They had existed for centuries, they had manifested a Protestant bias for centuries, but as yet they had been marked out by no separate designation; for the idea that they derived their name from dwelling in the valleys has now been abandoned by all competent critics. It is with the close of the twelfth century that their historical life begins. Then for the first time they burst upon our view, no longer as an obscure and nameless band, leading a hidden life, and holding an undefined faith, but as a fully equipped and regularly disciplined Church; guided by fixed principles, ruled by definite laws, and claiming an existence distinct from all beside, by assigning to its members the name of their leader— the Waldenses, the followers of Waldo.

It will be seen from this statement that we have adopted a highly eclectic position. We have done so, not that we may attempt the satisfaction of all parties, which proverbially pleases none, but solely in order that we may satisfy a difficulty in our own minds. This is one of those subjects in which we have felt ourselves between the horns of a dilemma. On the one hand, we lean strongly to the belief that the dwellers in the valleys of Piedmont manifested a Protestant tendency at least three centuries before the date at which we have arrived. On the other hand, we are thoroughly convinced that the inhabitants of those valleys derived their name from the merchant Peter Waldo, who lived in the twelfth century. We have sought to find a meeting place for these apparently conflicting statements, both of which we believe to be facts. We have rejected, on the one hand, the notion that the name Waldenses signifies the dwellers in the valley, and we have assigned to those inhabitants no name earlier than the days of Waldo. We have refused, on the other hand, to admit, what in many quarters has been too hastily assumed, that the derivation of their name from Waldo proves that from him also they derived their existence. A name is not an existence. The name Protestant was first given to those who protested against the decision of a Diet held in the sixteenth century, yet in this respect they had been preceded by a long train of forerunners. Waldo gave his name to the Waldenses, but we have no reason to suppose that he gave them his nature; it is far more probable that, in an age in which the minds of men were moving consentaneously, he was drawn towards them by beholding in them a nature kindred to his own. What, then, was that Protestantism which, after slumbering latently in the valleys, woke to the voice of Waldo? If we were asked to describe it by comparison, we should say that it was nearer to the Protestantism of Zwingle than to that either of Luther or of Calvin. Unlike Luther, it was averse to ceremonialism; unlike Calvin, it did not yet possess a developed theology; but it breathed the free spirit of the Swiss reformer, —it desired only air and ventilation and room. Whether, like Zwingle, it denied the inherent efficacy of the sacraments, we cannot tell; we should think it certain that to the priesthood it denied the monopoly of their administration. Indeed, this whole movement was originally rather anti-hierarchical than anti-Catholic. It opposed the temporal power of the Papacy; it opposed the multiplication of rites; it opposed the exclusive place of images in religious teaching; it opposed the ignoring of individual judgment, implied in the influence of the priesthood; and it opposed the tendency to confine the interpretation of Scripture within the hands of a clerical caste. These were truly Protestant elements; yet they did not exhaust Protestantism, did not yet touch that article which Luther declared to be the test of a standing or a falling church. It was impossible that at this particular era the doctrine of justification by faith should have conveyed to the Waldensian mind any but a repulsive meaning. The formula which would have expressed the religious orthodoxy of that day was justification by faith in the authority of the hierarchy,—an intellectual assent to the doctrine that the Catholic Church had received its power from God. It was precisely this intellectual assent that the Waldensian mind was weary of. It longed for something more than dogmatic belief; it wanted religious life. It seemed a slender ground of church-membership that a man should merely assent to the existence of a superior authority; it seemed as if a condition so wide would make room in the kingdom of heaven for the very extremes of morality. And so to that intellectual faith, which was the mark of current orthodoxy, the Waldenses opposed the necessity for a life of personal piety. They declared that the organ of divine vision was not the far-seeing intellect, but the pure heart; that the acceptable gift to Heaven was not a judgment willing to admit any proposition, but the offering up of a broken and a contrite spirit. They declared that the individual man had a burden of his own to bear,—a burden which no church-membership, founded on intellectual agreement, could remove,—a burden of personal responsibility for his thoughts and words and actions; and they pointed to the sense of this personal responsibility as a surer ground of admission into the kingdom of Christ, than any intellectual conviction that the kingdom of Christ was hierarchical. It is this endeavour after a Christian life which has invested the history of the Waldenses with its highest glory. They struggled to reach that light of purity which their hearts had pictured, and in which their imaginations beamed; and their struggles were not all in vain. Never since the days of the Galilean fishermen, had humble birth and adverse circumstances been ennobled by a morality so pure, by an integrity so stainless, by a sincerity so profound. A man might have walked from one end of these valleys to the other, laden with treasures of silver and of gold, and assuredly he would have emerged from their recesses unmolested and unharmed. This is, to our mind, the proudest triumph of the age of chivalry. We have seen with admiration how the knight could stoop to relieve the wants of the peasant; here the peasant himself has become the knight, who will not stoop to touch unlawful gain. The dwellers in the valleys were nature's chivalry; they mustered a moral force which all the armies of Papal Rome, and all the horrors of Papal torture, were ultimately unable to repel, and which eventually breathed a new and higher life into the very heart of its enemies.

We come now to the second body of insurgents against the Papacy. If the Waldenses occupied the valleys of society, the Albigenses may be said to have stood upon its heights. Their movement was the speculative side of the romantic impulse. It originated amongst the knights of Provence and Languedoc, and was patronised by Raymond of Toulouse, and other nobles of weight and influence. The Albigenses comprehended a multitude of sects, differing considerably from each other in their theological opinions, but there were certain intellectual features common to them all. Lord Macaulay, in an incidental sentence of one of his essays, has expressed his opinion that their theology was a mixture of Calvinism and Manichæism. This no doubt is substantially true; but the real point for investigation is, how two such elements as Calvinism and Manichæism could rest side by side in one system. They are clearly antagonistic elements. Calvinism says, 'God does all;' Manichæism says, 'There exists from eternity a material principle of evil, repugnant to the nature of God, independent of Him, and unconquerable by Him.' Is there any explanation by which we can account for the union in one theology of opinions so dissimilar and so discordant? We think there is, and we take the explanation to be this: each of these doctrines contained a spiritual truth, which had not been sufficiently emphasized by the hierarchy of that day. The spirit of Calvinism, abstracted from its dogmatic aspect, is the sense of an infinite, divine presence; the spirit of Manichæism, divested of its extravagance, is an overpowering sense of the horror of sin. Each of these elements had been diluted by the Church of the hierarchy. The sense of God's infinite presence had been weakened by the intervention of the image; the sense of the horror of sin was in the act of being blunted, by a practice of widespread prevalence — a practice which through the whole twelfth century had been growing in extravagance, but which had its germ in the past, and was destined to have its fruit in the future; we mean the granting of indulgences.

In the days of the far past, when the spirit of Christianity was struggling to preserve itself in separation from the spirit of paganism, it admitted of no compromise on the part of its adherents. Those who through stress of persecution were tempted to lapse from the faith, were seldom received back into the fold until they had passed a long probation and undergone a heavy penance. It became customary, however, to make an exception to this rigour in the case of the sick, the old, and the infirm. These could not be expected to endure the flagellations, the fasts, and the pilgrimages which were commonly prescribed as the evidences of repentance; and that religion which is essentially the soul of humanity, was unable, even in the interest of stern justice, to show itself inhumane. Accordingly, to those aged or infirm penitents there was granted an indulgence, or what in after ages came to be called by that name; the Church remitted their penalty, and received them back by an act of ecclesiastical grace. Even in these cases the Church was anxious to receive some impersonal equivalent, where such an equivalent could be obtained,—it expected pecuniary donations in lieu of personal penance; but these were the days of Christianity's poverty, and beyond their individual sufferings, the delinquents had in general nothing to offer in recompense. Thus far the practice of indulgences had its root in pure humanity; and had it ended there, its effect would have been comparatively harmless. But it did not end there. The time came when the Church and the State united into one kingdom, and the waves of a new civilisation began to sweep away many old forms altogether, and to

bear some into other modes of life. Amongst the
latter of these was this practice of indulgences; it
continued to live in mediævalism as it had lived in
the primitive centuries, but it existed no longer as
the product of Christian humanity, but as the fruit of
a theological dogma. We have seen how strong was
the mediæval tendency to dwell upon the divine side
of the Master's person; we are now to see how that
tendency was transferred to the Master's work. His
atonement was looked upon as something too majestic
to include the venial sins and foibles and frailties
of humanity, too grand to have any concern with the
little petty weaknesses which belong to human nature.
These were all bad and worthy of punishment, but
they were too earthly to be comprehended in a divine
scheme of salvation. Christ's work was a redemption
from the punishment of eternal death, and a remission
of those mortal sins which lead to eternal death; the
treatment of trivial diseases might be left to human
physicians. Even mortal sin had two hemispheres
of punishment,—one in eternity, the other in time;
Christ's work compassed the former, it was too great
to touch the latter. The remission of a sinner's
eternal punishment was one act; the remission of his
temporal punishment was a very different act: the
one sprang from God, the other was a question for
the hierarchy. Nor was it anywhere stated where
the temporal ended, and where the eternal began.
In a religion which fixes the final state of the soul at
death, the grave is the boundary-line between the
transient and the everlasting. But mediævalism did

not fix the final state of the soul at death. It allowed the disembodied spirit, whether of saint or sinner, to be pursued by the voices of time into that 'bourne whence no traveller returns;' as if to tell him that, though escaped from earth, he was still overshadowed by the wings of the hierarchy, and remind him that though the million debts had been discharged, the uttermost farthing had not yet been paid. So, by the light of later decisions, we are taught to interpret the scope of mediævalism; and seen in that light, we cannot deny that it presents an aspect of appalling power. We see the priesthood invested with a retributive authority, which not only stretches over all the kingdoms of the earth, but enters even into the world of the departed,—an authority from which there is no appeal either to earth or heaven, and no possibility of evading, even by the act of death. Truly the empire of the Cæsars was in comparison with this the sceptre of a child.

It was here that the opportunity arose for the revival of that ancient practice of indulgences, which had its birthplace in the Christian Church of the first centuries. The hierarchy had been entrusted with the power of inflicting temporal punishments; must it not also have the power to remit those punishments? Christ's work had only removed the penalty of eternal death; but Christ's merits went beyond His work; the intensity of that spirit with which He performed it was more than was required to accomplish salvation. Here, then, was a treasury of grace unappropriated, a power still available for action; He who had redeemed from everlasting punishment, might be granted an additional boon—the remission of His people's temporal sufferings. The intensity of His spiritual sacrifice would have been sufficient to accomplish this, had it been the work assigned Him to do; ought He not to receive it as a reward for having outrun His mission? The hierarchy asked that question, and they proceeded to answer it in their own favour. On the ground of Christ's super-abounding merits, they had the claim to be intercessors with Heaven for the remission of earthly penalties; they held the chains of human sorrow, they could loose as well as bind. They aspired to the proud prerogative of claiming from the tribunal of heaven the forgiveness of the men whom they favoured, and they declared that such intercession could never prove in vain. They aspired to a prouder eminence still: to fill up that which was behind in the sufferings of Christ, to do that which He had not done, to remit that which He had left unremitted, to grant exemption from temporal penalties in the name of His unappropriated merits.

But, now, on what principle was this intercession made? Was it that the leaders of the hierarchy had good evidence that the men whom they recommended were sincere penitents? Was it because the objects of their favour had, as in the Church of olden times, signalised their repentance by an act of outward penance?—the indulgence was expressly designed to obviate such a necessity. Was it that the priesthood had direct knowledge that the private characters of their votaries had passed through a stage of reformation? They granted indulgences at one sweep to all the crusading armies of Europe, men whom they had never seen, whom they did not know by name, and of whose individual conduct they were in absolute ignorance. It was an altogether different evidence which the priesthood demanded; it was the service of the Church, either by arms or money. Now, we must not misrepresent this feature of Catholicism. It was not that the priest accepted money, or accepted the service of war, as the price of that forgiveness which his intercession had procured; every Roman Catholic in the world would repudiate such a statement, and no Protestant has a right to charge him with holding a belief which he professes to repudiate. But the question which the Albigenses probably asked, and the question which we are inclined to ask with them is this, In what respect was this service a test of repentance? That which tests the moral nature, must surely be of a moral character. The possession of wealth, the possession of lands, the possession of physical strength and warlike enthusiasm, were great advantages to their possessor, but they did not involve of necessity an upright heart or a good conscience. The willingness to use these gifts in the cause of the Church might possibly have sprung from the ardour of religious zeal; but in an age when the favour of the Church was the pathway to outward prosperity, the fact might readily have admitted of more than one interpretation. We do not charge the hierarchy with all the effects of their system, we charge with those effects only the system itself; but in this view we must say that the basing of indulgences upon a material standpoint was a regress to pagan elements, which tended to deaden that conviction of evil which the spirit of Christianity has quickened in the heart of man. That was what the Albigenses thought when they supported Manichæan doctrines. They felt that sin was made too little of; and through the excess of their reaction, they made too much of it. They felt as if the leaders of the hierarchy were claiming power over it; and in their revulsion of feeling they made its power independent of God. They felt that the sense of its prevalence was being frittered away by the delusion of an easy conquest; and in the strength of their aversion to such a doctrine, they declared it to be unconquered and unconquerable, either by God or man.

It is now time to resume the thread of our narrative. It was not to be supposed that a movement so pronounced and so dangerous as that of the Waldenses and Albigenses would be permitted to pass unchallenged by the Church of the hierarchy. It was clear that the weight of priestly displeasure must fall upon the latter. The Waldenses were somewhat protected by their own poverty and humility; the Albigenses were standing prominently upon the heights, and could not possibly elude the eye. There was the less possibility of this from the present circumstances of the hierarchical Church. At the time when the Albigensian movement had reached its consummation, the Papal throne was occupied by one of the greatest intellects that ever filled the chair of St. Peter.

Lothario Conti, better known by his pontifical name of Innocent III., was a man who would have been distinguished in any age, but who in his own age was remarkable. Like Hildebrand, his education had been enriched by a diversity of experience. His career as a student was brilliant, and in the course of that career he passed with distinction through the learned institutions of Paris, Bologna, and Rome. He rose immediately into Church preferment; in the flower of his youth he had attained the lofty rank of cardinal, and at the age of thirty-seven he found himself seated on the Papal throne. His elevation to that dignity was instantly followed by an elevation of the dignity itself. His commanding talents, his brilliant scholarship, his literary eminence, his far-sighted policy, his sincere piety, his unblemished morality, his indomitable and inflexible zeal for the promotion of that cause which he believed to be the truth, all contributed to render the Papal power conspicuous in the eyes of the world. Never, perhaps, has the authority of a single man exerted, in the course of so few years, so potent an influence over so wide an area. He was pontiff at thirty-seven, and he died at fifty-six years of age, but during that period he dominated the world. There were few lands of the earth which the rod of his empire did not touch. It waved over Italy, it directed the succession of Germany, it interfered with France, it gave law to Spain, it reorganized the affairs of Norway, it claimed the sovereignty over England, it sent its commands into Armenia, it ruled the Latin kingdom of Jerusalem; nay, through the temporary conquest of Constantinople by the French and Venetians, it abolished for a time the distinction even between East and West. There was scarcely a sovereign of the earth who did not bow submissive to that rod. It kept young Frederic II. under its protection in Italy, and placed him afterwards on the throne of Germany. It compelled Philip Augustus of France to do justice to his injured wife. It prevented the king of Leon from marrying within the prohibited degrees. It demanded and obtained the oath of fealty from the king of Aragon. It opposed with success the pretensions of the Norwegian usurper Swero. It made the king of Armenia accept his dominion as a Papal gift. It deprived John of England of his crown, and conferred it upon Philip Augustus; and then, revoking the grant, restored it again to the suppliant delinquent, as an act of sovereign mercy; further than this the power of human empire could not go.

A potentate of such genius, backed by so powerful an organization, and commanding an influence so wide in its extent, was not likely to tolerate any heretical effort to subvert his authority. Innocent III. was not a cruel man; for the poor and weak he showed ever a kindly consideration, and Dean Milman even applies to him the attribute of gentleness. But the relation in which heresy stood to that age was one which precluded any treatment of it, however severe, from incurring the imputation of cruelty. The Church and the State had ceased to be merely united; they had become absolutely one, as they were in the pagan days of Augustus and Tiberius. The Church was the State, and the State was the Church; all political offences were violations of religion, and all religious offences were violations of State law. The heretic was therefore a criminal,—a man who had outraged the law of his country, and whose punishment for that outrage was demanded by every principle of justice. The Albigenses had put themselves in this position; they had set up their judgment in religious matters in opposition to that of the hierarchy, and had thereby publicly declared themselves the voluntary violators of national law; they were guilty of treason, and the punishment of treason was death. Nevertheless, when Innocent III. drew the sword, when he proclaimed a crusade against the Albigenses, and offered a plenary indulgence to all who should embrace his cause, he committed, in our opinion, the one political blunder of his life. We have already expressed our conviction that, from the Papal point of view, all crusades were political blunders; expedients successful for the time, but tending ultimately to weaken that authority which they were devised to sustain. It has proved emphatically true of all Churchmen, that 'they who take the sword perish with the sword.' When the spirit of Christianity resorted to physical force, it fell back upon the weapons of paganism; and the weapons of paganism, which had conquered the men of its own day, were utterly unable to subdue the lives of mediæval Christendom. Even the wars with Mohammedanism were the result of a mistaken policy; but by what name shall we designate the policy which could turn the sword against the school-life of the Christian Church? None knew better than Innocent that the Waldensian and Albigensian movements were reactions against a real defect in the spiritual life of the hierarchy; he proved this by instituting two new monastic orders, whose office was to foster piety. He ought to have left this new spiritual element of the orthodox Church to fight the battle alone with the spiritual element of the heretics, abiding by Gamaliel's counsel, and trusting to the triumph of that cause in whose justice he so implicitly believed. He did not do so; he prepared to vindicate his spiritual position by material weapons, and thereby eventually he lent strength to the opposition, and lowered that moral influence which ever goes far to decide the battle.

CHAPTER XXIX.

LAST TRIUMPH OF THE TEMPORAL PAPACY.

THE war upon which the Church of the hierarchy now entered was not so much a fierce struggle as a prolonged massacre. The odds were too unequal. The sons of the rising renaissance, bred in the lap of luxury, and domesticated by the amenities of social life, were no match for the sturdy warriors of the North, whose home was the camp, and whose music was the roar of battle. The Waldenses had indeed been inured to poverty, and in this respect they had the advantage over the natives of Southern France; but theirs had been a poverty which had rather necessitated patient endurance than active exercise; they had never found the opportunity of struggling with their condition, and therefore they were not strong. Accordingly, the crusade of the hierarchical Church was little more than an assault on the one hand, and an almost unresisting death on the other. The thought of leniency, of mercy, of compassion, never entered into the heart of the Papal party; they had a commission from Heaven to execute, and they performed their bloody work with the utmost Stoicism. No Smithfield fires of persecution, no Bartholomew massacres, no Bulgarian atrocities, surpassed the enormities of those deeds of cruelty which the crusaders perpetrated upon their hapless victims. They seem to have acted upon the principle, which is repudiated by the criminal jurisprudence of modern times, that it is better that ten innocent men should perish than that one guilty should escape. When they had taken a town by assault, they proceeded to execute their work of death without discrimination. In every such city there was always a multitude of orthodox Catholics mixed up with the Albigensian heretics; but to distinguish between them would have required a sifting process, which could only have begun when the force of passion had subsided. But this force of passion was looked upon as itself a divine impulse—God's command to avenge the breaking of His laws. The crusaders had no desire that it should cool down into calm policy, or subside into lukewarm prudence; they welcomed it as the evidence that they were Heaven's commissioners, they gave full play to it, they revelled in its influence. They followed up indiscriminately their work of slaughter; all who inhabited the captured city were sacrificed without distinction,—orthodox and heterodox alike went down beneath the sword of the conquerors. 'Kill them all!' they cried; 'the Lord will know His own.' It is not too much to say, that never since the institution of the Christian Church had the history of that Church appeared in so unfavourable a light. The spirit of Christianity appeared to have changed places with the spirit of paganism; to have mounted that very throne of materialism from which paganism had been deposed. In truth, however, such a statement by no means represents the case. The spirit of Christianity had in itself as much life as ever, but it had been dominated by the spirit of paganism. It had been conquered and imprisoned by a resurrection of the old forces of heathendom; a resurrection which renewed the idea of an empire in which the king was priest, and in which the priest was king; an empire where Church and State were not united, but one, and in which all difference had vanished between material force and spiritual power. The school-life was at war with the schoolmaster, and the schoolmaster had become the tyrant; the ward was at variance with the guardian, and the guardian had become the despot. The spirit of Christianity was assailed by weapons foreign to itself. The policy which the Papal party pursued towards heresy was precisely consistent with that policy which, in the granting of indulgences, it had pursued towards penitence. It tested penitence by a material standard—the provision of resources in money or in war; it applied to heresy also a material standard—the power of the sword and the horrors of the outward battlefield. It would have been well if the Papal party had paused here. War, however dreadful, is by its very nature evanescent, and tends to exterminate itself. But the Papacy proceeded to render perpetual that revival of pagan force which would naturally have been transitory. It proceeded to invest the acts of that day with a lasting significance, by the perpetration of a deed which has left an indelible stain on the history of mediæval Europe, the foundation of that institution which has associated the Christianity of the Middle Ages with the worst days of the Roman empire—the tribunal of the Inquisition.

It is only fair to state, that the best Roman Catholic writers are at one with Protestants in repudiating this system. It is only common justice to avow that, according to the best writers, Catholic or Protestant, the Inquisition, in its Spanish or most malignant form, became in the fifteenth century a purely political institution, passed from the hands of the Church into those of the State, and was thenceforth regarded by the Papacy as an object of aversion. This is the view of Ranke, of Guizot, of Leo, and of Llorente. But while we accept, and accept with gratification, the opinion of these eminent authorities, we cannot close our eyes to the fact, that the way to such a transference had been partially necessitated by circumstances. The Papacy of the fifteenth century was no longer the Papacy of the thirteenth; its material glory had departed, its unity was broken, its temporal power was rapidly passing away. It was no longer able to enforce its physical penalties by physical weapons; the State had obtained the empire over it, and as the voluntary servant of the State it could alone be strong. In such circumstances, it was easy to relinquish a possession which it had not the strength to support, and no sacrifice to part with that whose potency had lost everything but the name. At the period in which we now stand, it was all the reverse. The ecclesiastical power ruled the world. Upon a throne, exalted above all the dynasties of the earth, sat a potentate who incarnated in his own person the majesty of empire and the authority of priesthood; in whose right hand was a sword, and in whose left a cross; whose will was the law of humanity, and whose law was the destruction of human will. Around his person all objects met together in an artificial unity. All ages met there; the paganism of Augustus and Tiberius sought to thrust itself upon the Christianity of the monk and the cloister. All nations met there; East and West had for a time united, and Europe had established itself in the heart of Asia. All ranks met there; the Papacy was the head of a republic, in which any man, however lowly, might rise to heights of stupendous power. At the opening of the thirteenth century, the Papacy was absolutely supreme; the originator of every movement, the breath of every wind that blew, it moved the sceptres of sovereigns, it sharpened the swords of armies; apart from this power, the world could do nothing. And it was precisely in this age of unbroken Papal dominion that the Inquisition emerged into being. One word, one gesture, one look, from the pontiff would have crushed it at its birth; but that word was not spoken, that gesture was not made, that look was not given. Nay, it is impossible to conceive that without the direct mandate of the pontiff such an institution could ever have existed at all; and all history points to the conviction that it proceeded from such a mandate. It had its germ in the brain of Innocent III.; its expansion in the Council of Toulouse, which was emphatically a hierarchical council; its maturing in Gregory IX., who formed the inquisitors into a distinct court; and its full development in Innocent IV., who gave to that court its complete organization. The Inquisition was really a continuation of that crusade which Innocent III. had proclaimed against the Albigenses; an attempt to render perpetual that exercise of physical force which had been brought to bear upon religious questions. The spirit of the Inquisition was a crusading spirit. It started from the principle, that the accused should be considered guilty until he was proved to be innocent. The heretic was in reality judged beforehand. He was not permitted to confront his accuser, he was not suffered to see the witnesses against him, he was not even allowed to know the precise offence with which he was charged. The reason of the last prohibition, indeed, is probably not far to seek; the inquisitor in all likelihood did not himself know. He had in his mind the impression of a vague general accusation of heresy, which he was called upon by his office to substantiate in detail; but to get those details, he was in general obliged to trust to the testimony of the unfortunate culprit. The heretic was asked to confess, he commonly replied that he had nothing to confess; he was thereupon, for an indefinite period, remanded to prison, his effects were seized, and his friends immediately went into mourning. The custody of the grave, the enclosure of the coffin, the trammels of the winding-sheet, were not reckoned more secure than was the grasp of the inquisitors. It was felt instinctively, that in the pleasant light of the sun, in the busy haunts of men, in the scenes of social intercourse and domestic enjoyment, the victim of ecclesiastical displeasure would appear no more. When next he came before the tribunal it was after a long lapse of time, when the sympathy of public excitement had died away, and when he himself was regarded as one among the dead. He was interrogated as to the whole course of his past life; if his answers were unsatisfactory, if they conveyed the notion of a mental reservation, or suggested the thought of something yet to be explained, the blank left in his information was filled up by physical torture. If in his agonies he uttered words of self-condemnation, the utterance was accepted as a full confession of guilt, dispensing with all need of further inquiry; and he was handed over to the authority of the secular arm, from whose grasp he by no means came forth until he had paid the uttermost farthing; sometimes by death at the stake, sometimes by death on the scaffold, and occasionally by life as a galley slave, which was worse than death itself.

In estimating the horror of this institution, we ought, if we can, to separate between the system which produced it and the individuals who inflicted it. The individuals were not of necessity, or in themselves, cruel men. Innocent III. has been honoured by the ascription of gentleness; his commissioner, Dominic, the very founder of the institution, was by nature by no means hard-hearted. The inquisitors were, for the most part, in all other relations of life, capable of the average amount of humanitarian sentiment; we can quite well imagine one of them, on his return from an inquisitorial examination, shedding genuine tears over a spectacle of suffering, and feeling real sorrow for a tale of distress. But in this particular relation of life the inquisitor felt it his duty to let his heart become adamant. When he dealt with religious heresy, he was precisely in the same position as is the modern judge who pronounces sentence of death on the criminal convicted of murder. Murder is not so revolting to the modern heart as was heresy to the mediæval, for heresy was itself regarded as the murder of the soul. And just as it is the duty of the judge to abstract the prepossessions of individual feeling from his review of legal evidence, so the inquisitor felt it to be his duty, in conducting a trial for religious heresy, to steel himself against the promptings of humanity, and be stern in the service of God. The barbarity of the Inquisition was far too deeply rooted to be the result of mere personal cruelty. It had its source in something more radical than the passions of the heart; it sprang from an error of the intellect. The intellect is the road to the heart, and a man's intellectual belief is the measure of his moral action. The Inquisition sprang from the revival of the pagan idea, that force is the test of greatness, and that strength is identical with virtue. It arose from the resuscitation of that belief which once dominated the world, but which the Christian spirit had surmounted; the belief that the possession of power is the evidence of divine favour, and that resistance to such power is resistance to divine will. Above all, it emerged from the conviction that all forces, religious or political, were forms of one great force,—the paramount authority of the State ruler; and that where a religious force was in opposition to the paramount authority, it ought to be crushed by the hand of the ruler, and extinguished by the fires of persecution. Nay, in this respect, we have no hesitation in saying that the paganism of mediæval Christendom was a vast advance on the paganism of the second century. The paganism of Nero, of Trajan, of Marcus Aurelius, of Antoninus Pius, of all the emperors up to Decius, never seems to have resorted to an organized persecution. It persecuted merely from the anger of the moment, roused into temporary wrath by some passing incident or transient suspicion. Its earliest persecutions were but the outbursts of popular fury, venting blindly its disappointment upon those whom it imagined to be the authors of a famine, or the causes of a pestilence, or the occasions of a national reverse; they swept in swift gusts across the sea of human life, and then as quickly subsided into a settled calm. But the persecutions of mediævalism were no popular outbursts, no ebullitions of vulgar anger, no manifestations of mere superstitious fury. They were intellectual devices, planned by human reason, devised by calm judgment, methodized by careful deliberation, and carried out with systematic precision. They came from the spirit, not of Nero nor of Trajan, but from the more developed spirit of Decius and of Diocletian; they exhibited paganism in its full strength, in its perfect consolidation, not as a mere feeling of the heart, but as a thought which had obtained the empire over the judgment, the imagination, and the reason of mankind.

It was in strict pursuance of this pagan principle that the Church of the hierarchy proceeded every day to give fresh emphasis to the fact of its independent existence. The Waldensian and Albigensian heresies had been movements of the laity; it was imperative, therefore, that the laity should be made to feel more keenly than ever the Brahminism of Christianity: the predominance of a sacerdotal caste, whose province it was to rule over them, but whom they themselves were unable to approach by any conceivable efforts. They must be made to feel how great, how impassable was that gulf that yawned between them and the hierarchy; how unapproachable were those privileges which the priesthood enjoyed as a birthright; how unassailable was that power which the Papacy derived directly from the King of kings. To this end pointed all the measures of the age: the fourth Lateran Council of 1215 made it obligatory that confession should be offered to a priest; the Council of Toulouse, in 1229, forbade to the laity the Scriptures in the vulgar tongue. It seemed for a time as if humanity were about to surrender all rights except that of submission. The Albigenses in every quarter were repressed; the Waldenses buried themselves again in their mountain fastnesses; the kings of the earth bent low and touched the dust. During the last three decades of the first half of this century, there stood one solitary figure breasting the torrent of despotism, a figure so conspicuous by its erect attitude amid the crouching of all other forms, that it has survived the mists of ages, and still lives in modern memory: it was Frederic II., Emperor of Germany. If Innocent III. was the most remarkable of mediæval pontiffs, Frederic II. was the most remarkable of mediæval kings. He combined those qualities, which in the sovereign of any age are rare, which in a sovereign of the Middle Ages are scarcely to be found: military genius and intellectual acquirements. Struggling with insurmountable difficulties, contending with hopeless odds, oppressed through life by foreign and domestic foes, assailed even by the ingratitude of those of his own household, this man yet obtained over the heart of Europe the victory which he could not obtain over its dominions. His foundation of the University of Naples; his encouragement of the medical school of Salerno; his accessibility to all the learning, the art, and the poetry of his day; his personal merit as an author, so rarely found in any sovereign, ancient or modern; his possession of those knightly accomplishments which spring as much from the heart as from the intellect; his ability to speak six languages, at a time when few men could correctly speak their own; above all, his defence of national freedom against ecclesiastical supremacy, at a season when ecclesiastical supremacy was universally conceded, conspired to make him then, and have conspired to render him still, an object of undying interest. We have more than once in the course of this work been tempted to draw historical parallels; it seems to us that here we may draw another. We have always felt that there are many points in which Frederic II. of Germany resembles his illustrious namesake of Prussia. Both lived at periods of extreme political conservatism, which yet contained the germs of coming revolution. Both spent their early years under the influence of a restraint which was far from agreeable: the Prussian king under that of a stern father, the German emperor under that of a rigid pontiff. Both emerged from that restraint, with theological opinions which, to say the least, were free-thinking. Both surrounded themselves with the company of the most illustrious literary men whom their age had produced. Both aspired to be themselves worthy to rank amidst that company, and sought to win a personal niche in the temple of literary fame. Both were animated by an ardent patriotism for their mother-land,—the one for Italy, the other for Prussia. Both struggled to secure the welfare of that land, through wars, and privations, and dangers,—sometimes inspired with hope, and sometimes sunk in despair; but in hope and despair alike unyielding still. In the result of their lives, indeed, the parallel broke down. Frederic of Prussia, after being beset by the armies of continental Europe during seven years of alternate victory and defeat, came forth with the palm of the conqueror, and returned to his capital in triumph. Frederic of Germany, after thirty years of struggle, after courage not less conspicuous, and heroism not less signal, sank, weary, by the wayside, and died in the heat of the day. Yet it may be doubted if the memory of the German emperor did not receive as proud a triumph as the person of the Prussian king. For long years he was cherished in the hearts of his people. There was a strange expectation floating ever through the land, that one day he would rise from the dead and finish that work which he had begun,—that even death had only vanquished him for the hour, and would be forced to give him back again to complete the liberation of his country. It was one of those anticipations which, while delusive, and even absurd, in the letter, are yet in the spirit prophetically true. The spirit of Frederic did not die; it was crushed, it was buried, but it was not dead; it was to rise again in a greater leader, and to pursue its work of liberation under higher and more spiritual impulses.

Meantime, however, the death of Frederic extinguished the last spark of opposition to the temporal power of the Papacy, and the pontiff cast his eye over the kingdoms of the earth, and called them all his own. And, now, let us look once more at this gigantic power, which has arrived at its full stature. It will be our last look; never again through all the ages shall we behold it in such splendour. A few brief years and its glory will be departed, its unity broken, its authority despised, its armies disbanded, its fulminations received with ridicule and contempt; it has arrived at the summit, and will soon begin to descend. Yet how proud is that summit at which it has now arrived! If ever the mere force of will could be an object worthy of veneration, it must be the force of that Papal will which raised the See of Rome from a simple bishopric into an empire well-nigh co-extensive with the world. Standing on the brow of the mountain, we view with amazement the steepness of that ascent by which the Papacy has climbed to power. We see it at the foot of the hill, as yet only meditating its upward journey, — claiming, indeed, an honoured place amongst the bishoprics, but rather for its association with St. Peter than for any merit peculiar to itself. We see it advanced one step on its journey, aspiring to priority amongst the episcopal dignities, claiming the uppermost room at the feast and the chief place in the synagogue. We see it progressing farther still, seeking to transform the Church into a representative monarchy, of which itself should be the head and centre. We see it then making strides of advancement, no longer satisfied with being head of a representative monarchy, but aspiring to the sovereignty of an absolute ecclesiastical dominion. We behold next its revulsion from the authority of the State, its refusal to render unto Cæsar the things which were Cæsar's, its claim to an independent existence and to a separate empire. Last of all, we witness the greatest of all its pretensions: the attempt, and the successful issue of the attempt, to subordinate the State itself into the position of one of its vassals—to hold the Church and the world alike within its sway; to rule with an undivided sceptre, unrivalled and alone.

Such was the proud pre-eminence to which the Papacy had now attained, a pre-eminence towards which all its footsteps had been bent, and which all its measures had been designed to achieve; the last step of the Isidorian decretals had been reached when the State acknowledged the pontiff as its sovereign lord. And yet in this hour of triumph, the causes were already in preparation which would hasten the hour of downfall. From this epoch of the Papacy there issued two distinct streams,—a stream of spiritual experience, and a stream of outward circumstances,—unconnected in their course, but tending towards one common ocean. Both were steadily and surely to flow towards the same goal—the emancipation of the school-life, and the opening of a higher age; both were to progress towards one end, and pause not until their waters should be lost in waters mightier still. We intend to follow the course of each of these. We begin with the stream of spiritual experience, whose windings we shall trace in what remains of this and in the two succeeding chapters. We recur to a remark which we made at the close of Chapter xxviii. We there pointed out that Innocent III. was conscious of a spiritual want in the hierarchy, which had given colour to the Waldensian movement; and we saw that, with the view of remedying that want, he had instituted two new monastic orders. These orders were the Dominicans and the Franciscans, names which have been immortalized in subsequent history. We have said that they were instituted by him; to speak with strict accuracy, we should rather say that the one was originated, and the other utilized by him. The Franciscan movement was in its germ really spontaneous, and therefore more directly allied to the spirit of incipient Protestantism. Indeed, the fact that either of these orders should have been confirmed by the pontiff, points, in our view, to the conclusion, that the existing want of the Church had been felt by earnest minds within its pale. The heart of Christendom, even of orthodox Christendom, looked out upon the Waldensian movement with a strange feeling of admiration mingled with its fear. It beheld a company of men seeking to realize the ideal of that apostolic life which the world had long surmounted, and it asked, not without a sense of pain, where such an ideal was to be found in the bosom of the hierarchy. Where was now the morality which divine lips had proclaimed, in the sermon on the mount, to be the highest standard of conceivable perfection,—the morality which had its root in poverty of spirit, and its fruition in the power to exist in persecution? Where was that self-denying spirit which had gone forth on its missionary journeys without gold or silver or purse, making no provision for the morrow, and trusting to the divine strength of the hour? Where was that singleness of heart which had ennobled humble fishermen, and poor tent-makers, and despised tax-gatherers,—which had made heroes of the world's weak ones, and kings of the men whom paganism would have held as slaves? Where, finally, was that unselfish society which had all things common, which called nothing its own, which lived only in the community of its members,—that society in which the individual repudiated the glory of personal riches, and valued wealth alone as a means of making wealthy? These days were all gone, and in their room there had crept into the Church of the apostles the lust of the flesh, and the lust of the eye, and the pride of life; the desire, at any price, for all the kingdoms of the world, and the glory of them; the willingness, on any terms, to purchase outward power; the preference, on every side, of the seen and temporal to the unseen and eternal. Ought these things so to be? Was not the spirit of Christianity being crucified afresh, and put to an open shame? was not paganism itself being restored to a firmer throne, and placed upon a stronger basis? Surely these despised dwellers in the valleys were not entirely wrong.

Such was the cry that went up from the earnest minds of Christendom; the Papacy heard it, and answered it, and its answer was the institution of the Dominicans. It seemed to the Papal power that there lay open to it a course by which it could restore the fervour of apostolic days without diminishing its own material grandeur. Without being itself missionary, might it not be the sender forth of missionaries? without being itself poor, might it not commission to evangelize the world a new band of disciples, possessed of no worldly substance? Had not the first apostles gone forth at the command of a divine head to teach all nations, to baptize all men in His name? And was not the Papacy the representative of that divine head? was it not the vicar of Christ on earth, the vicegerent of God below, the visible manifestation to the world of the power that rules in earth and heaven? Why should not the pontiff still send out his missionaries to preach, to convert, to comfort, to support the weak, and bring down the pride of the strong? Why should not these missionaries, in obedience to a command which still represented the divine, lead lives of poverty, of privation, of toil, trust for their subsistence to the benevolence of the souls they cured, and find their highest joy in making others glad? And so, as an attempt to work out this thought, the Dominican order arose, an order which sought to transplant the shores of Galilee into the plains of mediæval Europe. They, like the apostles of old, were commanded to go and teach all nations. They, like the seventy disciples, were enjoined to take for their journey neither silver nor gold nor apparel. They, like the listeners to the sermon on the mount, were told to take no thought what they should eat or drink, or wherewithal they should be clothed, but to trust for their nourishment to Him who fed the ravens and clothed the lilies. And it was marvellous how warmly the world welcomed them; a welcome which proved beyond all controversy how deeply had been wanted such a manifestation of the Christian spirit. In a very few years the pagan ideal grew dim, and the Christian ideal of self-sacrifice began to resume its sway. These sons of voluntary poverty were the observed of all observers, and the admired of all admirers. They multiplied day by day; their ranks were hourly crowded with new recruits; their influence was yearly expanded over all society, until they came at last to mould the counsels of kings. They stretched from sea to sea, and from shore to shore. They passed into France, and secured a chair of theology in the University of Paris; they went over to England, and founded a monastery at Oxford. They planted monastic institutions in every nation of Europe, in nearly every nation of Asia, in many parts of Africa, and eventually in the new world of America; they revealed, for the first time in history, the practical power which dwelt in Christian mediævalism.

But whatever the Dominicans were, that were the Franciscans with a tenfold intensity. Theirs, as we have seen, was originally a more spontaneous movement, and to this extent it was nearer to Protestantism. Their character and history have been strikingly epitomised in the life of their founder, Francis of Assisi. That life connected two moral worlds,—the world of romance, and the world of religious earnestness. He was born in the palmy days of the French renaissance,—the days of chivalry, of knightly accomplishments, of the love-song, the joust, and the tournament. He was bred on the lap of luxury; his father was in trade, and had acquired great possessions; and the facilities which such wealth afforded gave the youth easy access to the society of the opulent and the cultured. Into that society he plunged with avidity; in its atmosphere of polished gaiety he found a congenial home. He joined in all the pageants of the age, was foremost at the tilt and the tournament, was conspicuous in the feats of chivalry, was distinguished above his fellows in the accomplishments of the knight and gallant; so thoroughly, indeed, did he breathe the French spirit, that his original name of John was superseded by that of Francesco, or the little Frenchman. Amid this life of gaiety, a discerning eye might have detected a germ of the future; even in these days he was never known to turn a deaf ear to the cry of distress, and he was ever as lavish in providing for the pleasures of others as he was in indulging his own. Suddenly over this fair scene there fell a black cloud; Francis was prostrated on a bed of sickness, and the shadows of death seemed to be drawing near. The world, and the pomp of the world, faded from his vision, and, in communion with his soul, he stood alone. The crisis passed; he recovered, and the world came back to him, but it came back with a changed countenance; its glory was departed, its gold had become dross, its garments were moth-eaten, its pleasures were dust and vanity. From his bed of pain he arose a new man, — an earnest, devoted, self-denying man. From that pride which chivalry had engendered, he sank into the profoundest humility, into the deepest conviction of his own utter nothingness. No sooner had it become a conviction than it passed into action; if he was in reality poor, why should he seem to be rich? He dedicated all that he had to God. He exchanged his clothes with a strolling mendicant, and wore ever after the meanest attire. He abjured all family ties; he resigned his claim to the paternal inheritance; he begged his bread at the gates of the monasteries. His example became contagious; in a little time he had gathered a small company around him, and to them he unfolded his rule of life. But his own life was larger than his rule; it brimmed over with enthusiasm for the welfare of humanity. In the glow of that enthusiasm, he felt his individual nature to be lost. As a man with a strong end in view knows not how many miles he travels, nor feels the weariness that is creeping over his frame, so Francis of Assisi, travelling over the road of life in pursuit of his brother's good, knew not how hard he toiled, and felt not how arduous was the way. He sent a mission to Morocco to convert the Moors; he went in person to the East to ask from the Sultan some indulgence for the Christian captives; he wrought with his own hands for the building of churches at home. Nor was it only in spiritual matters that he desired the health of his brother; his was a practical Christianity. He went among the lepers in the hospital of Gubbio, and there, in the presence of the most loathsome disease which humanity has ever encountered, he tended its victims with an assiduity and a tenderness which no relative dared to manifest; stooping to the most menial offices, and ministering to their deepest necessities, alike of body and of soul. And let it be observed, that this instinct to supply the temporal wants of human nature was no ephemeral impulse, arising from the momentary excitement that stirred a single man; it was a principle of life, which the founder of the order communicated to all his followers. In proportion as these followers multiplied, the spirit of active benevolence increased. In the next century, Europe was ravaged by one of the most terrible pestilences which have ever desolated its shores; strong lives were stricken in a moment, and the world in its terror forsook them and fled. But in that hour of danger one band remained stedfast at the post of duty; fearless amidst the fearful, firm amidst the wavering, calm amidst the panic-struck, resigned amidst the despairing, the Franciscan friars tended the last moments of the plague-stricken, and there died of their dauntless band 124,000. There have been noble battlefields in the history of mediævalism,—fields which have displayed the courage of human nature, and the instinctive chivalry which dwells in the human heart; but, to our mind, the noblest, the proudest, the most heroic of them all, is that vast field of mediæval Europe, where, in the path of duty, and in the enthusiastic love of man, the 124,000 Franciscans lay down to die.

It was when the life of Francis drew near its close that there occurred that remarkable episode which has excited the admiration of one party and the ridicule of another. In an ecstasy of prayer, in a moment of rapt enthusiasm,—when the world, and the objects of the world, had completely lost their hold over sense and brain,—he was confronted by a mysterious heavenly stranger, bearing a sword in his hand. He approached the eager suppliant, and imprinted upon his body five distinct wounds, the same which Christ had received in the agonies of crucifixion. We have no doubt at all that the vision was subjective, we have equally little that the wounds were unconsciously self-inflicted; a frame attenuated by intense thought, wearied with long watching, worn out with fasting and with voluntary penury, might well present distorted impressions to a highly-imaginative mind. Yet it does not seem to us that the matter is a subject for ridicule; we are rather inclined to recognise in it the prophecy of coming development. Whence this eagerness of Francis to appropriate the wounds of Jesus? Was it not really an eagerness to appropriate more of His human nature? We have seen how the sense of His divinity had almost absorbed the thought of His humanity; we have seen how His human presence had been supplied by the presence of the Virgin Mother: was there not here the longing for a return, a desire to go back to the earthly life of the Master, and to see Him as He was in the fashion of a suffering man? The longing expressed by Francis of Assisi was to find more vehement utterance in after days.

The death of this man was consistent with his life; in the last scene of all, his humility reached its climax. He felt the end approaching, and he prepared to meet it in that attitude which he had maintained through his whole career. As if death itself were not a sufficient mark of human poverty and helplessness, he desired to be carried out to the church and laid on the bare ground; in that posture, so expressive of his sense of human nothingness, the founder of the Franciscans closed his eyes and fell asleep. His memory did not die with him; he was greater in his death than in his life—more honoured, more influential, more potent. For the first time since the days of early Christianity, a gentle, self-denying life achieved by self-sacrifice an influence which armies by conquest failed to win. Looking back upon him through the ages, it is not at once easy to say what precise place he should occupy in history; not easy to separate his character, alike from the extravagant adulation of his friends and the unjust detraction of his foes. Of his personal sincerity, his piety, his earnestness, his self-denying zeal for the welfare of humanity, there can be no doubt; and that the method by which he exhibited these qualities was carried to extravagance, there can be equally little. It is, indeed, a very simple process to say, that this man was a 'delirious fanatic;' nor do we in the least object to the expression, provided only it be conceded that it explains nothing. We want to know what was the fever and what was the fanaticism? Fevers frequently spring from social neglect; fanaticism is not seldom the result of social reaction. The fanaticism of Francis was emphatically so. The moral atmosphere had long been impure, and the elements which conduce to life had been looked upon with contempt. When the reaction came, it came furiously, driving helplessly before it the minds and hearts of men, stringing up the nerves into excitement, and firing the blood into fever. Francis of Assisi was the first fruit of this reactionary movement, which, in relation to the hierarchy, was almost a Protestant movement. He burned with that sense of individual responsibility which had well-nigh been buried in the collective unity of the Church. He glowed with the spontaneous fervour of a life which had awakened to the joys of personal religion. He expressed that spontaneity in a collection of Italian hymns, the earliest written in the dialect of his native country; hymns brimming with the enthusiasm of the love of nature, the love of humanity, and the love of God. And if, in the reaction from long torpor, he felt too deeply the awfulness of human responsibility; if, in the revolt from hierarchical pride, he was overweeningly impressed with the duty of self-abnegation; if, in short, in the suddenness of his waking, he was surprised into an excitement which disordered the balance of his mind, the fault lay with the system he had surmounted, and the virtue was all his own.

CHAPTER XXX.

SEARCH FOR A RULE OF CONDUCT.

WE proceed to trace still further the development of that remarkable moral movement which had already taken its rise in the Catholic Church, and was now widening towards the mighty sea. The Dominicans and Franciscans, in common with other monastic orders, were bound by a threefold vow of chastity, poverty, and obedience. In their case, however, the vow seems to us to have had a special significance. It united them to three ages of history: one in the far past, one in the generation that was fading, and one that had its being in the vigorous life of the present hour. The vow of poverty connected them with the far past; with the days when the gospel was preached to the poor, and when the common people heard it gladly. The vow of chastity connected them with that age of chivalry, which was already dying; the age when man transferred to woman a reflection of that holy light which he had caught from the ideal vision of the Virgin Mother. The vow of obedience connected them with the iron present; with the temporal power of the Papacy, with the indomitable strength of the hierarchy, with all that reminded them that they were the subjects of an absolute dominion. It was not long, however, before it became evident that one of the two parties lived in the past alone; not long ere the Dominicans and Franciscans revealed a chasm in their midst. Both had vowed poverty, but to each of them it had been a different vow; to the Dominicans it was the ordination to an official ministry, to the Franciscans it was the consecration to a personal life. The Dominicans thought it sufficient not to be rich; the Franciscans deemed it imperative to be in absolute need. The Dominicans abjured the luxuries of life; the Franciscans denied themselves almost its necessities. The Dominicans were well content to possess as an order that wealth which they could not hold as individuals; the Franciscans refused to the community the possessions which they held sinful in the man. A difference so considerable, and threatening day by day to become more marked, was not likely to be contemplated by the Papacy without anxiety. The Pope interfered to restore harmony. He claimed for himself all the possessions of both orders; but he told them that they might freely use that which they could not own, might dwell in the lands and in the castles which belonged to their master, and might live sumptuously as guests while yet in themselves they were penniless and destitute. The reconciliation between this world and the world to come savoured somewhat of sophistry, and was not likely to convince any one not desirous to be convinced. Accordingly, some believed and some doubted. The majority of the Franciscan order succumbed to the lenient interpretation, and resigned themselves to the enjoyments of the present world; but there parted from the midst of them a stream which never returned, a band who held fast by the rigid rule, and whom no threats nor promises could draw again within the dominion of the Papacy. They claimed to be the true followers of Francis of Assisi; their fervour supplied the place of their original numerical weakness, and their number itself was augmented day by day. Scattered up and down through many lands, hunted by hierarchical persecution and Dominican fury, stamped by so many epithets of contempt that their individuality has been almost lost to history,—appearing at one time under the name of Spirituals, at another as Brethren of the Free Spirit, now as the Fraticelli, now as the Beghards, and now again as the Beguini,—they held through all opprobrious names one common unity of nature, and one simultaneous attitude towards the Papal power. It was an attitude of defiance; a defiance not sufficiently wide-spread to constitute a revolt of the school-life, yet revealing a weapon of attack which no scholastic revolution had as yet dared to wield—the power of the pen. For the first time the Papacy was attacked by literature. In the early part of this century there had appeared a remarkable book, of unknown authorship, which bore the name of *The Everlasting Gospel*. To be the production of an unscientific age, it was a work of extraordinary merit; for this, if for no other reason, that it recognised in human history a process of development. It started, as all books of that day started, from certain theological premises, which were assumed to be true; and then, proceeding from the divine to the human, it showed how the nature of man reflected the nature of God. There were three persons in the Trinity, and each of these had a distinct manifestation: the Father was the manifestation of power, the Son of wisdom, the Spirit of goodness or inward purity. Each of these manifestations had occupied in turn the sphere of human history. The first age had been that of the Father; it was the age of power, of physical strength, of temporal dominion, of material majesty, of government by the rod of fear. The second age was that of the Son; it was the period of wisdom, of revelation, of light,—the period when men had ceased to be mere mechanical instruments, and were desirous to examine and analyse the objects which lay around them. But there either had begun to appear, or there was shortly to appear in the future, a third and higher manifestation—that of the Holy Spirit; a manifestation which must supersede those of the Father and the Son, and reign with an empire unfading and imperishable; the manifestation of goodness, of purity, of love, of the heart unsullied, of the mind at peace, of the life made beautiful, of the will of earth harmonious with the will of heaven: this was the perfect fruit of the gospel tree. It was this remarkable work which Gerhard, one of the recusant Franciscans, now sought to use as a weapon against the hierarchy. He published an exposition of it, in which he proceeded to apply its statements to the features of his own age. Two of the epochs were already past. The age of power had yielded to the period of reason; and the period of reason itself was yielding to another age. A new day had dawned for the world; the proclamation of the gospel of love, the gospel which made all men equal, which levelled the distinction of rich and poor, which forced every man to feel his inherent poverty. The angel of that everlasting gospel, whose coming had been predicted by the seer of Patmos, had already been flying through the air, bearing its universal tidings; that angel was Francis of Assisi. He had been sent to proclaim the essential brotherhood of man, the breaking down of that middle wall of partition which the hierarchy had raised, the abolition of priestly caste, the establishment of Christian equality—an equality whose bond of union was the sense of destitution, of poverty, of nothingness. This had been the work of Francis, and it must go on until its task was done. All barriers must be broken, all restrictions must be cleared away, all hindrances to a united brotherhood must be swept into oblivion; and that age of wisdom, which had been claimed as the exclusive possession of the priesthood, must yield to the age of love, which was as universal as the Spirit of God. This was bold language, but bolder remained behind. Scarcely had the hierarchical world recovered breath from the surprise of this assault, when John Oliva followed up the attack of Gerhard by an attack more acrimonious still. If Francis was the apocalyptic angel, Papal Rome was the apocalyptic Babylon; Babylon drunk with the blood of the saints, Babylon on whose head were to be poured all the phials of the wrath of God. Here the spirit of antichrist had its seat, here the prince of this world had his throne, here the Son of man was crucified afresh, and that holy name blasphemed to which every knee must bend. The sword of heaven was drawn, and the saints were hurrying onward to the field of Armageddon, for the day of the Lord was at hand, and the measure of the city's transgression was almost full.

But while the Franciscans were thus resolute in the demolition of the old landmarks, they were in dreadful unrest as to what they should substitute in their room. They had cast out from their hearts what seemed to them to be the unclean spirit; its departure had left them empty indeed, but neither swept nor garnished. They felt clinging about them all the old corruptions of their nature; and in the absence of that which they had once believed to be a source of strength, the feeling was beyond all measure painful. There is something almost tragic in the efforts of these men to find repose. They exhausted every means and appliance to drive out or starve out the old nature: they wore the meanest garments; they ate the coarsest food; they wrought at the most repulsive labour; they engaged in the longest pilgrimages, and they found all in vain. They resorted to more terrible remedies: they fasted until life was almost extinct; they did penance till death itself would have been pleasure; they lashed themselves with merciless fury, that they might reproduce the figure of baptism by blood; they exposed themselves to the anger of all the elements—to the burning fire, to the keen wind, to the freezing water, to every medium in nature by which they might obtain the washing of regeneration; and again they found it all in vain. There is not, to our mind, a sadder spectacle in all history than that of this moral discomfiture; its sadness is too deep for tears, and too eloquent for description; it is humanity weighing mediævalism in the balance, and, in spite of all its glories, finding it wanting.

Whence sprang this unrest? It is a question of vast importance, intimately connected with the moral development of human nature; and we shall offer no apology for making a brief inquiry into the sources of its being, and the secret of its power. It seems to us that the unrest of mediævalism took its rise from three distinct causes: from a just and genuine reaction, from a mistake as to the design of religion, and from a very defective system of moral philosophy. We must glance in turn at each of these. And, first, it is evident that the unrest of mediævalism had at least part of its origin in a reaction which was genuine and just,—a reaction against that tendency to deaden the sense of sin which had been fostered by the increasing practice of indulgences. The Franciscans felt, and felt truly, that no high spiritual nature could be satisfied with such a remedy,—a remedy which was applied only to an unaffected part, and did not touch the seat of the disease. They felt, at the same time, that a nature of feeble spirituality would be rendered by this practice more spiritually feeble still, more blunted to the sense of guilt, more blind to the charms of virtue, more deaf to the voice of conscience; 'from him would be taken even that which he had.' In the strength of this reaction, the Franciscans magnified sin, felt its power more intensely, experienced its bondage more keenly, and looked more despairingly upon the prospect of obtaining emancipation from its fetters. And by one of those strange coincidences which frequently occur to remind us of the unity of human history, these poor Franciscans, in upholding the enormity of man's corruption, received an ally from an unlooked-for quarter—from the opposite side of the social ladder, from the courtly literature of the romantic age. That brilliant renaissance of the human mind which had its birth in the south-east of France, was beginning to grow weary of its home. The spirit of French literature was rapidly dying; the golden age had already given place to one of silver, and the age of silver was gradually yielding to that of iron. Chivalry had lost the dew of its youth, and minstrelsy had lost the clearness of its song; the spirit of the renaissance turned its eyes away, and looked out for another home. And for that spirit another home was indeed preparing. Along the banks of the Arno, on the site of those plains where of old the strolling merchants had erected their tents of temporary shelter, there had sprung up, with the birth of the free cities of Italy, a city fairest of them all—the beautiful, the cultured Florence. If Rome was the mistress of the world, if Venice was the mistress of the ocean, Florence was the mistress of the garden; it was into her lap that all the others poured their precious fruits. She was the repository of the world's treasures, the custodier of the world's wealth, the refiner of the world's silver; she received the stores of earthly merchandise, and she gave them back again in visions of outward beauty—in noble architecture, in finished sculpture, ultimately in perfect painting; she was already the favoured child of nature, she was soon to be the cherished companion of human intelligence. It was to this city of Florence that the renaissance of France was winging its flight; but Florence was by no means ripe for receiving its spirit of freedom. She had bowed her neck to the hierarchy; she had become the handmaid of Papal Rome; she had experienced those corruptions which flow from luxury, and that deadness of conscience which springs from a too easy forgiveness. She was pre-eminently in want of a preacher, and her first preacher was bound to be at the same time her earliest martyr. In point of fact, it proved so. A great preacher was at hand, a Boanerges, a son of thunder; whose pulpit was a cleft of Parnassus, whose text was the bottomless pit, whose message was the destruction of evil, whose inspiration was the spirit of poetry. Looking back through the distance, we see his gigantic figure clear against the clouds of six centuries; the first poet of his own age, the second to none of any age—the immortal, the immortalizing Dante. His life had been singularly moulded by female influences, as if from very childhood the purest ideal of the mediæval heart had sought to claim him for its own. Having lost his father in very tender years, he was thrown upon the guardianship of a wise and upright mother, to whom he probably owed the first planting of those seeds which in after days bore so rich a harvest. But to this influence there was added another, so powerful that Dante himself has called it the awakening of a new life within him; we allude to that attachment to the child Beatrice, that love so chaste, so pure, so unstained by the meretricious or the sensual, which yet was strong enough to direct the current of his life, and absorbing enough to hold him above the waves of temptation. This Beatrice, originally the personal object of his devotion, became in time a typical being; the type of stainless purity, of womanly tenderness, of self-sacrificing love, even of the Virgin Mother herself. When he comes to unfold his revelation of the soul's destiny beyond the grave, it is Beatrice who appears to him as his guide into the regions of resplendent light. On the poet's wing he has two flights to traverse: one into the regions of the lost, the other into the abodes of the blessed; his pioneer to the one is Virgil, his conductor to the other is Beatrice. Virgil is paganism, Beatrice is Christianity; Virgil is human reason, Beatrice is divine revelation; Virgil is the brow-beating strength of man, Beatrice is the calm, enduring, self-denying power of woman. He was weary of the paganism, weary of the materialism, which had buried the soul; weary of the rites and ceremonies which had made worship an act of the hand rather than of the heart; weary, above all, of that magical salvation which could profess to free a soul from sin, and yet leave it steeped in the depths of its corruptions. He felt that his countrymen wanted to be roused into terror; pagans in heart, they could only be assailed by pagan weapons, and the strongest of all pagan weapons was the sense of fear. To awaken that fear, to stir the echoes of human responsibility, Dante led Italy down into the recesses of that awful world where dwelt the spirits of those from whom all hope had fled. He made no attempt to soften the terrors of that state; he presented it to the eye in its full horror, and in its utmost repulsiveness. As we descend with him down the ever-contracting circles, as we pass with him through the ever-increasing miseries, we feel how terribly such physical representations of the consequences of evil were calculated to awaken the Italian world of that day; and we recognise in the great poet a man whose mission was more than poetry, who was sent to be a forerunner of Savonarola, to tell his countrymen that, in spite of hierarchical indulgences, and in spite of Papal absolutions, sin was a dreadful disease, a disease whose progress was destructive, and whose end was death. That was the message of Dante, and we know how his countrymen received it. We know how that befell him which has befallen most prophets: to be 'without honour in their own country.' We know how his native Florence cast him out, and how, through all his remaining years, he wandered a fugitive and an exile, seeking rest and finding none. We know how his dust reposes far from that city which would have gladly paid him in death the honour she denied him in life; these events are amongst the commonplaces of history. But the reformation which Dante began was not one which could be quenched by the extinction of a single life, however noble; it was a movement in the air, and Dante was, after all, only one of its melodious instruments. It took hold more or less of all his contemporaries; took hold prominently of his beloved friend Giotto, the painter, sculptor, and architect of his day. In his picture of the 'Triumph of Death,' we seem to catch the echoes of Dante's *Divina Commedia;* in his figures of Chastity and Obedience, we seem to hear again the tones of the poet-reformer; Obedience, in the true spirit of the Florentines, bows her head to curb and yoke, but Chastity stands apart in a rocky fortress, unassailed and unassailable. All this demonstrates that the air had been impregnated with the new spirit, that humanity was becoming more and more restive under the chain, that individual responsibility was every day asserting afresh the claim to let its voice be heard, and that the sense of individual sin was each moment waxing deeper and stronger, refusing to be drowned in the Papal waters of forgetfulness.

Here, then, was the first source of that unrest which permeated the mind of the Franciscans. It arose from reaction against that tendency to moral lethargy which had been created by the hierarchical spirit. The individual had been so long taught to think of himself as merely a part of the Church, that he had grown forgetful of his own individuality, and of all that moral responsibility which individuality involves. He had been so long taught to think of himself as dependent on the hierarchy for spiritual blessings, that he had ceased to remember that channel of personal appropriation by which alone any blessing can become our own. The Franciscan movement was a revolt against this belief. It was a waking up of the individual to the awfulness of his own being, the untransferableness of his moral nature, the solitariness of his soul before God, the responsibility which he had to bear undivided and alone, and, above all, the terrible weight of guilt and sin for which that responsibility called him to account. What wonder that, in the immediate perception of such a vision, in the sudden and instantaneous awakening to a thought which had been suppressed for centuries, the opening experience of the human mind should have been one of unrest and misery?

But there was a second source of this unrest: it had its ground in a mistake of the mediæval world concerning the design of religion. We have become familiar with the platitude that religion is designed to make man happy; in mediæval times, such a statement would have been neither a platitude nor a commonplace, but a very fresh proposition, worthy of being discussed, and open at least to qualification. For there had gradually crept into the heart of mediævalism, the notion that the design of religion was itself to produce unrest; no man ever said so in so many words, but the belief lies at the very root of the system. It is impossible to study the morality of that age without being convinced that the men of the thirteenth century, those men at least who were in search of a rule of life, estimated the merit of an action by the difficulty involved in its performance. To perform a work from which the nature of the man revolted; to do what he very much wished to leave undone; to toil through his task with temptations at every turn inciting him to throw it aside; to struggle up to the attainment of his object in opposition to every natural instinct and every individual propensity, —this was to be a virtuous man, this was to win the crown of holiness. But to do good from the impulse of nature; to enter into life without passing through the strait gate and the narrow way; to manifest the fruits of a spiritual growth without experiencing those hindrances which generally obstruct the progress of the seed; to perform a religious deed because religion had become the very breath of the soul's atmosphere, —this was passed over without admiration, and spoken of without praise. If a man should offer up his life to prove his concurrence with the law of sacrifice, he would be esteemed worthy of the highest commendation; if he should offer up his life because his love of humanity was stronger than the love of life, and stronger than the fear of death, he would assuredly have been assigned an inferior place in the temple. Or, to descend to a less elevated platform, if a man came in contact with a gold coin, and after sore temptation decided not to appropriate it, he would be reckoned essentially moral; if he passed it by without experiencing the slightest temptation, his position would be less exalted amongst the ranks of the virtuous. Now in all this there is a manifest confusion of thought; the confusion of that which is worthy of praise with that which is worthy of admiration. The man who abstains from touching the piece of gold in opposition to the prompting of his whole nature, is an object of greater praise than the man who is never tempted at all; but why so? It is because the latter stands upon an eminence higher than praise,—praise would insult him; he is following his nature, and to commend him for following his nature would be to suggest a suspicion that the act was not natural. The truth is, that just in proportion as we cease to view a good work as meritorious, so much the nobler does that work become. We commend a work of genius because genius is not common to humanity; if genius became common to humanity, it would no longer be an object of commendation, but its universal possession would lift man himself to a higher level. So is it with virtue in the individual mind. At first it has to struggle with the natural life; and the struggle is fierce and keen, sometimes inclining to the flesh, and sometimes to the spirit. But if the spirit faint not, it will conquer at the last, and the virtue will become no longer meritorious, but natural,—as natural as the breathing of the air, as natural as the vision of the sunbeams. The seed which was sown in tears will be gathered up in joy, the bread cast on the waters will come back to us after many days, the life lost in the shadows will be found again in the sunshine. When a man arrives at this stage, the natural has become one with the spiritual; heaven and earth have met together. He would no more dream of congratulating himself on his merit, than he would dream of considering himself heroic because his heart rejoices in the morning sunlight, or because his mind grows pensive beneath the silent stars; virtue is as much his life as sense or memory, and virtue, like sense and memory, is to him not a merit, but a gift.

Now, if it be so, it follows that the struggles of virtue, so far from being its crown, are the proofs of its incipiency; that the feeling of sacrifice experienced in its performance, so far from constituting its glory, marks in reality its distance from full development. When that which is perfect has come, that which is in part is done away; the sacrifice ceases whenever the human will has rested in the divine will. We have always felt how grand is that touch in the Hebrew Scriptures, where the patriarch, offering up his son on Mount Moriah, is allowed at the last hour to resume his gift. It is a true picture of the history of all sacrifice. If persevered in, it loses its pain, loses its very sense of loss,—its death has no sting, its grave has no victory; the absolute goal of religion will be reached when a man has ceased even to desire the gratification of his individual will in separation from the divine life. Yet, strange to say, this was the very point which the mediæval world did not see. That world magnified the sacrifice as a sacrifice, and valued the religious life in proportion as it was a life of struggle, until in the thoughts of men unrest became the summer ripeness of the soul, pain its maturest fruit, the endurance of privation its richest harvest. Men weighed themselves in the balance, and found themselves wanting if they did not find the traces of suffering and mortification. To produce those traces, they courted the severest penances, and sought the bitterest lacerations; and the only spiritual joy which they knew was the melancholy satisfaction that they had actually and intensely succeeded in rendering themselves unhappy.

We come now to the third source of that unrest which we have found existing in the heart of mediævalism. Its first was the genuine reaction from a superficial view of sin, its second was a mistaken estimate of the design of the religious life; but it had a third, in one sense more radical than either of the others: a very defective system of moral philosophy. We have become so habituated to think of sin in the abstract, and of virtue in the abstract, that we find great difficulty in realizing the mediæval position. That position did not contemplate either vice or virtue as abstract principles; it viewed both of them only as collections of separate acts. Sin was the aggregate number of a series of evil deeds; virtue was the aggregate number of a series of good actions. The whole conception of vice and virtue was numerical. The mediæval mind did not contemplate the law of God as giving sanction to a pure life, but as ordaining the observance of certain definite commandments. The modern Christian reads the Bible that he may catch the impress of the divine life; the mediæval Christian who was able to read Latin, read the Bible that he might count those precepts which he was expected to obey. God's moral law to the world was by no means contemplated as infinite or absolute. It comprehended a limited number of commandments, all of which a man might keep; nay, which by very strenuous labour a man might surpass. Let us suppose that the New Testament was found to contain a thousand distinct precepts,—the number was large, but not infinite; it was quite possible that a human being might not only exhaust them all, but add to them a new commandment not involved in any; by reason of this ten hundred and first precept, he had got beyond the standard even of divine law—he had performed a work of supererogation.

It may be said, In all this where do we find any ground for unrest? It may be foolish, it may be childish, it may be unphilosophical; but is it not at least comforting? To tell a man that God requires from him something less than absolute perfection; that he is not bound to rise to the standard of stainless purity which he beholds in the divine life; that he is not expected to be perfect as his Father in heaven is perfect; that he is only called upon to keep a limited number of commandments, so limited that they may be counted by a human mind, compassed by a human life, transcended by a human imagination, and actually surpassed by human action,—this is surely a solace to a frail perishable being, conscious at once of his own corruption and his own natural impotence. To tell the weary traveller, who is exhausted by climbing the mountain, that he has only a few more peaks to pass ere he shall gain the final summit, is manifestly a source of greater strength than would be the information that the summit was far away, and the points of ascent innumerable. So, in like manner, would not the mediæval traveller, climbing the difficult hill of human duty, be stimulated more to prosecute his course by learning that the course was not immensely long, than he would be by discovering that it almost transcended possibility?

Nevertheless, a deeper examination must lead us to the conclusion, that in the spiritual region it was not so; that mediævalism would have received far more rest from contemplating Christianity as a perfect life, than it ever could derive from viewing it as a series of numerical commands. Christianity demands a perfect life, yet the germs of that perfection may be reached in a moment. In the breath of the infant's life there are involved all the possibilities of manhood; in the soul of simple childhood there are wrapt up all the powers of the philosopher, and all the susceptibilities of highest genius. Now, the life of religion is love. We might write upon tables of stone a thousand moral precepts, directing a human soul how it shall act towards its brother, and we might see that soul, by long and laborious efforts, able at last to exhaust them all; but if we were to erase the writing, if we were to destroy the tablets, if we were to leave the moral precepts a blank, and if in their room we were to kindle within the man himself the tiniest spark of love, in an instant the new life would outstrip the stereotyped acts of years, and would bound to the goal on wings of earnest fire. There is no rest in mechanical morality; it is at best but manual labour, it is the work of the anvil; the only repose it can bring is that of physical exhaustion. It is as if one, in obedience to direction, were to strike with weary hand the notes of a musical instrument, producing in their combination a harmony he never intended, and which, even when produced, he fails to appreciate. The only work of supererogation is the life of love; for it is this alone that transcends the limits of law, and transforms the badge of servitude into the joy of voluntary service.

It was this thought which at last, though late, the mediæval world was beginning to realize. It had tried in the furnace all the external rules of human morality, and had found them all impure. The rule of Benedict, the rule of Dominic, the rule of Francis, had one after another passed in review; each for a moment had seemed to supply the emergencies of the hour, and each had proved in the sequel vanity and vexation of spirit; they had brought no rest, they had contributed no joy. And the heart of the mediæval world shrank back from a touch so cold, and recoiled from forms so dead. It wanted a life—a life deeper than the natural life, deeper than the rites and ceremonies of the visible Church, deeper than the hollow pageantry which passed too often for religious devotion.

It wanted a hidden communion between itself and the fountain of its being; a communion which would be interrupted by no intermediate agencies, and marred by the presence of no outward witnesses; a communion in the solitary silence of the soul, whose joy would be known to itself alone, and whose converse would be heard by no ear but that of the listening spirit. And, in answer to that want, there was rising a new movement of religious life; a movement noiseless as the summer air, silent as the working of gravitation's law, yet mighty in its silence, and irresistible in the power of its attraction; a movement which was to carry the spirit of Christianity many steps nearer to the object of its labours, and to bring it almost within sight of the promised land: we allude to that phase of thought which men have called mysticism. It was not that now for the first time it had made its appearance. There never was an age of the Christian religion, there never was an age of any religion, in which there were not to be found some lives imbued with the mystical spirit. It beamed out in many of the hymns of Brahminism; it flashed forth in some of the deepest aspirings of Platonism; it was taken up in due season into the light of Christianity. It appeared in some of the writings of Paul; it tinged the Alexandrian school of the second century; it came forth with Origen in the third, with the monk Dionysius in the fifth, with Scotus Erigena in the ninth, with Bernard of Clairvaux in the twelfth, and with Bonaventura in the earlier half of the thirteenth century. This system has never at any time been left without a witness. But while undoubtedly it is so, while no single age can be found which is not represented by at least one mystical mind, it is now that for the first time we discover what may be called a river of mystical life; a river continuous and unbroken, forming a distinct feature of the moral landscape, and resting not until it has mingled its waters with those of the great ocean. We see it rising with the close of this thirteenth century in the speculative, almost pantheistic, mind of Henry Eckart; swelling into greater breadth in the sublime and beautiful life of John Tauler; progressing in its course in the self-forgetting creed of Ruysbroek; and at last reaching its culminating glory in the publication of that work which of all others, next to the Bible, has been dearest to the heart of European Christendom, that book called the *Imitation of Christ*, which always by the popular voice, and now, after long discussion, by the general consent of the learned, has been ascribed to Thomas à Kempis. From that day mediæval mysticism gradually disappears; but it disappears only as the forerunner vanishes when that prophet has come for whom he has prepared the way. Mysticism, as Ullmann remarks, was the true forerunner of Protestantism; its work was preparatory, its struggles were but the prelude to a mightier conflict. It was imperative that it should fade; but it faded only into a stronger light, a light whose harbinger it had been, and whose day it had predicted. Its mission, indeed, was not precisely the mission of the Baptist in the wilderness; it had less of the thunder and the earthquake, more of the still small voice. Its object was not to stimulate to revolution, but silently to prepare the ground for future revolution. The mystic claimed no new system of theology, attached himself to no party, ranged himself under no sect; he was to be found amongst all parties, he was to be met with amidst all scenes. He aspired not to destroy the Catholic religion, but to spiritualize it, to deepen it, to show that its roots were more firmly fixed in human nature than even Catholicism itself had ever dreamed. He aimed to bring out, and he succeeded in bringing out as none had ever done before, the Protestant yearning that lies at the heart of Catholicism, the desire for individual life apart from the life of the collective Church. A system so vast in its scope, so deep in its soundings, so high in its designs, and so far-reaching in its historical results, ought not to be passed over without a separate consideration.

CHAPTER XXXI.

DISCOVERY OF A NEW WELL-SPRING.

THE movement called mysticism, at which we have now arrived, was a silent protest of the school-life against being retained in school. We say a silent protest, for it did not rebel, it only felt rebellious. It neither strove nor cried, neither did any man hear its voice in the streets; its dissent was expressed inwardly, in the secret places of the heart. It is therefore in no sense to be regarded as an ecclesiastical revolution; it certainly never regarded itself in this light; it professed to be in strictest harmony with Catholic truth. But it sought to place that truth upon a new basis, and by that attempt, while not revolutionary itself, it prepared the way for revolution; it was an internal preparation for those events of outward history which were to change the aspect of the world and transform the spirit of man. What mysticism objected to, was not the receiving of Catholic truth, but the receiving of Catholic truth in the form of a school lesson; it wanted emancipation from scholasticism. It was essentially an anti-school movement, a reaction against the studies and the modes of study that were prevalent in the class-room. It desired separation from the class that it might enjoy individual meditation; it craved the liberty to think in solitude, to commune with its own heart, to stand face to face and alone with those mysteries in which it lived and moved and had its being. When we come to examine its position in detail, we find that mysticism constituted a threefold reaction; it was a reaction against school morality, it was a reaction against school authority, and it was a reaction against school theology. We must advert briefly to each of these.

First, then, mysticism was a protest against the morality of the school. It was not that it believed the morality to be bad or hurtful, it simply believed it to be defective. We have seen in the previous chapter what was the character of the Church's moral teaching; it was the attempt to win salvation by the observance of a definite number of precepts. Mysticism proposed to blot out the handwriting of all the precepts, to destroy the tablets on which they were written, and to write a new law upon the heart itself. It said, Why stand ye all the day gazing up into heaven, seeking to reach the ascended Christ by the steps of a moral ladder rising line upon line, and precept upon precept! He whom ye seek is already nigh you; dwelling in your hearts, and waiting for recognition by them! Ye have only to turn your eyes inward, and you will behold His glory; ye have only to look on Him, and immediately you will be likened unto Him! Cast but a glance upon His infinite brightness, and your heart will catch fire, and His brightness will become your brightness! It may be only a spark, but the whole fire is potentially in a single spark, and all daylight is enclosed in the first beam of dawn! The light has already come to you, but you are looking too far to find it! You are seeking it on the summits of Mount Sinai, while all the time it is at the door of your spirits; you are striving to reach it by outward acts, while in reality it is itself that must act through you! Your motto in the past has been, 'Do this and live;' your motto in the future must be, Live, and you will be compelled to do! There is a life which is touching your life—the life of infinite love; receive it, and it will become your own! Gaze upon it, and in your gaze you will be transfigured into its glory,—you, and the world with you; 'old things shall pass away, and all things shall be made new!' You will cease to number the precepts of human duty! You cannot distinguish the drops of the ocean from the ocean itself, no more can you distinguish the acts of love from that ocean of love in which they dwell! Love breathes in one word the language of all the precepts, concentrates in one sound the voice of all the commandments; it is the soul of the moral universe; it at once fulfils and overleaps the law!

That was what mysticism said to the world. A doctrine very trite and commonplace to modern ears, but which must have sounded wondrously fresh to men who had lived so long under the shadow of Sinai. And this protest of mysticism against school-morality was intimately connected with its second protest against school-authority. Morality had been viewed too much as the mere obedience to an outward command; mysticism came to ask if the belief in Christianity itself had not been made to rest too much upon the basis of external authority? The ground for the acceptance of Christian truth had been the universal consent of the Church; and as the Church had become an absolute monarchy, its universal consent was likely to be determined by the one and supreme will of the sovereign pontiff. In the sense of universal consent, there is a confidence; whether it be the consent of churchmen, or the consent of the *vox populi*. Let a mandate be given as the result of concurrent agreement, it will be received as having a higher basis than mere outward authority; the concurrence itself will constitute a presumption in favour of its rectitude. But let all confidence be destroyed that there has been any concurrent agreement, let there be borne in upon the mind even the suspicion that this seeming harmony is the result of collusion, and that this collusion is itself the result of a command issued by one human will, the mandate will then be received only as an arbitrary law—a law which may be good or which may be bad, but which is to be estimated neither by its goodness nor by its badness, but simply by the strength of the authority which has imposed it. Now that was the goal to which the mediæval world had come. It had grown suspicious of the absolute monarchy, and between suspicion and aversion there is only a step. Thou shalt! thou shalt not! had become weary sounds in the ears of a generation which had seen the rise of the Italian renaissance, and read Gerhard's exposition of *The Everlasting Gospel.* Everywhere there was a heaving of reactionary life,—underground, suppressed, half-smothered, but potent still. The first impulse came from the Teutonic mind. If Italy was the home of Christian art, Germany was the nursery of religious reform; Eckart, Tauler, Ruysbroek, and all the leading mystics were Germans. Let it not be thought, however, that this German mysticism proclaimed in so many words, that the days of authority must end; it was too cautious for that, nor was the world yet ripe for such a message; what it did say was, 'Destroy this temple, and I will raise it again.' It said, Even if the hierarchy were to pass away, even if the Papal voice were to lose its power, even if the universal consent of the Church were disunited and broken, Christian belief would not be left without a reason for the hope that was in it, for it had a 'building of God, an house not made with hands, eternal in the heavens.' God was Himself the light of the soul, and in God's light the soul must see light. Behind the veil of sense, behind the forms of time, there was a temple in the pure heart where the altar fires were ever burning, where day and night ascended the incense of a deep devotion, where every thought was a spiritual song of praise. There, face to face, God met with the human spirit, and the human spirit lost itself in God; lost its meanness, lost its littleness, lost its human nothingness, and was absorbed into the very heart

of the divine life; its pride broken, its selfishness
crucified, its darkness dispelled, its weakness banished,
its path lighted for evermore. It no longer required
the illumination of the outward eye, it had no need
of the sun nor of the moon to guide it; God was its
light, and it could dispense with outward evidences.
Heaven and earth might pass away, Pope and hierarchy might cease to be, Rome with its hallowed
associations might sink beneath the waves, the records
of all the councils constituting the proofs of universal
consent might be consumed to ashes; but this inward
evidence, 'this life that never shone on sea or shore,'
this testimony which was independent of all the
Fathers, older than all the councils, more fundamental
than all the creeds, must remain an imperishable
possession—a word which would not pass away.

But there was a third protest uttered by mediæval
mysticism; it was the protest against school-theology.
It was not that mysticism was opposed to all or any
of the doctrines of the Catholic Church, it professed
to be in strictest harmony with these doctrines. But
it objected very strongly to having Catholic truth or
any other truth presented to it in the form of a school-
lesson. With the multiplication of rites, with the
reverence for images, with the pomp and pageantry
of ceremonial representation, with the gorgeous ritual
which attracted the eye and charmed the sense, with
the incense and the vestments and the music and the
æsthetic culture; in short, with the external helps of
religion in general, this movement had little sympathy.
It did not say they were wrong, it did not say it

disapproved of them, it did not say men ought not to follow them, it simply did not sympathize with them; it moved on a different plane. It was quite ready to admit that these outward observances had their place in religious development, it was quite ready to recognise their utility to a primitive age, it was quite prepared to see how powerfully they might influence the transition which every religion must make from the child into the man. But, conceding that they had been helps to the opening school-life, conceding that they had proved beneficial in illustrating abstract truths to minds unaccustomed to abstract reasoning, did it follow that their lives should be extended beyond the conclusion of that work which had been given them to do? The school-life of the Christian spirit was now far advanced, ready even to vanish away in the light of a higher life; was it fitting, was it reasonable, that what was good for the boy should be held binding on the man, and that a mode of tuition which was necessary to an incipient intelligence, should, when that intelligence was expanded, be deemed essential still? Yet this was precisely the attitude which the hierarchy had assumed; nay, the importance of ritualism had been made to increase with the advance of mediævalism; it had once been contemplated only as a help, it had now come to be viewed as possessing a magical efficacy. It was at this point that mysticism interposed its voice. It said, You stamp our doctrine as vague! you call us mystics! but is not the name more applicable to you? Do you not profess to have a mystical power residing, not in the heart, which would at least be a legitimate place for it, but in certain outward forms, in certain ceremonial acts which are connected with the life of religion by no other bond than that of long association? Our mysticism, be it false or true, comes at least from within; the communion we seek is a communion between soul and soul, we admit no intermediate agencies between our spirits and the infinite spirit! Such a communion is incapable of expression in earthly language, and therefore it must be mystical; but to seek mysticism in painted symbols and gilded forms, is surely a movement back to the days when men worshipped the fetich! Such was the spirit in which mysticism contemplated the religious life of the hierarchy. It viewed that life as the survival of a past age, an existence superannuated and behind the day. It had once been beneficial, it was now merely ornamental; it had once been an element of progress, it was now only a memory of the past.

There was another point in the school-theology with which the spirit of mysticism had little sympathy. It will be remembered that while the schoolmen were commanded to believe implicitly whatever the will of the Church should dictate, they were allowed, after having believed, to substantiate their belief by proof; forbidden to use reason as a source of religious truth, they were yet allowed to employ it as the messenger of Faith, the handmaid whom Faith sent to gather up her treasures. But if mysticism was opposed to the acceptance of truth upon mere outward authority, it was not less strongly opposed to the endorsing of that authority by the steps of a logical demonstration. It held mathematical proof to be just as foreign to the nature of Christianity as was the mere imperative mandate of an external voice, and it regarded both as foreign to it for the same reason; because both belonged to a different region of human nature. The true province of authority was to regulate the actions of the body; it could have no control over the thoughts even of a slave. The true province of reason was to regulate the acts of the daily life; its sphere was the order of nature, and its task was the discovery of nature's laws. But here, within the heart, was a region independent of natural law,—a region which owned no atmosphere but the atmosphere of heaven, and no light but the light of God,—a world beyond sense, and beyond the conditions of sense. Into this world reason dared not intrude, its objects were beyond the reach of reason, it was their glory to be irrational. The kingdom of God could not be reached by a scaling ladder, could not be gained by the steps of human demonstration; it must be seen by an inward sense, beheld by an eye that never gazed upon the visible landscape, heard in its deepest music by an ear that never listened to the sound of earthly voice. It must be mirrored in a light to which all human demonstration would be darkness,—a light in which vision was one with knowledge, and in which knowledge was one with intuition,—a light before which grew dim the authority of all councils and the decretals of all pontiffs, and in whose clear and stainless beam the most perfect reasoning of the greatest mathematical genius seemed but the lisping of the child and the groping of the benighted traveller. Such was the claim of mysticism,—the claim to a faith whose pride it was to be irrational, not beause reason was opposed to it, but because reason was beneath it. It sought an evidence of things not seen, but it sought that evidence, not in the things that *were* seen, for it felt that the spiritual world could only be approached by the spiritual nature, and that the objects which transcended sense and time could only be perceived by an eye which had been closed to the impressions of the visible and the temporal light.

We have now examined all the leading points of reaction which the mediæval mystics presented to the spirit of the hierarchy, and it must be acknowledged that they were of vast importance, and of far-reaching significance. Why, then, did not the reformation come? With so much in the atmosphere of the age to favour its appearance, should we not have expected that it would have recognised its opportunity? Was there anything to have prevented John Tauler from having been Martin Luther? These two men had much that was in common. Both were Germans, both lived in seasons of religious reaction, both were endowed by nature with extraordinary gifts, both possessed that power of pulpit eloquence which more than all other powers is calculated to sway the masses and mould the mind of the religious community, both were gifted with that lively and picturesque style which renders the gravest subject interesting and attractive to the most superficial intelligence, both denounced the vices of their age—the sins of pope, priest, and people—with a fire and a vehemence which did honour alike to their moral and their physical courage, and both, in return for such denunciation, were objects of Papal suspicion and aversion. Nay, if we were to confine ourselves to the mere personal qualities of the men, we should say that Tauler ought to bear the palm. He was a more cultured and a more amiable man than Luther, though probably the superior amiability was the result of the superior culture. In self-sacrifice both were equal, neither of them ever for a moment took his personal safety into account. Luther went to the diet of Worms, and Tauler, like the Franciscan friars, administered dying consolations to the victims of that great pestilence which swept the Europe of the fourteenth century. Yet, with such analogies in their character, their destinies were very different; the name of Luther is a household word,—how few ordinary readers ever heard of Tauler? The reason is plain; the name of Luther is connected with a work, and it is the work that gives glory to his name; the name of Tauler has nothing to rest upon save the memory of his own beautiful life. But the question recurs, Why was it so? why did not the reformation movement which ennobled the memory of Luther forestall him by falling into the hands of Tauler? why did not the birth of Protestantism antedate itself by a century and a half? The question is a very important one, and we intend briefly to consider it. The fault clearly does not lie with Tauler as a man; it becomes, therefore, of great consequence to inquire whether there lay not some real deficiency in that system of mysticism of which he was the noblest representative. We make the inquiry in a purely historical spirit. We have studied above all other studies to render this work strictly scientific and impartial, free from the influence of all polemical bias, and in the interest of no theological school. We therefore consider the question simply as a matter of historical fact, and with that calm and dispassionate judgment which one ought to bring to the problems of history. In this light, then, we ask if there was any essential particular in which the theology of Martin Luther differed from the theology of John Tauler; in other words, if there was any doctrine possessed by Protestantism which did not find a place in the system of mediæval mysticism? Should we be compelled to answer that question in the affirmative, we shall have reached the probable solution of the failure of mysticism as a religious life to lift the world into a higher atmosphere, and we shall have discovered at the same time that element of power which gave to the Protestantism of the sixteenth century the widespread celebrity and success which the mysticism of the fourteenth had failed to win.

Let us see, then, what were the leading features of mediæval mysticism. Hitherto we have looked at the system only on its negative side, have considered what it was not, what it opposed, what it refused to be; we must now see what it was in itself. It is well known that the mediæval mystics recognised three essential stages of spiritual life,—three periods of progression through which every man must pass in his journey from the realms of darkness into the happy land of Beulah. There was the stage of purification, the stage of illumination, and the stage of ecstatic union. First of all, the soul had to be purified; corruption could not inherit incorruption, the darkness could not comprehend the light, even though it shone amidst it. There must be a process of cleansing, a washing of regeneration, an obliteration of selfish and worldly passions, and the impartation of a new moral life,—a life of purity, a life of charity, a life of spiritual beauty. Next came the light, the light of the new heavens and the new earth,—the light in which the soul stood transfigured and gazed without a veil into the face of God; after purification came illumination. Then, lastly, even this triumph was superseded by a triumph greater still; illumination was followed by ecstatic union. The soul which had been transfigured in the light of God was lost in the light of God, ceased any longer to have a separate being, but merged its own little light in the glorious effulgence of the heavenly sun until it became absolutely blended with the infinite life,—one with Him in being, one with Him in purpose, one with Him in will. Such were the three phases of mysticism. It will not be denied that they open up a picture of spiritual experience, all of which is beautiful, and much of which is true. But the precise question for our consideration is not so much what was truthful or beautiful in the picture, as what in that picture was adapted to meet the wants of the age? In this light let us examine, one by one, the three mystical stages. The first requirement is that of purification, a good heart, an upright life. But we ask, as a matter of historical fact, Was the first element of mediæval unrest the absence of this purity? was the immediate desire of the world of that day the attainment of this good heart and this upright spirit? It may be answered that it ought to have been; that is a question of moral philosophy, and the only question for us is one of fact. It is indeed difficult to conceive how men can desire that which they have never perceived by any sense external or internal, difficult to imagine how those who have never felt the power of spiritual purity should see any beauty in it that could make it an object of desire. The infant cries before he has ever tasted food, and he cries from the feeling of hunger; yet the infant is altogether unconscious of that particular remedy which is to remove his unrest, all he can be conscious of is the unrest itself. In like manner, if we could imagine a world absolutely destitute of the life of spirituality, we might well conceive that world to be subject to a perpetual hunger; but we could not well conceive it to be conscious of that spiritual nourishment which would supply the void and foster a new vitality. Spiritual purity can only be desired by those who are already partially or latently its possessors. It is indisputable, however, that the mediæval world had a deeper unrest than that of the unconscious infant; it was no vague indefinite craving that it manifested; it wanted a special object, and it knew what that object was. It was not sufficiently spiritual to desire spirituality; but even had it seen the beauties of holiness, it would have felt that it had no right to appropriate these beauties until it had removed the preliminary cause of all its troubles. That cause was the sense of a violated law; the conviction that, being evil, it was under the reign of chastisement; the consciousness that no sunshine could be bright in the present until the accumulated clouds of darkness had been rolled away from the past. What the mediæval world wanted primarily, wanted as the first step of the ladder, wanted as a possibility of seeking any other good, was the proclamation of an atonement for sin. To prove this, we do not need to go deeper than the very surface of mediæval history. What was the most pernicious moral element in the history of the Middle Ages? It was, as we have seen, the granting of indulgences. But why were indulgences granted? It may be answered, Because the priests found them profitable to the funds of the Church. We ask, then, Why did they find them thus profitable? It is the demand, and not the supply, which needs to be accounted for. Even in the most corrupt days of the Roman hierarchy,—even in those days when indulgences were sold for the purpose of building churches, —the very avidity of the people to buy them proved beyond all controversy, that whatever political motives may or may not have influenced the priesthood, the masses were swayed and dominated by an overwhelming desire to bury the flaming sword of justice which they believed to be hanging over them. The practice of indulgences would not have lasted for a day, would not have filled the ecclesiastical coffers for a week, would not have been remembered in history for a single year, if there had not been a heaving mass of human beings throbbing, palpitating, panting with the eagerness for a cancelled past. They had violated God's law, could they be pardoned? they had insulted the majesty of Heaven, could they obtain forgiveness? they had incurred the sentence of condemnation, could they escape the endurance of earthly penalties and of purgatorial pains? And let it not be forgotten, that to men suffering from this species of unrest the hierarchy in the granting of indulgences presented an apparent remedy—a bad remedy, a remedy worse than the disease, a remedy which alleviated the moral pain by destroying the moral nerve, and relieved the fear of punishment by undervaluing the power of sin, yet not the less a genuine attempt to meet the emergencies of the time and satisfy the wants of the masses. How did mysticism act in this emergency? How did the religion of the higher life propose to deal with an unrest so wide-spread in its prevalence and so definite in its cause? It did not profess to deal with it at all, it simply ignored it. Now we have no hesitation in saying, that sublime as mysticism was in many of its doctrines, noble as were its aspirations, pure as were its impulses, it yet allowed the hierarchy to gain the advantage over it in this one respect. The hierarchy, by the granting of indulgences, manifested at least an interest in the fears of the multitude trembling at a bar of judgment; the mystics, by ignoring the subject altogether, interposed between themselves and the masses a gulf of philosophical contempt which prevented, and must ever have prevented, them from becoming the leaders of a popular reformation They showed to the famished crowd the spreading of a rich banquet, but it was spread on the top of a mountain too steep to be climbed by the multitude. The man of daily toil, oppressed with the memories of unhallowed deeds and unkind thoughts, unable to find leisure for reflection on the mysteries of life, and incapable of such reflection even were the leisure found, conscious only that he had done those things which he ought not to have done, and left undone those things which he ought to have done, and that thereby he was liable to the penalty of transgressors, was not likely to find much solace in the mystical exhortation of John Ruysbroek, to lose himself in the 'infinite brightness.' That would have been to him very like a plunge from Scylla into Charybdis. It was just the infinite brightness that he most feared. He wanted to know how he, a poor sin-stained man, could stand before the brightness of God without being scorched by it; that fear mysticism did not allay, did not attempt to allay. But Lutheranism did. When Martin Luther swept away indulgences, he held up in their room a thought which, if accepted, would render indulgences superfluous—the idea of a penal sacrifice for sin which was commensurate with all time. Whether that thought be or be not the ultimate revelation on the subject, has been the great question of dogmatic theology, but about the power which it exercised over the masses there can be no question at all; it supplied a moral vacuum in the heart of mediævalism, a vacuum which indulgences had only partially filled, and which their removal left void altogether. Luther came from the people, and therefore he spoke to the people; Eckart, Tauler, and Ruysbroek came from the schools of the philosophers, and their language had only meaning to those who were already initiated in philosophic mysteries; their wellspring was too deep to be reached by a thirsty world.

This, then, is the conclusion at which we have arrived, on the first head of mystical doctrine; we find that, in beginning their teaching with the proclamation of the beauties of virtue, they did not meet the special ground of that unrest which was rampant in their age. If we pass now to their second head, that of illumination, we shall find that here they are in strict conformity, not only with Lutheran doctrine, but with the doctrine of all evangelical churches. Purification first, illumination afterwards; to do the will, and thence to know the doctrine, is the order of spiritual life which is prominently set forth in the fourth Gospel, and which is implied in all parts of the Christian creed. Thus far mysticism has presented nothing which admits of legitimate question; its error hitherto, if error there be, has been one purely of defect, of inability to adapt itself to the incipient stages of moral life. That of all positive possessions purity is the first, is undenied and undeniable by any spiritual mind. That the best road to the attainment of religious light is that which leads along the thorny path of duty; that the best cure for religious scepticism is the performance of honest work; that the best way to know the doctrine is to do the will, or, as the mystics put it, that purification is followed by illumination, is also a statement which will find advocates for its truth amongst all the churches. It is when with mysticism we make the transition from illumination into ecstatic union, from the light of God into the life of God, that we are disposed to pause and ask where we are going? Union with God is indeed the goal of Christianity; but an ecstatic union, a union which lifts the soul right out of humanity, a union which involves the destruction of all earthly conditions, is a destiny upon whose threshold one may be pardoned for wavering. It is marvellous that a system comparatively so Protestant should have been utterly unable to emancipate itself from that dominant idea of mediævalism, the idea that the divine and not the human Christ was the just object of contemplation. Mysticism had transcended image-worship, had transcended Virgin-worship, had transcended all intermediate worship, had aspired to enter into the Holy of Holies, and to see the very face of God; but it never dreamed of seeing that face in the human portraiture of the Master. Humanity, even glorified humanity, was looked upon as a perishable garment, a vesture which must be folded up and laid aside at death, that the spirit might be clothed anew. That the human life of

Jesus could be that light in which the spirit of man must dwell, that the human side of Christ's portraiture could furnish an eternal ideal for the soul of man, never entered into the thoughts of the mystic. The destiny he contemplated for the soul was one which involved the practical annihilation of its present nature; the Christ he desired for the spirit was one whose light was too glorious to be earthly, too divine to be human, too majestic to be consistent with an individual existence; a light in whose unearthly brightness the world and the objects of the world must melt away; a light in whose all-embracing radiance the flickering taper of the individual spirit must be lost and overshadowed, and in whose infinite range of power the feeble spark of humanity must go out and be extinct. In such a system, to be lost in God was individually to be lost altogether; to be suffused with the infinite brightness was to part with finite beauty; to see the face of God was to know no more the face of man.

If we ask now, What was the practical consequence of such a system? there clearly can be but one answer; it was eminently calculated to paralyze practical effort. If humanity was but a garment, why toil for it? if the finite was necessarily perishable, why waste so much time upon its welfare? if the world was ready to pass away, why should not we already withdraw ourselves from the world? Such was the legitimate conclusion, and the only conclusion, to be drawn from the premises. When we say that mysticism tended to be unpractical, we do not mean that all the mystics were unpractical men. It has been well remarked by Professor Flint, of Edinburgh, in his Baird Lecture for 1877, that it is unfair to impute to the adherents of a system the holding of those opinions which necessarily flow from it. It is one of the glories of our human nature that it has occasionally the power to become splendidly illogical, beautifully inconsistent, sublimely unreasoning. There never was a more practical man than John Tauler, none more devoted to the temporal welfare of his fellow-creatures, none more bent on the amelioration of the outward circumstances of humanity; but he was so, not by reason of his system, but in spite of his system. Mysticism, as it appeared in the mediæval world, led logically to a separation from that world, to a want of sympathy with its requirements, to a repudiation of its deepest interests. We have only to take the sublimest work of all its series; that of Thomas à Kempis on the *Imitation of Christ*. Rich in spiritual life, full of deep thought, high in religious aspirations, beautiful in its portraiture of virtue, it yet portrays a virtue and describes a religion which may be for other worlds, but can find no place in this. It is essentially an ascetic work,—a work which breathes the spirit of that early Christian age, when men, disgusted with the vices and the vanities of a pagan world, and ignoring the possibility of conquering that world for God, retired into the deserts and into the mountains, and prayed for the coming of the end. Mediæval mysticism in its last and grandest literary effort seemed to have accepted as its destiny the proclamation of the regress of humanity, and to have sounded over the field of progress that dolorous trumpet of retreat which informed the powers of this world that they had won the battle over virtue.

And yet, after all has been said, was there not in this very regress of mysticism the emanation of a strongly Protestant element? Whence this rupture with mediæval reality? Whence this flight alike from the religious and the secular forms of Catholic life? Whence this retirement of the soul within itself, this eagerness to close its outward eye upon surrounding scenes, this absorbing desire to bury even from its thoughts the world in which it lived and moved? Did it not spring from the deep conviction that mediævalism was no longer able to fill the heights and the depths of its being; that Catholic life, with its rites so imposing and its forms so beautiful, was yet no longer adequate to meet the requirements of a nature desiring a perpetual temple, and craving for an endless worship? Was it not the confession that, after weighing in the balance the pretensions of the hierarchy, the deepest spirit of the mediæval age had found them grievously wanting? unable to stem the torrent of human passion, unable to lighten the burdens of a single weary soul. Mysticism gave up the finite, because in the finite world of that day it saw nothing worth perpetuating; it gave up human nature, because in the lives around it, it had failed to find the glory of human nature; and it sought to forget the light of the natural sun, because the light of the natural sun lit up a scene at variance with the light of God. If we cannot join in the unqualified admiration of Ullmann, if we cannot regard this system as the direct anticipation of Protestantism, we can assuredly regard it as a movement which made for Protestantism; a movement which recoiled from the world because the world was too small for it, and which sought rest in the impressions of the individual heart, because the united heart of Catholicism had become cramped and frozen.

In a vastly different department of human study we see at the same period a similar rupture with reality. It would seem as if the mystical spirit had affected the students of nature as well as the students of mind. There was rampant in this age what might be called a scientific mysticism. Amongst the many victims whom the Church offered up to the fury of the Inquisition, no class were more numerous than those who read the stars. Astronomy was passing over from the hands of the Mohammedans into the hands of the Christians, but in their hands it was becoming romantically young again. God had made the stars to give physical light to the earth; why should they not lend it spiritual radiance too? God had made the stars to rule the outward night; why should they not rule the deeper darkness of the soul? Was there not a connection between the heavens and the earth,—a mutual affinity, a responsive sympathy, whereby the impressions of the one were repeated and imprinted on the other; and by this connection, by this affinity, by this responsive sympathy, might not man, gazing into the night, read his destiny, already photographed in the heavens, and learn by letters of golden light that work which had been given him to do? Nor let any man despise this youth of the astronomic science. Astrology, with all its absurdities, had both an intellectual and a moral basis. Intellectually, it was the groping after a truth which all science in every age is ever freshly unfolding; the unity of this vast universe, the sympathy of all its parts, the interdependence of all its members. Morally, it was the groping after an object far less attainable but not less exalted—the knowledge of the unknown future. It was the desire to pierce the clouds which confine the horizon of the human spirit, to get beyond the trammels which imprison alike sense and soul, and to catch but a glimpse of that promised land which to the imagination of every age is waiting for us in the future. And in this moral aspiration there was again manifested the same dissatisfaction with existing objects which we have seen permeating the mystical spirit, the same desire of the individual life to break away from that collective life where its individuality was dwarfed, the same Protestant impulse to receive its own revelation, to commune with its own universe, and to read its own destiny.

Nor was this search for the unknown limited to the act of star-gazing. To that age the geography of the earth was itself a mystery; humanity had not found the wings on which it could fly from shore to shore. A few Venetian merchants, a few Florentine adventurers, had indeed, in the interests of commerce, undertaken voyages from which they received more than commerce,—a knowledge of other climes; but mankind in general were ignorant of everything beyond the boundaries of their native land, and thoroughly conversant with nothing not included in the boundaries of their native village. The dawn of light in this direction came in the desire to know. The spirit of mysticism, which had shed a mysterious glory over the innermost regions of the soul, diffused a like glory over the unknown regions of the earth. Those lands never visited by the European traveller appeared to the imagination of that world to be blazing with gorgeous palaces, laden with luscious fruits, watered by rivers wandering o'er sands of gold, lighted by suns that never set, and painted by summers whose rosy hue never yielded to an autumn. They were lands of light, of love and joy; lands which death rarely visited, where sorrow seldom entered, but where man basked for ever in the sunshine of perpetual day. These gilded anticipations of a glorified world, already hidden in the far distance, had no other ground in fact than that enchantment to the view which distance proverbially lends; the lands were fair to contemplate, just because they were unknown. Yet the Utopian dream was not without its practical utility; it awakened the longing, and the longing awakened the action. It stirred up in the heart of man the desire to transcend his narrow limits, to burst the prison doors, and traverse the face of the world. It was during this fourteenth century that there came into prominent use an instrument which was singularly to facilitate the satisfaction of his thirst for enlargement, an instrument whereby man could steer his way on seas from which had receded all sight of land, and guide his course at will, independent of helps from the shore; that mariner's compass, known to the nations of remote antiquity, but lost amid the waters of western civilisation, and only lately rediscovered by mediæval Europe. The position of that Europe was in striking analogy with the position of its incipient voyagers; it too had need of a mariner's compass. It was about to enter upon a sea from every side of which the vision of the land would vanish; a sea bounded far away by a new earth, and ultimately to be overhung by new heavens too. Already the arms of the frith were widening, already the headlands upon either side were growing fainter and less prominent, already the old landmarks were beginning to disappear, and the murmur of what seemed to be a chaos of waters was every moment becoming clearer. Europe must find a new compass, a new object on which to rest its gaze, a new index to point its way, for the old earth was about to vanish, and the revivified earth was not yet come.

CHAPTER XXXII.

DECLINE OF THE TEMPORAL PAPACY.

WHATEVER may be thought of the connection between the silent progress of the stars and the noisy events of earthly history, there can be no doubt of the connection between the events of outward history and the silent progress of the human soul. While the mind of man had been thus noiselessly expanding, while the unuttered longings of his spirit had been going up ever more and more, there had been occurring, in the region of the outward world, a series of incidents surpassing in their suddenness, startling in their novelty, and transcendently important in their results; incidents which were co-operating with the unspoken desires of the human mind, and hurrying on the world towards its destined goal. It cannot be said that these events were directly caused by the moral aspirations we have been exhibiting in the previous chapters. It is a saying which has become proverbial, that incidents never happen as we expect them. Europe had been undergoing a gradual process of religious revolution; yet the crushing stroke at the Papacy was to be made, not by religious revolution, but by political freedom.

Germany had all along been the champion of this political freedom; it was Germany that had stood face to face with Hildebrand; it was the Germany of Frederic II. which had opposed the last barrier to the absolute monarchy of Rome; yet the final blow at the temporal Papacy was to be struck, not by Germany, but by a nation which has never left the Catholic fold — the kingdom of France. In these respects, the order of history baffled the calculations of man, and wrought out the ends of humanity in a way which humanity had never contemplated. To the consideration of this great political revolution we must now briefly turn.

Never did the temporal power of the Papacy seem more triumphantly manifested than in that hour when Benedict Cajetan ascended the Papal throne by the title of Boniface VIII. His inauguration was marked by peculiar splendour, signalized by unwonted pomp and pageantry. Two sovereigns, the kings of Hungary and Sicily, held the reins of his horse as he rode to the Lateran, and stood afterwards, with their crowns on their heads, serving him in the courses of the table. Never perhaps in history has such an appearance of power been followed by so quick, so ignominious a transformation. The very swiftness of the transition proves that the spectacle of magnificence was a counterfeit, an attempt to resuscitate in form a glory which had passed away in fact. Nevertheless it was this empty pageant which Boniface made the key-note of his pontificate. He assumed a double crown, to represent the fact that he was wielder alike of the temporal and the spiritual power of the world. Had not Hildebrand uncrowned a German emperor? had not Innocent III. uncrowned a king of England? why should not he also assert that prerogative which his ancestors had won? But Boniface had forgotten two important circumstances which distinguished his case from that of either Innocent or Hildebrand: his own personal character, and the distinctive character of his age. Hildebrand and Innocent III. had both been men of the highest principle; pure in intention, upright in action, zealous in duty, and stainless in morality. Boniface, after all deductions have been made from the statements of those who were actuated by personal enmity, seems to have been a man of whom no sacred office could reasonably be proud. Dante, in his *Divina Commedia*, has honoured him with a prominent place in the future world; but it is in that region of the future where those souls are believed to dwell whom through all the ages hope shall visit no more. If one half of what is written of him be true, it must be confessed that he was well worthy of it. His enemies, and they comprehended the best men of his time, charged him with every vice under the sun; every species of infidelity, every form of corruption and bribery, every kind of debauchery and immorality, every quality and propensity which is capable of dwelling in a bad heart. Nor does it seem to us that the source of these accusations materially weakens their force. Hildebrand had all Europe openly arrayed against him, Innocent III. had most of the kings of Europe arrayed against him in their hearts; yet the enemies of Hildebrand and of Innocent never imputed to either of them the charge of immoral lives; on the contrary, it was their stainless moral lives which gave them an indomitable power even over the minds of their adversaries. And it was the want of that stainless purity which made Boniface so contemptible in the eyes of his enemies; when he threw off the life of rectitude, he divested himself of that which to every pontiff has been his strongest armour. It was because he had lost his personal sanctity that he lost the respect of Europe; with that sanctity, even without a soldier, he might have been the greatest of monarchs; without it, even with an army at his command, he must have proved the weakest of kings.

But in aspiring to the pretensions of Innocent and Hildebrand, there was another element which Boniface had ignored: the changed character of the age in which he lived. The world into which Boniface was born, was not the world in which he now dwelt. There had been growing up in the interval a new social power,—a power distinct from that of either king, knight, or baron,—the power of the people. It was not yet very strong, but it was daily prophesying its strength, and its prophetic voice was ever in the direction of religious freedom. Kings had begun to discover that in the rise of this new force they would have a powerful ally in their struggle with hierarchical domination, and they had become correspondingly eager to assert their regal claims. At the opening of the fourteenth century, Europe possessed two of the ablest sovereigns that ever filled a throne; Edward I. of England, and Philip the Fair of France. They had features not altogether unlike; they were both physically handsome, both personally brave, both intellectually vigorous, both capable when roused of an implacable resentment. On the whole, the English monarch was amenable to the softer traits; he had been in the wars of Palestine, and had caught somewhat of the spirit of chivalry. In his youth, he had defended his father's crown against that great revolution which ended in the permanent establishment of a House of Commons; and although it was his hand that saved the crown, there are not wanting some indications that, to a certain extent, he sympathized with the objects of the rebellion; he learned from it, at all events, a lesson which he never forgot. None loved arbitrary power more than the first Edward; but none saw more clearly that the days for arbitrary power had passed away, that the principles of Magna Charta, rightly interpreted and fully evolved, must lead to the suppression of all despotism, and the confirmation of all individual rights. Accordingly, through his whole reign, it was the object of Edward Plantagenet, as it was afterwards the object of Elizabeth Tudor, to discover in what direction the winds were blowing, and to trim the sails in harmony with them, to catch the popular voice and give effect to it; and where the popular voice was raised against his measures, to desist from these measures with the best grace he could command. It is true that as yet the popular voice was chiefly the utterance of the barons; but we have already seen how the power of the barons presupposed the privileges of the vassal, and in proportion as feudalism declined, it became more and more evident that the voice of the vassal must have weight in framing his country's laws. Edward, on his part, seemed more desirous for the extension of his kingdom than for the extension of his kingly prerogative. He aimed to erect the throne of England into the throne of the British Empire. He was already in possession of Ireland, and he was eager to complete the union. His design was not wholly unsuccessful; he permanently conquered Wales, he temporarily conquered Scotland; at the time of his death he was actually sovereign of a united Britain. But if he desired to keep Britain united in himself, he was determined to keep it separate from all others. He had studied so closely to meet the currents of public opinion, that he had become beloved by his people, and he felt that here lay at once his own strength and the strength of England. He refused to admit that he was the vassal of any sovereign, secular or spiritual; he refused to admit that his kingdom was dependent on any power either of Church or State; and he maintained an attitude of bold opposition to all the pretensions advanced by the Roman See.

But England was too insulated in position, either seriously to disturb Boniface, or seriously to be disturbed by him; it was on the continent of Europe that the great battle was to be fought between Papal absolutism and political freedom. On the throne of France there sat a sovereign who was by no means disposed to hold the reins for any pontiff. Philip the Fair had ascended that throne when a youth of seventeen. He had come into a kingdom circumscribed on every side, beset by enemies all around, and virtually dominated by its own vassals; in a very few years, by talent, by intrigue, by courage, and by policy, he had made it a formidable power in the councils of Europe. He had obtained Navarre, Champagne, and Brie by marriage; he had possessed himself of a great part of Flanders by the sword; he had surprised, for a time, even out of the strong grasp of the English Edward, the important duchy of Guienne; he had extended the northern and eastern boundaries of the French nation very nearly to the measure of their present limits. If the aim of Edward I. was to establish a united Britain, the aim of Philip the Fair was to establish a united France— to be sole and undisputed sovereign over all his dominions. There were two elements which retarded the realization of this plan—the temporal pretensions of the pontiff, and the feudal insolence of the French barons; the breaking down of these barriers was the task which Philip contemplated as the mission of his life. He seems to have felt that, in order to effect either object, there must be raised into prominence a third power in the nation; that same power which had begun to rise in England with the institution of a House of Commons; that same power which had begun to issue from the universities in a current of intellectual life. It was from that despised company whom, two hundred years before, a French writer had stigmatized as a herd of slaves, that Philip the Fair resolved to seek a new source of strength for the nation,—a strength which, while inevitably it must restrain the arbitrary power of kings, must free them at the same time from the dangers incidental to an unchecked reign of feudalism,—a strength which, as it flowed from the very heart of liberty, must support the authority of the crown in maintaining national freedom against the claims of an absolute Papacy.

It was not long before the ideas of Philip and of Boniface revealed their mutual antagonism. The protracted wars of the French king had exposed him to heavy expenses, and to meet these he was obliged to resort to severe taxation. He saw no reason why any party in the State should be exempted from bearing the burdens of the State. That the clergy should be allowed to exercise temporal privileges, and should yet be held free from contributing to the temporal wealth of the nation, was a notion that, to the mind of Philip, seemed contrary to all the laws of nature. Accordingly he enacted that the public taxation should be shared equally by the clergy and the laity; that the priest, in so far as he was a man and a Frenchman, should regard himself as a citizen of his country, subject to civil law, and bound to lend his support to the temporal good of the community. Such a mandate struck at the very roots of Papal absolutism, and could not be suffered to pass unchallenged. The clergy had hitherto acknowledged no sovereign but the pontiff; it was in attestation of that doctrine that Thomas à Becket in England had submitted to privation, to exile, ultimately to death itself. Boniface issued his command to the French clergy to pay no respect whatever to the enactment of Philip, to hold themselves the subjects of heaven, and ignore the tribute to Cæsar. Philip retaliated in a very practical manner; he issued a decree that neither money nor valuables should be sent out of the country, and the effect of this mandate was to cut off a main source of the Papal revenue. Boniface despatched his legate to France, hoping to overawe the king by a representative of the Papal presence; but he had mistaken the character of the man with whom he had to deal. The legate indignantly remonstrated, arrogantly declaimed, and insolently reprimanded; Philip replied by ordering him to prison. An act so daring, an act in the view of that age so sacrilegious, could not do otherwise than startle the heart of Europe; but when a man takes a strong step, his only chance of success is to follow it up by a stronger. Immediately after the imprisonment of the legate, Philip convoked an assembly of the States of France. That was perhaps the most remarkable Parliament which the French nation had ever seen. It was composed, not from one class, but from all classes. The king was there to represent the state-power. The barons were there to represent the power of the aristocracy. Last, but not least, the deputies from the towns were there; no longer as a 'herd of slaves,' no longer as a patronized class permitted to eat the crumbs which fell from their master's table, but as a real legislative body forming an integral part of the social system, and holding a prominent place in the political decisions of their country. And the conduct of that Parliament was as remarkable as its composition. With one voice, the French nation homologated the acts of their king, declared that his quarrel was their quarrel, his interest their interest, his freedom their freedom, said that they would stand by him to the last extremity, that no Papal interdict, no bull of excommunication would alter their sentiments or shake their allegiance; and that in the face of the whole opposing hierarchy, they would maintain and defend the independence of their native land. The spectacle is fading in the mists of five hundred years; but even through the shadows of the past, its moral grandeur reaches us, and enchains our admiration. It is not the question of a disputed taxation, it is not even the interest of an anti-Papal movement which impresses us; it is the vision of one united nation emerging bodily from the night of superstition; defying interdict, defying anathema, defying everything save the love of country and the thirst for political freedom. Never before had the history of mediæval Europe exhibited an attitude so determined, and a course so uncompromising. Proud Germany had quailed before the thunderbolt of Hildebrand, Norman England had crouched repentant beneath the lash of Innocent, France alone had remained undaunted and unwavering. The German struggle of investitures had been in great measure the struggle only of a personal ambition, the will of one sovereign contending with the will of another. The controversy with John of England had in no sense been national; it was but the strife between the claims of a pontiff, and the individual pride of a European potentate. The war with Philip of France was originally the contention with the pride and avarice of Philip himself; but the moment he was supported by the voice of the States-General, it became in the highest sense a national war. It was no longer by the caprice of a solitary despotic will that the pontiff was assailed, no longer by the personal ambition of a French king, nor even by the secret cabals of a French ministry; it was by the voice of the French people, by the sentiments of the national heart, by the opinions of the public mind. He was opposed by the whole life of the nation, and the moral force of such an opposition was more formidable than would have been the coalition of all the sovereigns, and the marshalling of all the armies.

Boniface felt that this moral force must be counteracted by a similar movement on his own part. Accordingly he assembled a council at Rome, which supported his view of the question. With the consent of this council, Boniface issued one of the most remarkable bulls which has ever proceeded from the chair of St. Peter,—a bull which expressed in the most daring and presumptuous terms the utmost stretch of Papal ambition,—terms which Hildebrand at the height of his power, and Innocent in the zenith of his glory, would never have dared to use. The

Isidorian decretals had all along contemplated the absolute power of the Papacy. Hildebrand, unconsciously to himself, had been working towards that destiny even while he imagined that he was securing only a spiritual empire. Innocent III. had consciously and deliberately ascended the throne of universal dominion, and claimed the sovereignty alike of Church and State, of king and priest, of the temporal and the spiritual world. But neither the Isidorian decretals in their prospective anticipations, nor Hildebrand in his strivings to realize them, nor Innocent in his actual realization of their dream, had ever for a moment contemplated making the absolute power of the Papacy an essential doctrine of Christianity; that was left for a rasher and a weaker man. It is true, the pontiffs of the past had pronounced sentences of excommunication, but they had done so on the ground that they had been constituted custodiers of the divine government on earth. Whatever motives of private resentment may secretly have mingled with their actions, they had nominally inflicted punishment, not on account of a personal insult to themselves, but on account of a spiritual principle which they alleged to have been infringed. But the bull called *Unam Sanctam* which now issued from the deliberations of Boniface and his council, presented to the world a view of the subject which in form at least was altogether new. In that bull it was proclaimed that, considered in itself and for its own sake, the belief in Papal absolutism was necessary to salvation; that to separate between the temporal power of the civil magistrate and the spiritual power of the pontiff was to enthrone Satan side by side with God; that to distinguish between the political empire of the kingdom and the ecclesiastical empire of the Church was to revive the Manichæan heresy, to go back to the days of Parsism, to worship two principles of nature, the one good, and the other evil.

On the receipt of this remarkable document, the French king issued two commands: the first was, that it should be publicly burned; the second, that those of the French clergy who had supported it, should have their property confiscated. In both of these enactments he was seconded by the voice of the nation. Did France at that moment believe itself to be a nation of infidels? did the king of France at that moment believe himself to have shaken off the fetters of all religious faith? did the eyes of united Europe, contemplating the scene, shrink with horror from an act of sacrilege? On the contrary, Philip professed then and ever to be the strictest of Catholics; France, in the very act of following his footsteps, declared herself to be a true daughter of the Church of Rome; and mediæval Europe, so far from instituting a crusade against a heretic nation, looked on sympathetically, and secretly rejoiced. These facts are alone strongly suggestive. They show that the bull of Boniface was not regarded as a legitimate exposition of the doctrines of Catholicism; that in framing that bull, he had transcended the limits of all decretals and of all councils; that he had added to the subject-matter of the sacred writings a doctrine which even in germ was not contained in them; and that he had subordinated the interests of Catholic truth to the gratification of his own individual passions. Had the sense of all this not been strong in the heart of Europe, the heart of Europe, in beholding the attitude of the French people, would have thrilled with indignation. A hundred years before, the Waldenses had been persecuted for a rebellion not half so great; two hundred years afterwards, the Lutherans were persecuted for a rebellion originally no greater. But at the present juncture, Europe felt that in the very bosom of the hierarchy, in the very central figure of the hierarchy, there was being perpetrated a most portentous heresy,—a heresy which, if promulgated, would shake the thrones of the world to their foundation, would extinguish the last spark of temporal power, would quench the waking life of political freedom, would repress the movement of culture that was issuing from the walls of the universities, would arrest the growth of the spirit of Christianity itself, and forbid its further increase in wisdom or in stature. Catholic Europe felt this, and therefore for once, Catholic Europe refused to be Papal; it stood a neutral spectator of the scene, stood with the sword undrawn and the sympathy unexpressed for either side, but waiting the issue of events, hoping for the triumph of secular liberty, and allowing the onward development of humanity to unwind without hindrance its mighty destiny.

The burning of the Papal bull brought out the thunderbolt; that thunderbolt which in the hands of

Hildebrand had brought an emperor to his knees. Boniface issued that long-delayed sentence of excommunication, whose very delay was calculated to render it more imposing and terrible. Excommunication had been to the Papacy what in an after age the Old Guard was to Napoleon; an unfailing source of strength, which turned the scale of battle even at the eleventh hour. Nor had Boniface any reason to conclude that its thunders would be less potent now than they were when a German emperor stood uncrowned before them at the Castle of Canosa. But Boniface had only been observing the surface of the world, and beneath the surface all was changed. Excommunication had lost its power. The thunder still rolled, but it rolled no longer as the voice of God; the lightning still flashed athwart the sky, but it flashed no longer as an angry gleam from the eye of the Almighty. The world had gradually been retiring into the inner chamber of the soul, had been listening to voices more directly divine than those of any natural majesty, had been slowly though surely learning the lesson that physical force is not spiritual power. The minds of men had changed, and silently the times had changed with them, and the evidence for the transformation was shortly to appear; the thunderbolt which brought the emperor to his knees brought the arms of Philip to the gates of the Roman capital.

If a sentence of excommunication did not utterly crush, it was inevitable that it should embolden; itself an extreme step, it drove its victim to extremity. Instead of being prostrated, Philip prepared for war.

Boniface had now played his last stake; he had launched his imaginary thunders, but he had no real ones. A formidable enemy was on his track; where could he find resources to meet him? Casting his eye over the western world, he could discover no friend. France was already in the field, England was hostile in spirit, Sicily had ceased to hold the reins, Italy was secretly disaffected, Germany was restive and ready to rise at a moment's notice. He remembered the days of Hildebrand, he remembered how that enterprising pontiff with all his genius had been unable to protect his capital, and he felt that the task must be still more hopeless now. He resolved not to abide the issue; he fled from Rome. He had a country-seat at Anagni; thither he repaired, hoping to be overlooked in its obscurity. His hope was fallacious. The French general Nogaret surrounded him with a band of soldiers, and no man drew a sword in his defence. He surrendered, and the temporal Papacy surrendered with him. They put him on a steed with his face to the tail, and, loaded with every species of ignominy, they led him back to his capital; that capital into which, nine years before, he had ridden in so different an attitude and under such contrary auspices. There they imprisoned him, and for two days he remained in the closest custody. Into the agony of those two days the eye of history cannot penetrate; the effect they produced upon the pontiff alone reveals their horror. He seems to have believed that a scheme had been formed against his life. He refused to taste food lest it should contain poison, and his physical strength became exhausted. But all this time the inward passions of the man were blazing with a lurid fire. Impotent rage venting itself in imaginary acts of vengeance, chagrin feeding upon its own disappointment, malign hatred wreaking its fury upon victims beyond its reach, the mortified pride which even in ruin shrank from acknowledging that life had been a failure,—all at one moment preyed upon his famished frame. At the end of two days the populace rose and released the pontiff, but they released a raving maniac; his nerves had been unstrung, and reason had fled. For a month he raged in wild delirium, and then the fire of the burning spirit consumed its outward tabernacle, and with the loss even of the empire over his own soul, the last of the temporal pontiffs passed away.

It was the determined resolution of Philip that he should be the last; accordingly he prepared to take such steps as should place the Papacy entirely under his control. He raised to the vacant throne Bertrand of Bordeaux; a Frenchman, and therefore supposed to be interested in France; a creature of his own, and therefore certain to be the tool of all his measures. The new pontiff, who took the name of Clement v., was immediately confronted by two commands of the French king, in both of which he obsequiously acquiesced. The first was the suppression of the Knights-Templars. That order had been originally devised as a body-guard to the Pope. In the days of chivalry it had shared in the prevailing spirit, and had become rather adverse to the Papacy; but now that chivalry was gone, it was in danger of going back again to its first love. For chivalry had departed from knighthood and had gone down into the valleys; gone down to ennoble the paths of the humble Waldenses, gone down to illuminate and beautify the acts of the self-denying Franciscans. The order of the Knights-Templars had become demoralised, and a demoralised order supporting by military force a demoralised Papacy was a consummation devoutly to be deprecated. We have therefore no hesitation whatever in justifying this act of Philip; we believe their suppression to have been demanded by the interests of the rising civilisation. But when we consider the method by which that suppression was effected, when we review the spectacle of merciless persecution in which they were extinguished, we are unable even now to withhold our surprise and horror. That Philip should have confiscated their wealth was perhaps in a measure just; the Templars had taken the oath of poverty, and had no right to the possession of riches. In any case, however, such a confiscation can awaken no surprise, for it was in strict keeping with that avarice which was ever the overmastering passion in the heart of the French monarch. But if Philip was avaricious, he was not cruel for the sake of cruelty; nay, he has performed one act in the direction of benevolence which has conferred as much honour on himself as benefit on humanity; we allude to the abolition in France of that terrible institution which had disgraced mediæval civilisation, and thrown a blemish over the history of a church which in many of its aspects is worthy to be admired—the deadly tribunal of the Catholic Inquisition. This Philip abolished, and for this humanity is his debtor. Yet it is not too much to say, that the Inquisition in its fieriest days, in the days when it hunted down the unfortunate Albigenses with a more than pagan fury, never surpassed the ferocity of hatred, never transcended the horrors of torture, with which Philip pursued the Templars on to the bitter end. They were driven from city to city, they were hunted from hiding-place to hiding-place, they were stripped, they were spoiled, they were lacerated, they were burned in hundreds. That they were guilty of one-half the crimes alleged against them we do not believe. They were transparently a demoralised order, but they ought to have borne their punishment *as* an order, and not as individual men; nor was any further punishment than suppression demanded by the circumstances. We must not forget, however, that in these deeds of seeming barbarity Philip acted not alone; that here, as ever, he was in strict alliance with the voice of his people; and that if odium there be, France has elected to share it along with him. The spectacle of a united nation, a brave, generous, and humane nation, consenting with one mind to institute a relentless reign of death, may perhaps encourage us to hope that there were features of the case which to us of later times are no longer visible, and that there were grounds for a national severity which have disappeared from our view in the obscurities of a long-vanished age.

The second command which Philip imposed upon the new pontiff was one which involved far less cruelty, and occasioned in its execution far less noise, but which, like many noiseless proceedings, was powerful in its influence and potent in its results; it was the command that henceforth the capital of the Papacy should no longer be Rome, but Avignon. The requirement, on a superficial view, seems trivial; in reality, it was a blow which struck at the very roots of the Papal dynasty,—a blow compared to which the suppression of ten thousand orders of knighthood and the disbanding of all the Papal armies in Europe would have been but the touch of a feather. If it be true that Paris is France, it is still more profoundly true that Rome is the Papacy. The concentration of France around the prosperity of Paris is at best a political and social fact; the concentration of the Papal life around the prosperity of Rome is the result of a religious association as close as that which connects the sacred service with the consecrated walls of the cathedral. Even in pagan times we have seen how the Roman Empire centred in the welfare of Rome; we have seen how Nero, when he would break the spirit of that empire, had to attempt the work of subjugation by setting fire to that capital which had given birth to its heroism and its patriotism. The classic associations of Rome had not died with paganism, but to these associations there had been superadded another stronger still, that of Christianity itself. Rome was the chair of St. Peter, the seat of the chief apostle, the bishopric assigned to him who had received the power to bind and to loose on earth, and on whom, as on a stedfast rock, the Master Himself had promised to build His Church. To Rome, in a long unbroken line of witnesses, had been entrusted the keeping of the oracles of God, the transmission from age to age of the sacred traditions, the preservation of the apostolic light to all generations; Rome had been to the Roman all that Jerusalem was to the Jew. To transplant the Papacy from Rome was to destroy Jerusalem. It was to accomplish without bloodshed and without struggle all that Nero had attempted to accomplish by fire; it was to rob the capital of that sacred association which was now its only claim to majesty; it was to rob the Papacy of that possession of the capital which was now its only claim to empire. Yet this, and nothing less than this, was the design of the French monarch, and that design he accomplished bloodlessly and effectually. Without a struggle the pontiff yielded; gave up his sacred capital, gave up its hallowed memories, and took up his court at Avignon, to serve as the slave of his master, under the immediate glance of his eye. And now there began for the Papacy that long and dreary period of the seventy years' exile; that period which Italian writers call the Babylonish captivity, which Protestants perhaps would be more apt to call the captivity of Babylon. For ourselves, we are quite willing to admit the parallel between the position of captive Rome in Avignon and the position of captive Israel in Babylon. Mediæval Rome and ancient Israel had both been carried into a foreign land, and they had both experienced that fate for the same reason. Israel had forgotten that its strength lay in its theocratic power; it had aimed at a purely temporal dominion, and had lost sight of the object of its worship in the forms which symbolized Him. Rome had forgotten that the apostolic mission which it claimed had, in the hands of the apostles, been a spiritual work—the proclamation of peace on earth and goodwill to men; and it, too, had lost sight of the object of its worship in the images by which it represented Him. Therefore Rome, like Israel, passed over into bondage, and the Papal reign was overshadowed by the temporal power of kings. The successors of St. Peter entered upon a long and ignominious captivity; a captivity which wore out the heart by the expectation of a deliverance it so bitterly deferred, until at last it was closed by a catastrophe yet more dismal, and by a fate more ignominious still.

The history of those seventy years may be described as the history of an intellectual thaw. Everywhere the ice of outward restraint was melting, and the waters of long-imprisoned life were rushing over it. The renaissance which had risen in Italy with the muse of Dante diffused itself more and more, and Petrarch sang its sonnets and Boccaccio told its tales; Flanders caught the glow and burst into a life at once of æsthetic and of civil freedom,—the one blazing out in the triumphs of art, the other in that violent insurrectionary movement which appeared in the followers of Jakob van Artivelde. The French peasants received the infection, and rose with that brutal licence which in the first stages of political revolution the populace are apt to mistake for liberty. But stretching through all ranks, from knight to peasant, from lofty to obscure, there was a power permeating society which was calculated alike to confirm the freedom and to calm the violence; that power was the life of the universities. The universities were to the secular world what the Church was to the ecclesiastical; both were republican institutions, into whose fold, without distinction, could be admitted all who desired the privilege; within whose precincts rich and poor might gather side by side and listen to the words of earthly or of heavenly wisdom, and from whose precincts rich and poor could emerge with advantages which, intellectually at least, were not unequally shared. From these universities the captivity of the Papacy lifted a chain. The Sorbonne of Paris gave rein to that speculative tendency which had ever secretly characterized it, and in proportion as the Papacy declined, waxed bolder day by day. Oxford, from her thirty thousand students, poured forth every year streams of intellectual life, and sent out into the world of history men who were to shape its course and direct its way,—the subtle, powerful, hair-splitting Duns Scotus; the anti-Papal, rationalistic, half-sceptical Occam; the clear, judicious, legal-minded Bradwardine; the brave, enterprising, liberal-hearted Grostete; the earnest, zealous, life-seeking Richard of Armagh. We have said that the universities were inimical to Papal absolutism, we might have gone a step farther — the universities were inimical to all exclusive clerical influence, wheresoever manifested and in whatever sphere displayed. Their great work for society was the education of the laity, and the education of the laity meant inevitably the depression of clerical influence. Before their work had begun to bear fruit, the clergy had almost monopolized the learned professions,—they were statesmen, they were kings' counsellors, they were lawyers, they were physicians, they were philosophic lecturers, they were frequently everything but pastors, and many of them left their parishes to the care of delegates. It must be confessed that, if the parishes were sufferers, the public were generally gainers. If the clergy of those days had not monopolized the professions, the professions would for the most part have remained unappropriated; the laity were inadequate to conduct them, the mass of the people had received no training, and the churchmen shone like stars in a dark firmament. The clergy had up to this time been the sole supports of culture, and were therefore worthy of that respect and influence which humanity had accorded them. But with the development of university life there was coming a great change. The laity were becoming a power; not merely a fighting, or an agricultural, or a labouring power,—in these capacities they had always been distinguished. But, for the first time, the laity were rising into the dignity of an educational power. They were making strides of advancement over the path of human knowledge, they were growing in that knowledge which is most essential of all—the knowledge of their own souls, of their possibilities, their responsibilities, their powers as human beings, and the individual rights which flowed from the possession of such powers. By and by the learned professions became divided; they ceased to be a monopoly of the Church, they were parted amongst many lives. From the ranks of the laity there began to rise separate communities of students, each devoting itself to a distinct branch of study, and deprecating mutual interference; some followed the law, some healed the sick, some served in the cabinet, some lectured on the platform. The Church was thus driven more and more within its own province. The clergy, expelled from the exclusive empire over secular civilisation, were forced to become clergymen indeed, to devote themselves to their peculiar work, to limit themselves to their special sphere of operation. And while the Church gained by the change, the laity did not lose. They were left unfettered to pursue their investigations, to study the laws of nature apart from ecclesiastical jurisdiction, to meditate on the mysteries of mind outside the superintendence of the clerical eye. Science began more and more to be viewed in its own light, philosophy more and more to be studied by its own laws, while religion kept to the sphere of its own dominion, and allowed the secular world to tread its unmolested way. As the sum of the whole matter, those seventy years exhibited a diffusion of the arts of peace. That such a diffusion did not at once produce a diminution in the arts of war is transparent on the face of history. It was in this age of violent political changes, in this age when England, Scotland, France, Flanders, Italy, and Germany writhed in convulsive struggles, that Europe witnessed the introduction of artillery. Yet we are not sure that the introduction of artillery was not itself a messenger of peace. In proportion as the weapons become deadlier, the conflict grows shorter; may we not add that, in proportion as fire takes the place of sword, the conflict grows less bitter too? It is no longer the encounter hand to hand with an enemy whose every look is marked, whose every tone is heard, whose every stroke is seen; men fall in hundreds, but they fall by a scientific mechanism which is set in motion by a far-off foe. Above all, such an agency rubs off the gloss of war, divests it of those opportunities of personal heroism which have made it a sphere of chivalry, and reveals it in all its naked horror, in all its undisguised atrocity. So was it pre-eminently with the world of mediævalism. Chivalry ceased to find a home on the battle-field, and therefore it ceased to desire the battle. It passed over from the camp into the city, passed over from the scenes of physical power to the scenes of intellectual and moral strength, passed over from the ephemeral accomplishments of knighthood to embrace the less gilded but more valuable possessions of social life, to shine in the relations of the family circle, to adorn and beautify the thought of home, to contribute to the decrease of pauperism and the increase of comfort, to establish institutions of benevolence for the needy and of training for the ignorant, to redress the wrongs of the oppressed and down-trodden, and to seek everywhere for such political and religious reforms as might disseminate among the masses the seeds of life and light.

CHAPTER XXXIII.

THIRD REVOLT OF THE SCHOOL-LIFE.

THE changes we have been exhibiting in the previous chapter were as yet only of a political and social nature. The school-life, which was now the university-life, had been awakened into a sense of individuality; but it is not necessary that a sense of individuality should manifest itself in a religious form. Man has many outlets into the realization of personal responsibility; as yet the school-life of the Christian Church had found only one—the responsibility which flows from the right of citizenship. There was clearly something wanted higher and deeper than this. The members of the Christian school-life were not merely the citizens of a political constitution; they were the citizens of the city of God, and any reformation must fall short of the goal which did not lead them to realize this. When the spiritual force of a man is once aroused, its direction is commonly determined by circumstances, and so was it here. The life of the Christian Church was about to be diverted from a political into a religious channel by one of those sobering events which come to the world at large as personal calamities come to the individual mind. About the middle of the fourteenth century mankind was visited by one of the most dreadful pestilences that has ever touched the earth; it is known to posterity as the 'black death.' It is not too much to say, that subsequent history furnishes no parallel to the character of this malady. We read with horror the details of the Great Plague of 1665; some of us can remember with horror the terrible outburst of cholera in 1831. But the plague of 1665 was limited to London; the cholera of 1831, though widely diffused, was, in comparison with the mediæval pestilence, a mere trifle. This was a pestilence which made a sensible diminution in the population of the earth, which swept away from every country of Europe one-third of its inhabitants, which carried off from London alone 50,000 souls; which, beginning in the north of Asia, penetrated through every European capital and thinned every rank of society, from the residents in the palace to the peasants in the village. In an age which believed the earth to be the centre of the universe, in an age which was profoundly ignorant of the reign of law, in an age which made every unusual occurrence identical with the supernatural, it is not surprising that such a catastrophe should have been received by many as a direct judgment from Heaven. It is still less surprising, that in this or in any other age the perpetual presence of death should have roused men into a sense of moral earnestness. Here, in the midst of human ambition, in the midst of hierarchical claims and Papal aspirations, in the midst of the strife of kings for empire and of Parliaments for supremacy, there appeared a handwriting on the wall which proclaimed that these objects of human idolatry had been weighed in the balance and found wanting. Man was suddenly awakened to behold the nothingness of power, to see the emptiness and the vanity of the kingdoms of the world and the glory of them in the presence of the great leveller, death. And the levelling power of death had itself a moral suggestiveness; it drew nearer those ranks of society which feudalism had divided, it showed that the points in which they differed were as nothing in comparison with that great load of human frailty which they had all alike to bear. Men not only began to think earnestly, but they began to think unanimously. The sense of human brotherhood was kindled by the feeling of human nothingness in the presence of the great destroyer, who knocked impartially at the door of palace and of hovel; and the recognition of a common need, binding in unity the lives of men, was the origin of a bond of sympathy which knit the interests of the hamlet to the engrossments of the throne.

This current of moral earnestness running through humanity changed the tendency to political revolution into the desire for religious reform; in other words, it transformed what had been only a revolt of the State into a revolt of the school-life. The first symptoms of this revolt appeared in England. Here, the ravages of the plague had been specially severe. It had spared no class of society, it had removed two members of the royal family, it had carried off the learned Bradwardine from the Church, it had swept away multitudes from the marts of commerce and the scenes of agricultural labour. England being thus united in a common suffering, became united also in a common aim—the endeavour after a revived religious life. It was around the University of Oxford that this union centred, specially around one majestic form which occupied its theological throne; a form which, even in an age rich in its historical figures, has left all its contemporaries in the shade; the zealous, the illustrious John Wicliffe. His biography belongs to the history of England, and specially to the history of the mediæval Church of England. The point which concerns us is the work of the man; his place in human development, and his contribution to the growth of the Christian life. Great as Wicliffe was, he was not an originator; he followed the course of his times, and his life was the product of his times. It is therefore of importance to see what was that position which he occupied in the Church's pilgrimage, what stage of its journey he marked, what advance upon the past his life was designed to indicate.

Wicliffe derived his name from the place of his birth, a village in Yorkshire. It is remarkable that nearly all the great English Reformers had sprung from the northern counties. Cædmon had inaugurated the birth of Saxon poetry in Northumberland; Bede, the first of Saxon commentators, was a native of Durham; Alcuin, the greatest of Saxon educators, was master of the school of York; and Wicliffe was now to add another to the list. But if Wicliffe was born in that region, which had in days of old been the home of liberty, he was bred in that school, which in mediæval days had ever been esteemed the strongest guardian of its interest—the University of Oxford. With Oxford were associated the days of his youth, with Oxford were blended his hopes of greatness, with Oxford were shared his first literary triumphs. It is as Master of Balliol College that he makes his earliest appearance in history; before that time, he had led a hidden life. We know not the beginning of his spiritual struggles, we are unable to trace the rise of his Papal antipathies. When he stands before us, he is a man of thirty-seven, with a mind intensely spiritual, and a Papal antipathy, if not fully developed, certainly very clearly manifested. Doubtless, like other Englishmen, he had been impressed with the horrors of the great pestilence, roused to think of the nothingness of the outer world, and the awful reality of the inner. But he possessed a power which other Englishmen did not possess; he could rouse others to think. His lectures of 1363 opened a new era in Oxford. Students who had once been attracted by the subtlety of theological debate, or by the novelty of theological speculation, were now stimulated by the exhibition of that religious life which is deeper than all subtlety, and higher than all speculation. They listened to a man whose researches were made, not into the manuscripts of the doctors, nor even into the writings of the Fathers, but chiefly and primarily into the secret places of the human heart. At first, all Oxford, in the course of a few years all England, was thrilled. Never before had the heart of the English people been stirred so unanimously. A community of interest had made all ranks one. Edward III. was struggling with the Papacy to obtain the remission of that tribute which Pope Innocent had enacted from King John. The Duke of Lancaster, his brother, was animated by a personal admiration for Wicliffe, and perhaps also by a prepossession in favour of his doctrines. The Parliament was at one with the king in contending for the liberties of the nation. The best men in the Church were stimulated by that fervour which pervaded the moral atmosphere of the day. The burghers were in sympathy with a creed which seemed to recognise the individual rights of man. The peasantry themselves had been recently raised into enthusiasm by the publication of an anonymous work called *Piers the Ploughman*, in which the practices of the hierarchy were satirized, and the abuses of the Papacy held up to ridicule. With such a unity of sentiment permeating the land, Wicliffe found no difficulty in making his voice heard over its length and breadth. As by an electric current of sympathy, his words were borne far and near into the hearts of all, and irrespective of age or circumstance or station, they found a responsive echo in every mind. But perhaps the most singular fact is, that this impression should have been so enduring. That an age of religious revival should find representatives in all classes, is not surprising, but that such an age should be prolonged for many years, is contrary to general experience. In proportion as such movements are strong, they are commonly short-lived; in proportion as the fire burns fiercely, it is the sooner extinguished. But in the reformation of Wicliffe we have a very remarkable exception to the ordinary rule. From the time when he delivered his Oxford lectures in 1363, till the day when he was summoned before the Convocation of 1382, his influence never declined, and his star never paled. Although the Pope fulminated five bulls against him, although king and Parliament, archbishop and university, were alike importuned to silence his declamations, although thrice in the course of these years he was called to answer before an ecclesiastical tribunal of his country, his person remained unharmed, and his power continued unshaken. It is true that the final Convocation of 1382 did pronounce upon his doctrines the long deferred sentence of condemnation; but why? If we are not greatly mistaken, it was for reasons rather political than religious. In the preceding year there had been a great rebellion of the populace — a rebellion which aimed at nothing less than the destruction of monarchy and the establishment of a democratic constitution. Was it unnatural that in the public mind the political outburst should have been associated with the movement of religious reform? Connection between them there was none, except the connection flowing from the fact that, when the spirit of innovation has moved in one sphere, it tends towards a simultaneous motion in another. Yet the public might be excused for imagining a real connection between religious reform and political radicalism; at all events, they did imagine it, and the cause of religious reform suffered accordingly. From that day many of his best supporters walked no more with Wicliffe. As long as they believed his reformation to be in harmony with the interests of the State, they were enthusiastic in its cause; it was only when they conceived it to be politically dangerous, that they opposed themselves to its further progress. Were the ridiculous rebellion of Wat Tyler erased from history, we can see no reason why the transformation effected under Henry VIII. should not have found its accomplishment in the days of Chaucer.

Now, whence proceeded this long-enduring power of Wicliffe? It cannot be accounted for by mere enthusiasm, for that tends to expend itself. It cannot be explained by the exciting events of the religious world, for the excitement caused by historical incidents is by its very nature temporary and evanescent. It must clearly have its ground in some deeper source. If the movement of Wicliffe endured longer than the movements of his predecessors, it must have been because it contained some elements of strength which were wanting in previous efforts. And, indeed, we shall not look far ere we shall discover in the system of Wicliffe many elements which naturally made for permanence. There is one feature of this reform which on the very surface marks it out from all its forerunners. The keen eye of Wicliffe travelled over the organizations of the hierarchy, and in the perfection of these organizations it beheld the reason of that success which the hierarchy had so long enjoyed. Wicliffe saw that the Papacy had triumphed because it had never acted alone, because it had always surrounded itself with a body-guard of emissaries whose mission was to strike in its defence, to ward off the blows of its enemies, and to spread the reputation of its power. And Wicliffe asked why the sons of religious reform had not adopted a similar expedient? Papal Rome had its Templars, its Dominicans, its Franciscans; why should not reforming England institute an association of reformers who should accomplish for religious freedom what these orders had accomplished for Papal aggrandisement. Wicliffe answered that question by instituting the order of the Lollards. The meaning of their name has been lost in the lapse of ages, but the nature of their office is still clearly discernible. They were to be to mediæval Christianity what the first disciples were to opening Christianity; the diffusers of the message of peace, the preachers of the kingdom of righteousness, the baptizers into a higher faith and into a purer life. But Wicliffe knew well the evanescent effect of even the most eloquent preaching. He knew that while it was easy to rouse the passions of men, it was supremely difficult to imbue them with principles of action. He desired, therefore, to approach the people by a more certain avenue than the hearing of the ear. He desired to address them through a perpetual medium; a medium which would not vanish when the preacher's voice was withdrawn. To secure such a medium Wicliffe began, continued, and ended the distinctive work of his life; he translated the whole Bible into the English tongue, and put copies for distribution into the hands of his missionary Lollards. The work had more than a religious value; it marked a new era in literature. The English language was as yet only in its infancy; it had been born of the union of north and south, the amalgamation of the Saxon and the Latin races. But an infant language will perish unless it be nourished. There is nothing which tends so much to consolidate a new tongue as its embodiment in a standard work, for its terms thereby become the household words of all ages. The aristocracy of England had already received the instalment of such a standard in the first productions of one who was to bear the proud pre-eminence of being the father of English poetry. Chaucer was blazing in the literary firmament, and was shedding over the northern shores that light which he had caught from Italian skies. He had seen many lands, he had passed through varied circumstances, he had talked with all classes of men, and therefore to some extent he was a universal man. But the spirit which had most powerfully laid hold of him was the spirit of Boccaccio, of Petrarch, of the great renaissance of Italy; it was in him that the life of Florence first found a meeting-place with the life of England. Yet the poetry of Chaucer, just because it breathed the spirit of the renaissance, was better adapted to the higher than to the lower orders of society; it was the poetry of the king, of the court, of the knight, of the aristocracy, and as such it fixed the language only in the spheres of the great and noble. There was wanted a man who would perform for the middle and lower orders that work which Chaucer had accomplished for the higher, and that man was found in Wicliffe. He professed to do for the citizen and for the peasant what Chaucer had done for the knight and for the courtier; to give them a standard book,—a book in whose pages they would find food for meditation, yet food adapted to the simplicity of their daily wants; a book free from all verbal subtleties and removed from all scholastic definitions, but powerful in the plainness of its utterance, and strong in the directness of its meaning. In accomplishing that work, Wicliffe did for the English language even more than Chaucer; the poetry of the Italian renaissance could speak to the cultured, but the Bible had a voice alike for the refined and the unlearned; it bore the household words into every household, and made the language of England a universal possession.

But there is another element to be taken into account in estimating the ground of Wicliffe's prolonged popularity. It must be remembered that, while he professed to be a reformer, he never claimed to have advanced the development of Christian truth. Wicliffe disarmed suspicion by turning his eye, not towards the future, but towards the past, by contemplating as the object of desire not a progress, but a regress. If we were asked, in few words, to indicate to modern times the theological position of Wicliffe, we would point for answer to the Old Catholic movement of Germany. It seems to us that the attitude of Wicliffe in the mediæval world bears a strong resemblance to the attitude of Döllinger in the modern world. Wicliffe desired not to separate from the Catholic Church, but to lead back that Church to its primitive simplicity and purity. It is true he opposed the Roman pontiff with all the vehemence at his command, and in language neither measured nor ambiguous. 'The Antichrist,' 'the proud worldly priest of Rome,' 'the cursed clipper,' 'the wicked purse-kerver,' are amongst the choice epithets which he bestowed on the chair of St. Peter; the last two are obsolete, and exist only as survivals of mediæval passion. But if Wicliffe spared not the Roman pontiff, he would have been quite ready to reverence the Roman bishop. He objected to a Papal absolutism, he objected to a temporal Papacy of any kind, but he would have willingly acknowledged the bishop of Rome as the spiritual head of the Church; and in this he was a good Catholic of the olden time. Again, Wicliffe translated the Bible into English, and in doing so he was undoubtedly at variance with the law of his Church, yet that law was no older than 1229. Previous to the Council of Toulouse, it had been quite allowable to translate the Scriptures into the separate dialect of each country; the hierarchy did not encourage the process, but neither did they forbid it. It was only when the commotion excited by Peter Waldo's translation began to alarm the clergy, that they took steps to prevent the diffusion of the fire. Wicliffe, therefore, might well appeal to a time when

Catholicism was the religion of the world, and when, consistently with that Catholicism, the Scriptures might be disseminated among the masses; in this respect also he was a Catholic of the old school. His repugnance to the practice of indulgences led him to emphasize intensely the doctrine of predestination, as indeed, for the same cause, the Albigenses had done before him; but Wicliffe and the Albigenses alike could point to a time when the Catholic Church was a predestinarian Church, and could cite in proof of their averment that decree by which the Council of Orange homologated the doctrine of Augustine. Finally, Wicliffe challenged the belief in transubstantiation; but we have seen how slow in the Catholic Church was the acceptance of that belief; here, also, he could point to all the days which preceded Pascasius Radbert, and claim to be still a Catholic, though he rejected the later additions to Catholicism. Paradoxical as it may sound, the aim of Wicliffe was to lead the men of his age towards reform by leading them back to conservative principles, to purify Catholicism by forcing it to retrace its steps, to revivify the life of Christianity by restoring the life of the past. We know that in a future generation Luther made a similar attempt, we know that his first design was to reform by a conservative movement. In the days of Luther such a compromise was no longer possible, in the days of Wicliffe it was perhaps the best course which could be devised. Wicliffe made the nearest approach to a reformation which at the time could have been made with safety or success.

He held fast by the original standards of his Church, and he showed himself to be a man with whom the belief in church standards was a matter not merely of speculation but of life; yet in adhering to the essence he swept away the accidents, in holding fast by the original growth he opposed himself to all the accretions. He sought to present to the English people a Catholicism which was comparatively pure from its very primitiveness, and more accessible to reason because nearer to the historical sources of sacred truth; and the English people were at once attracted by the comparative purity, and relieved from apprehension by the manifest oldness of the faith.

It cannot be denied that the cause of Wicliffe was greatly strengthened at this period by a series of important events which occurred on the Continent. The seventy years of the 'Babylonish captivity' had now come to a close. The Papacy, weary of its long exile, had resolved at all hazards to return to its own land. To Gregory XI., the reigning pontiff at Avignon, it seemed that a time had come in every respect favourable for the resumption of Papal dignity. The France in which he sojourned was no longer the France of Philip the Fair; since the days of that monarch, its pride and its power had been brought low. Its fleet had been scattered, its armies had been vanquished, its territories had been dismembered, its king had been lodged a captive in the English capital. Of late, its fortunes had begun to revive, but their revival was slow and difficult. At best, all that France hoped to achieve was restoration to political independence; it was no longer in a condition to hope for the exercise of political domination. A nation thus fettered by adverse circumstances had ceased to present any formidable barrier to the return of Israel from bondage. Accordingly, Gregory XI. seized the opportunity, and set out once more for that sacred capital whose walls had grown more sacred by the endearment of long absence. His exodus was unmolested, and he arrived at his destination in peace; it is probable that, had he lived to reconsolidate his power, Papal Rome might have retrieved its fortunes, but these hopes were dissipated by his death within two years after his return to Italy. And now there opened a scene so humiliating and so dark for Papal Rome, that one, in looking back, cannot but marvel that the chair of St. Peter has passed through it and yet lived. The death of Gregory XI. was the signal for a great conflict; the cardinals of France and Italy strove for the election of the new pontiff. Italy had the claim of long antiquity, the claim of having been for ages the seat of the Papal throne. France had been in possession of the field for the last seventy years, and was not disposed without a struggle to surrender that advantage. An agreement on the subject was hopeless. The Italians elected an Italian, the French made choice of a Frenchman; the former assumed the title of Urban VII., the latter took the name of Clement VI. This was the beginning of the great western schism,—a schism which proved more injurious to the Papacy than all the seventy years of Babylonian bondage.

It was not merely that its physical strength was weakened by division; that was indeed a collateral result. The two pontiffs defied each other, reviled each other, anathematized each other, and at last, proceeding from words to blows, they engaged in a fierce conflict, in which the arms of Urban prevailed, and Clement was driven within the walls of Avignon. But this physical enfeeblement would not in itself have ruined the Papacy. Hildebrand, without an army, without a capital, almost without a friend, was still formidable in the eyes of his enemies. The glory of Papal Rome had all along consisted in the moral strength of its individual rulers; it had never been great or glorious when its bishops had been mean and despicable. The deepest fall which the Papacy experienced by the outburst of the western schism, was the decline of moral influence which that schism necessitated. The brightest feature of the Papacy had ever been its representation of the idea of fatherhood. With all its unconscious errors, and they were many, with all its deliberate faults, and they were not few, it had yet succeeded in representing to the eyes of the mediæval world the thought that that world was itself a vast family in the created universe, presided over by one common fatherhood, and linked together by the sympathetic ties of brotherhood. Europe was peopled by nations differing widely in manners, in customs, in laws, in institutions; separated by impassable mountains, and not less impassable seas, and if possible, even more divided by the differences of mental constitution and temperament. Yet these diverse nations had merged their diversities in a common unity—a unity external, artificial, rather material than spiritual, yet surely not undesirable where spiritual unity was not to be attained. They had gathered around one centre, as the family gathers around the household board; they had sat at one table, they had received their spiritual food from the hands of one father, and that fact had been to them a greater symbol of union than if they had inhabited one plain, and spoken the same language. The Papacy was the fatherhood of the Christian Church; that is and must ever be its proudest prerogative, because it is its oldest claim to antiquity. Before the Pope was recognised as the absolute temporal ruler, before even he was recognised as the source of spiritual power, he was reverenced as the father of Christendom; and to be the father of Christendom is an incomparably higher honour than to be sovereign of the kings of Christendom. But if the Papacy was built on the idea of fatherhood, the idea of fatherhood was built on the fact that the Papacy was undivided; its unity was essential to the very existence of the thought; let that once be broken, and whatever the Papacy might retain, it must lose its oldest claim to respect and veneration in losing the relation of fatherhood. The western schism broke this unity. There had been schisms before in the Papal Church, but these had proceeded, not from the heart of the Church, but from the efforts of kings and emperors to raise up rivals to the pontifical power; here was a division which had originated in the very heart of

Christendom, and which divided into two camps the collective nations of Europe. When each side could boast of such a multitude of supporters, it was clear that neither could have possessed a claim much superior to his rival; yet the very conception of a divided pontificate was suicidal to that office. It was destructive to its holiest element, the idea of fatherhood. It broke the unity of the household of faith; it destroyed the common meeting-place for the hearts of the distant nations; it made a partition in the temple, and divided the souls of the worshippers. The human race ceased to be one spiritual family when it ceased to hold one spiritual head.

And, indeed, at this time the Church had more than ordinary need of concentration; its very foundation was in danger of being shaken. We have seen how the doctrines of Wicliffe had permeated England; it was impossible that such doctrines should long be confined to England. In a very few years from their first promulgation, they had passed over into Bohemia, and there they found at once a congenial soil and an able advocate. The soil was one which had been long prepared for the seeds of political and religious revolution, the advocate was one in every respect qualified to be the spiritual successor of Wicliffe; that advocate was John Huss. There is, as it seems to us, a singular analogy between the outward life of Huss and the outward life of Wicliffe. Both were born into a world ready for revolt against conventionalism. Both were educated at the best and most liberal universities of their time; Wicliffe at Oxford,

Huss at Prague. Both rose to distinction in their respective universities, and ultimately delivered lectures to their respective students. Both subsequently passed from the life of the professor into the office of the preacher, and wielded the same power over the people which they had already exercised over the students. Both, in addition to the populace and the students, obtained access to the ear of royalty; Wicliffe as friend of the Duke of Lancaster, Huss as confessor to Queen Sophia. We are sorry to be obliged to add one parallel more: both were arrested in their career by the suspicion that their Protestantism would interfere with the political constitution of empires. Wicliffe's movement was suppressed by Convocation, because it was suspected of connection with Wat Tyler's rebellion; the movement of Huss was extinguished in blood, because it was accused of lending support to Ladislaus of Naples. In the case of Wicliffe, the political connection was imaginary; in that of Huss, it must be acknowledged to have been real, and this has always seemed to us a matter for regret. The circumstances may be stated in a few sentences. The Council of Pisa had made a laudable effort to put an end to the western schism, had deposed both the rival pontiffs, and had elected in their room Peter de Candia, by the title of Alexander v., thus temporarily restoring the idea of unity. Almost the earliest exercise of authority on the part of the restored pontificate was its proclamation of a crusade against the kingdom of Naples; and to obtain soldiers for the enterprise, it resorted to the usual expedient of granting indulgences to those who should serve. Huss raised his voice against this, and declared it to be a practice contrary to the spirit of Christianity. Though it is probable that he sympathized with the King of Naples, it is certain that his deepest motive was his genuine abhorrence of the practice of indulgences. But while his opposition to that practice was right in theory, we believe that in this instance it was erroneous in policy. To disorganize an army on the eve of battle was a dangerous political offence. Huss should have begun by attacking indulgences as they appeared in domestic life, and as they were granted to individual men; to attack them first in their political relations was an error of judgment, and an error which contributed to weaken the cause of the reformer. It seems to us that some explanation of this sort is required to account for the extraordinary virulence which was subsequently manifested towards him by the most liberal assembly that ever met in the mediæval Church. To that Council of Constance, itself an anti-Papal meeting, there could have been nothing in the doctrines of Huss so repellent as to lead it to condemn him to the flames. We are unable to find any essential point in which he was more heretical than his judges. Of the thirty-nine charges preferred against him at his trial, he positively denied many, and refused to admit the heresy of those to which he confessed. He belonged to the school of Wicliffe, but not more so than did the Council of Constance. Huss does not appear to have adopted the views of

Wicliffe which touched most nearly on heresy; he assuredly did not deny the doctrine of transubstantiation. It seems evident, therefore, that his subsequent judges must have been embittered against him by certain acts of his life which cast a shade over his doctrines, and gave to these doctrines an appearance of danger which was not inherent in themselves. The attempt to interfere with a military arrangement which had existed, and been a source of strength for two centuries, might well have excited alarm even in men who were no friends to the abuse of indulgences; it was too sweeping and too radical a measure to be attempted at once with safety, and the boldness of the aim wrecked the cause of the reformer.

There was, however, another element which increased the danger of Huss' position. He had the misfortune to possess a friend whose zeal outran his discretion. Jerome of Prague was, in many respects, the greater man of the two. He had more learning, and he had more eloquence. His life was, in a more strict sense than that of Huss, stimulated by the breath of the universities. Huss had studied at Prague; Jerome, after completing his studies there, had passed through the universities of Heidelberg, Cologne, Paris, and Oxford, thus receiving the impressions of many lands, and extending by varied sympathies the range of his knowledge of men. Yet, if Jerome was superior to Huss in the gifts of nature, he was inferior to him in its graces. Bold, generous, earnest, enthusiastic, pervaded with the spirit of piety, and with the spirit of the incipient reformation, he was yet deficient in those solid moral qualities which are necessary to constitute a great leader. Surpassing Huss in eloquence, he fell beneath him in judgment; transcending him in knowledge, he did not equal him in that calmness which knowledge ought to bring. His mind wanted a just balance; he took insufficient time to mature his measures, he acted ever on the impulse of the moment, and his momentary impulses were not seldom outrageous. He was not satisfied, like Huss, with condemning indulgences; he trampled the relics under his feet. He was not satisfied, like Huss, with inveighing against the monks; he cast some of them into prison, and threw one of them into the Moldau. Jerome was among the reformers what Peter was among the apostles. He was courageous, and he over-estimated the influence of his own courage; he was zealous, and he allowed his zeal to warp his judgment. He attempted to walk over the sea of human passions, and then recoiled from the danger created by his own temerity. He arrived first at the door of the sepulchre; but when he looked into its ghastly depths, he shrank back from the spectacle, and allowed another first to enter. Jerome and Huss both travelled over the road to martyrdom, but they travelled over it at a very different pace. Jerome beheld the grim shadow of death standing in the midst of the fiery furnace; he beheld it, and he ran with alacrity to meet it; yet, when he stood within the reach of that terrible hand, his courage quailed for a moment, and he retreated in dismay. Huss, too, looked upon the ghastly spectacle, and went forth to encounter it; not perhaps with alacrity, not certainly with eager haste: he did not run, but walked to the goal; yet, when he reached the opening of the furnace, he arrested his progress not a moment, but slowly, deliberately, and stedfastly walked into the arms of death. He that was last became first.

Such were the characters of the two great leaders of the Bohemian movement. In the meantime, that movement was greatly facilitated by the continued dissensions in the hierarchy. The temporary unity, which had been established by the Council of Pisa, had failed to produce peace. Alexander v. had died shortly after his election, and had been succeeded by John XXIII.; but the new election was the signal for a re-assertion of the old claims on the part of the rival pontiffs who had been deposed. Accordingly at one moment there were three men in existence, each professing to be sole sovereign of the spiritual world, and each issuing his decrees as the inviolable mandates of Heaven. In such a Church there could be nothing but anarchy, and religious revolution was as likely to prosper as religious orthodoxy. It was in vain that Archbishop Sbinko burned the books of Wicliffe; the books of Wicliffe had already been re-written in the hearts of the people. It was in vain that he prohibited the preaching of Huss; the voice of the populace, of the court, and of the university obliged him to withdraw his prohibition. It was in vain that a mandate was issued summoning the reformer to appear before the Pope at Rome; he simply refused to go, and the sternest Catholic might have hesitated to pronounce his refusal an illegal act. Who *was* the Pope? who had the right to summon him? who really sat on the chair of St. Peter? who was the schoolmaster to whose training the life of the Church was subject? These were questions which even a believer in the Papacy might well have asked. And these were questions which the whole Church was about to ask. It was becoming clear to the most obtuse mind that a change was coming over the aspect of the world, that old things must pass away, that all things must become new. Two influences had been long at work,—the influence of physical power, and the influence of rising intelligence. For two centuries they had been dividing the Christian world, and their battle had been fierce and fluctuating. But now at last the physical power was yielding, and the intelligence was growing mightier day by day. Could the Church close its eyes to this fact? could it refuse to see the approach of that change which ere long must make itself felt? Such a course was no longer possible. The school-life was stirred by wild impulses towards freedom; in some respects towards licence. It was not prepared, indeed, to give the full rein even to its own impulses; there were counteracting motives which still bound it to the past. The memories of the school, the ancient sanctity which had encircled the person of the schoolmaster, the many historic associations of victory and renown which clustered around the bygone days, all contributed to render a rupture with those days difficult in the extreme. But the school-life felt that, if its impulses were exaggerated, they yet pointed instinctively to a real want; that, if its desires required to be moderated, they must not be suppressed. Whence, with all its reverence for the past, came that dissatisfaction which would not let it rest in the past? Whence, with all that power of memory which bound it to the former days, came that spirit of inquietude which urged it to break away from the old trammels, and travel in freedom over nature's fields? Was it not because the school-life was now too old for school, because the days for scholastic education were past, and the days for a new and higher education had begun? Slowly, yet surely, this conviction was forcing itself upon the heart of Christendom. Day by day it was becoming more apparent that the rules which had been admirable in former years, had lost their power and had lost their usefulness. Day by day it was growing more evident, that the customs and the employments which had been congenial to a period of transition, had become repulsive to an age whose transition was almost perfected. The modes of thought and the systems of discipline that had been sufficient to guide the scholar through the school, were no longer sufficient to guide the youth through those dangerous avenues which lead to manhood; and the life of the Christian Church awoke to the conviction that a new mode of tuition must be opened, in preparation for the new heavens and the new earth.

CHAPTER XXXIV.

CLOSE OF THE SCHOOL-LIFE; THE NEGATIVE REFORMATION COMPLETED.

THE school-life had now arrived at a definite conviction, the conviction that it was too advanced for scholasticism. It accordingly determined to proclaim its majority, to declare itself capable of self-action, to assert its right and its power to be an independent existence. It was expressly with this design that the Church of mediæval Christendom convoked that great council which was to express its full voice and declare its united sentiment. The Council of Constance was one of the most remarkable assemblies which had ever met in mediæval Europe. Other councils had been convoked by the pressure of local circumstances or by the voice of Papal authority; this was assembled as the answer to a universal prayer which had been long going up from the united heart of Christendom. Its meeting arose from no local necessity, it was dictated by no private interest; it was necessitated by the common good, it was demanded by the longing of the entire Church. Men had looked forward to such a concourse, as benighted travellers look forward to the first ray of morning;

they wanted light, and they wanted no individual light but that which emanated from the combined lustre of all Christian minds; they felt that in the multitude of counsellors wisdom could alone be found. And the assemblage, in number and in quality, was worthy of that unanimity which had called it. Never had a council of the Christian Church embraced the representatives of so many classes of society, because never before had society itself so many classes to be represented. Humanity had become varied in proportion as it had become cultured. It could no longer be classified under the wide designations of aristocrat and serf, king and peasant; it had come to inhabit many mansions, each of which had to be described by its own separate name. Therefore this Council of Constance, as it professed to be the voice of universal Christendom, was compelled to include the representatives of every stage of Christian progress, and marvellously did it succeed in realizing its idea. As we cast our eye over the vast concourse which gathered there, we are struck with the immense varieties of opinion which that concourse represented. There stood Pope John XXIII., to symbolize the old things that were passing away, holding a firm grasp on the tottering throne, and refusing to let the sceptre go. There stood Sigismund of Germany, accompanied by a long train of German princes, to symbolize that victory of political power over Papal domination which was now at last secured, but which Henry IV. and Frederic II. had struggled in vain to win. There stood the ambassadors of nearly all the European courts, to indicate that all Europe participated in the triumph of political freedom. There stood the University of Paris, represented by its chancellor, Gerson, the worthy representative of a worthy university, combining the desire for Catholic purity with the earnest thirst for an increase of religious liberty. And there, too, were the leaders of what might be called the radical religious movement, John Huss and Jerome of Prague, men whose hearts were in the right place, but whose heads were too heated to await the natural development of the Christian life, and who, therefore, had been summoned to the council to stand their trial as heretics. Such were the elements which composed that vast assembly; elements which, if united and harmonious, must render its strength irresistible, and give to its measures the authority of law. Nor were the deliberations of that council marked by less harmony than was evinced in its social groupings; its voice was as the voice of one man. Its first great act was the assertion of its own power; without such an assertion, its proceedings would have been a burlesque, but the council knew where the foundation must be laid. It began by proclaiming the majority of the school-life, by announcing that the Christian Church was of age to be a law unto itself. There were three pontiffs in the field; the council deposed all of them, and elected a pontiff of its own by the title of Martin v. But the new pontiff no longer occupied the position of the Pope of former days; he was declared to be subject to the will of the council. At one stroke the Isidorian decretals were swept away, and that power which Hildebrand had striven for, and which Innocent III. had lived to realize, was seen to crumble into ruins. It was not merely that the Papacy was deprived of its temporal sovereignty among the nations; such a judgment it might still have borne with dignity, for Hildebrand himself had never in words laid claim to the empire of Papal absolutism. But the judgment of this council was a sentence annulling that power which of all others was most dear to the heart of the Papacy, nay, which constituted the very sinews of its strength and the very breath of its life—the power of spiritual headship. In making the will of the pontiff subordinate to its own decrees, the Council of Constance robbed him in a moment of the secret of his ascendancy, deprived him of the empire not only over the will of nations, but over the hearts of Christendom, and reduced him to a position very little superior to that which he had held in the days of Cyprian and of Augustine.

Thus far the acts of the Council of Constance had been in strict harmony with the growing Protestant spirit. There are, however, two measures of this council which greatly mar that feeling of exultation with which the Protestant reader contemplates its opening actions—measures, one of which, in the minds of all, the other in the minds of many, must attach to its memory an indelible stain. The first of these was the condemnation to death of John Huss and Jerome of Prague. It is impossible by any casuistry or by any special pleading to vindicate this act; in the case of Huss especially, it was an ungenerous, a false, and a shameful deed, because he had come to the council under the promise of a safe-conduct from the Emperor Sigismund himself. But although nothing can be said in vindication, a few remarks may perhaps be offered in explanation. The difficulty, to our mind, has always been, not to account for the condemnation of the men, but to account for the condemnation of their doctrine. We believe John Huss to have been up to this time as good, though perhaps not so discreet, a Catholic as John Gerson, yet the Council of Constance decided otherwise. It seems almost necessary to believe that the members of that council approached the articles of Huss under the bias of a personal prejudice against himself, and in the course of the previous chapter we have endeavoured to point out what in our view constituted the ground of such prejudice. We are acquainted with almost no theological statement which might not be interpreted heretically, if heresy were the object hunted for; and assuredly the somewhat heated utterances of Huss and Jerome might well have furnished heretical matter for those predisposed to find it. All difficulty must vanish if we once grant the predisposition, and if the view we have suggested be adopted, there can be no difficulty in granting it. Be this as it may, however, it is unquestionable that the Council of Constance did condemn the opinions of Huss and Jerome. And now for the first time in their lives, these men stand before us in the attitude of advanced Protestants—assume a position not unlike that assumed by Luther after the Diet of Worms.

They refused to accept the decision of the council; Huss refused throughout, Jerome after a temporary submission. That refusal transplanted both of them in a moment from the position of agitators for Catholic reform, into the position of agitators for Catholic dissolution. There was more heresy in the one act than in all the alleged opinions put together, and the act was a matter neither of interpretation nor of inference; it was a patent, clear, unmistakeable defiance of the highest tribunal of ecclesiastical power. The council had pronounced their opinions heretical. Jerome and Huss were unable to discover the grounds for that condemnation, yet their inability to see the truth of the judgment did not make it the less necessary for them as good Catholics to acquiesce in its justice. In the Catholic Church, as in all churches, the private sentiments of the individual may be frequently at variance with the collective voice; but in the Catholic Church it becomes incumbent on the individual, when he has heard the collective voice, to crucify his own individual sentiments. Huss and Jerome were called upon to accept the judgment of the council; they were not required to see its truth, much less to vindicate its truth; they were simply asked formally to acknowledge that its ways were higher than their ways, and its thoughts than their thoughts. That acknowledgment they declined to give, and thereby they ceased to be Catholics in any sense, approached more nearly to the standpoint of a developed Protestantism than any reformer had done since the opening of the mediæval world. But the

Council of Constance was not prepared for Protestantism; it wanted a liberalized church as far as Catholic liberality would stretch, but it would have repudiated the idea of abandoning its ancient landmarks. On this point, indeed, it was peculiarly tenacious, on account of its own somewhat equivocal position. It had produced a great innovation, alike in the Catholic Church and in the Catholic world; it had deprived of its sovereignty over both worlds the power which had held that sovereignty for two hundred years, and it had seated itself upon the throne from which its rival had been driven. Under these circumstances, was it not in danger of being reckoned a subverter of all religion, a leader of revolution, an inaugurator of universal anarchy? and must it not use all the influence at its command to counteract the impression and refute the charge? It was, we believe, for this reason that the Council of Constance was so eager to avoid the imputation of heresy, so anxious to be regarded as a standard of orthodox Catholicism; it found it safer in its present position to condemn the opinions of Huss than to incur the reproach of free thought by homologating ambiguous statements. But if the Council of Constance was zealous for the reputation of its orthodoxy, it was still more zealous for the recognition of its newly asserted authority. It is true of communities as of individuals, that they are more prone to assert their power in proportion as it rests upon a recently laid foundation; despotism often springs from the conviction of a doubtful title. It was the misfortune of Huss and Jerome that they were the earliest to defy the council. They threw themselves against that armour which had been newly sharpened, and which the wielders were eager to see in exercise; they rushed into antagonism with that pride which could not brook restraint in its first hour of possession. The sacrifice of their lives was as much a political as a religious offering; it was the proclamation to all the world that the Catholic Church meant to be obeyed.

We have attempted to explain what we cannot vindicate. We believe the burning of the Bohemian reformers to have been an act at once cruel and impolitic; but we do not believe it to have been an arbitrary act, and we have sought as briefly as possible to indicate what seem to us to have been the motives which prompted its performance. We come now to the second of those deeds which have cast a shade over the glory of this council; it was here that for the first time the cup was forbidden to the laity in the sacrament of communion. Vast as is the difference between the character of these two deeds, they have yet been placed side by side by the course of history. It was the prohibition of the cup to the laity which the followers of Huss took hold of as the rallying cry against the council. No doubt their real motive was the natural desire to avenge what seemed to them an act of deliberate murder; but they knew well that any opposition founded either on the affectionate remembrance of a leader, or on the desire to revenge his untimely fate, must inevitably lose its power as the years rolled on. Mere feeling could not protract a warfare, for feeling is calmed by time, and changed with temporal changes. The Hussites felt that, if they would preserve the name of their master, and maintain the integrity of his cause, they must lay hold of some real principle, must unite on some moral basis, must strike at some actually existing evil. The taking of the cup from the laity seemed to furnish such a point of attack, and the Hussites seized it. They could call it with truth a retrogressive act. They could point to the course of the last three centuries as a proof that the Council of Constance had arrested the advance of human development. They could declare the rights of the laity to have been guaranteed by a series of inalienable privileges, and they could affirm, without fear of contradiction, that the periods of greatest national prosperity had been the periods when the privileges of the people were most widely diffused. They could then turn to that council which professed to be a reforming council, and ask, not without an air of plausibility, if the new reform was to sweep away all the old reforms, if the people were to lose the position they had so hardly won, and if the sons of the hierarchy were once more to ride over the prostrate forms of the laity? Such in spirit was the line of attack adopted by the followers of the Bohemian leader. Yet, on calm reflection, we are not at all sure that its power was equal to its imposingness. The prohibition of the cup to the laity was certainly in form a retrogressive act, but it was only in form. It never occurred to the Council of Constance that the laity were suffering any wrong, or that they were losing any privilege whatever. The council had certainly a motive for the prohibition, but its motive was not the depression of the laity; it was the preservation of the blood of Christ. If there appears a strong Catholic element in the decree, it is seen not in the effort to infringe public freedom, but in the excessive prominence given to the doctrine of transubstantiation. The cup was believed to contain the veritable blood of the Master, and in the transmission of that cup from hand to hand, it was feared that the blood of the Master might be spilt; that alone was the motive which dictated the proceedings of Constance. The council forbade the cup to the laity, in order that the sacred element which the cup contained might not be trampled under the foot of the passer-by. Yet the council maintained that, in limiting the laity to the partaking of the sacred bread, it was depriving them of no privilege, and debarring them from no part of Christ's communion. The blood may be separated from the body, but the body cannot as a living organism exist without the blood. To partake of the sacred bread was really to have communion in both kinds, for the blood of Christ was contained in the body of Christ, and so metaphorically might the element of the cup be said to be contained in the elements of the broken bread. The laity, according to this interpretation, received all that they had ever received; and we cannot say that, conceding the truth of transubstantiation, the interpretation was itself either strained or unnatural. The innovation created for a time the great opposition of the Hussites; nor can we wonder that it should have done so, for the very forms of our religion become dear to us by long use, and the loss of one so hallowed could not be experienced without sadness. This act of the Council of Constance was the breaking of an old association, and no old association can be broken without a wrench to the moral nature. The Hussites therefore resisted the change fiercely and long, and had they continued united, they might perhaps have resisted it successfully. But as long as they were themselves believers in transubstantiation, they had not a settled principle on which to base their opposition; they were united only by individual feeling. A cord so loose could not bind their hearts together; they quarrelled, and broke up into hostile camps. Some professed to hold by the old rallying cry, and called themselves the Calixtines, or men of the cup; others retired into a solitary mountain, and strove to forget the world in the ecstasies of mysticism. The former ultimately went back into the bosom of the Catholic Church; the latter, in all probability, eventually mingled with those waters of popular revolution, which appeared simultaneously with the Lutheran Reformation.

It is not, however, in the followers of Huss that the deepest preparation for that Lutheran reform must be sought; it is in the life of the Catholic Church itself. We have now brought that life down to the close of a distinct period. We have traced the history of Christianity through the days of its childhood, we have traced it through the days of its school-life, and we have marked throughout that school-life the anticipations and foreshadowings of a higher stage of being. The Council of Constance may be said to have realized these anticipations; it was the proclamation of the Church's majority—the assertion of its capability of self-guidance and self-action. In the title of this chapter, we have called the close of the school-life the completion of the negative reformation. It will be seen from the whole course of this work, that we regard the Reformation, not as an act, but as a process, not as a great event which suddenly and unexpectedly flashed upon the world of the sixteenth century, but as the last stage in the maturing of a splendid life—the manhood of an existence which for centuries had been expanding towards the consummation of its being. If this view of the subject be true, it will follow that the Reformation which culminated in Luther had its beginning and its development in the bosom of the Catholic Church. We have endeavoured to mark throughout the history of mediævalism, the indications of this growing spirit of reform. We have seen it in its repeated revolts against conventionalism, in its repeated aspirings after a higher life, in the repeated evidence it yielded of dissatisfaction with the world in which it moved. It seems to us that the history of the Reformation ought scientifically to be divided into two great periods, which may appropriately be called its negative and its positive stages. The negative reformation begins with the image controversy, and terminates with the Council of Constance;

the positive reformation begins with the work of Luther, while the short intermediate period is a preparatory stage of transition. We have brought this history to the close of the former period—to the completion of what we have called the negative reformation. All completed stages of existence are appropriate seasons for reflection, times for retrospect, hours for self-measurement. Let us therefore pause here to consider how far the Christian life has advanced, to estimate that point of development which it has already attained, and to anticipate that point of development which it may legitimately hope to attain.

And, first of all, let us define what we mean by a negative reformation. When the mind of a human being is passing from one stage into another, it encounters two experiences: one of destruction, and the other of reconstruction. Before the mind of man can be attracted towards the new, it must be weaned from the old. The child cannot adopt the pleasures of youth, until he has ceased to relish the pleasures of childhood; the youth cannot adopt the pursuits of manhood, until he has ceased to find delight in that love of adventure which characterises youthful days. Now this destructive process, this weaning from the old, this rupture with the past which precedes our joy in the future, is what we call the negative reformation. We call it negative, because it creates a sense of void without immediately filling it; it destroys the old temple of worship, and leaves a blank on the spot where it stood. The negative reformation of the mediæval world was the revolt against absolute authority, the revolt against Papal domination, the revolt against the exclusive prominence given to rites, to ceremonies, to forms. It was the reaction of human nature against the restraints to its humanity; it was the rebellion of the school-life against the will of the schoolmaster. The negative reformation said: 'Thou shalt not;' it was not yet prepared to say: 'Thou shalt.' It had not determined what course it ought to follow; it had thoroughly determined what course it ought not to follow. It had not devised a system of truth which it could substitute for old opinions, nor had it an authoritative standard on which to base the formation of any system; yet it was convinced that the absolute will of a sovereign pontiff could no longer furnish such a standard, and meantime it preferred resting without an authority, to being subject to an authority whose foundation was on the shifting sands. It was a negative reformation, because as yet it had learned only what it could no longer retain.

The second point requiring illustration is the statement that this negative reform was fully completed before Luther entered on his distinctive work. It may seem singular that a statement so obvious should demand illustration, but in truth there is no subject on which there has been a more wide-spread misconception. Even in many standard books it is not difficult to find the traces of this misconception. If a man, for the first time, were to attempt to acquire a knowledge of the Lutheran Reformation from the pages of Hume's

History of England, he would inevitably be led to the conclusion that Luther startled the world into surprise by denying that Papal authority which had never been questioned before. He would inevitably be led to infer that the Lutheran Reformation was simply a revolt from old customs, and a declamation against old abuses, succeeding by reason of its boldness, and gathering strength by widening its invectives. Yet we have no hesitation in saying that, had this been the sole work of Luther, so far from startling the world by the surprise of novelty, it would have exposed him to contempt through its want of originality. Since the days of Philip the Fair, the hierarchical party had received nothing but invectives; there were reformers in every country, and every reformer did over and over again what Luther is here represented as having done as a novelty. We hear it frequently averred in popular and colloquial language, that Luther accomplished the reformation from Popery. Is it meant by this that Luther emancipated the Church from submission to the pontiff as a temporal power? The work was performed nearly two centuries before his birth by Philip the Fair of France. Is it meant that Luther freed the Church from subservience to the pontiff as an absolute spiritual head in matters of faith? The work was performed nearly seventy years before his birth by a decree of the Council of Constance. The truth is, that Luther did not accomplish what is popularly styled the Reformation from Popery—he accomplished a far greater work; that was only a work of destruction, his task was emphatically one of reconstruction.

At the very outset of his mission, Luther took it for granted that the negative reformation had been completed. When he was censured by Cardinal Cajetan, who professed to act under Papal direction, he appealed from the Pope 'badly informed' to the Pope 'better instructed.' He appealed to him, however, not as an authority, but as one good Catholic, conscious of his integrity, may submit his cause to another good Catholic whose high position in the Church is recognised; he felt that the approval of the pontiff would give him a moral support. When he failed to win that approval he appealed to a council; but in so doing he acted in strict conformity with the laws of the Catholic Church; there was nothing revolutionary in the measure, it was precisely that step which in all times of difficulty the Council of Constance had recommended future ages to adopt. Previous to the Diet of Worms, Luther was no more than a follower of the Waldenses, of Wicliffe, and of Huss; it was after his dissent from that Diet that his opposition assumed a positive character, and it is from that date his distinctive work begins. The work called the Reformation from Popery was a Catholic process. It had its origin in the Church of Rome itself; not in a sect of that Church, not in a heresy, not in a schism, not in the opinions of restless or eccentric minds, but in the very bosom of Catholicism, in the very heart of Latin Christianity, in the very soul of mediæval Europe. It was a reform effected by the Church of Rome while continuing to be the Church of Rome, wrought out by its own hands and devised by its own heart. The

Council of Constance may be said to have stamped with its imprimatur all the previous revolutionary movements of the school-life, to have acknowledged their justice, and to have upheld their necessity; when it abolished the absolute power of the Papacy, whether temporal or spiritual, it affixed its seal to the labours of its forefathers. Nor can it in any degree alter the place of this Council in the development of history, that the Œcumenical Council of 1871 has virtually reversed its decree. It is competent for any age to break away from the previous course of human development; in so doing it may alter its course for the future, but it cannot obliterate its line of progress in the past. We are not now considering the Œcumenical Council of 1871; we are considering the course of the spirit of Christianity through the world of Catholicism, and we must trace that course as it was, not as hereafter it may be. The conclusion at which we must arrive is this: that the history of the mediæval world is the history of a progressive school-life growing in wisdom and knowledge, gradually outgrowing the limits of scholastic education, and ultimately asserting its right and its power to be the arbiter of its own actions; the realization of that desire completes the negative reformation.

But there is a third point requiring illustration, and it is exactly the converse of the preceding point. If it be true that the negative reformation was fully completed before the distinctive work of Luther began, it is not less profoundly true, that before the beginning of Luther's work it never attained to any positive character, never reached a new principle of life, never extended further than the act of demolition. If we take a retrospective view of these mediæval efforts at reform, we shall be struck with the fact that not one of them approaches the standard of a positive reformation; they are all negative, they are all revolutionary, they all stop short at the mandate, 'Thou shalt not.' The first revolt of the school-life was, it will be remembered, the great image-controversy of the eighth century. We have seen how violent on that occasion was the outburst of the East against idolatry, and how its fire was fomented and fed by that kindred spirit of Mohammedanism which had just risen into life. Yet we have seen also that this image-controversy, powerful as it was in the work of destruction, was utterly unable to rebuild. It was prepared with fire and sword to destroy the idols in the temple, but it was altogether unprepared to place a new object of reverence on their vacant altar. The second revolt of the school-life was in some respects analogous to the first; this, too, was a reaction against the exclusive worship of the letter, only it came not from the east, but from the west; not from the Grecian plains, but from the Alpine valleys. Yet we have seen that even these Waldenses, with all their moral purity, and with all that high chivalry of nature which made their very poverty transcendently noble, were unable to reach the standard of a positive reformation. They were anti-hierarchical, but they were not anti-Catholic; they were weary of outward authority as a basis of faith, but they had not yet found any other basis on which they could rear the temple of truth. That great intellectual revival, which preceded, accompanied, and followed the Waldensian movement, was still less able to constitute the foundation of a positive reform. In so far as that revival bore any relation to religion, it was affected towards it with that spirit of scepticism which the sudden influx of intellectual light is apt to awaken in long darkened minds. Every negative reformation involves scepticism. Men would never part with the old if they had not learned to doubt its value; yet scepticism itself can never create, it can only destroy. The third revolt of the school-life was more radical and more prolonged than either of its predecessors. It was that revolution which, after having prepared its way by Franciscan unrest and mystical longing, burst forth with terrible power in the fiery utterances of Huss and Wicliffe. The image-controversy had been originated by the breath of kings; the Waldensian movement had sprung from the hearts of the peasantry; the reformation of Huss and Wicliffe was supported by the whole mass of mediæval society,—by king and peasant, by priest and layman, by the unlettered sons of the village, and the most learned sons of the most learned universities. The image-controversy died after a century; the Waldensian movement was within a few years driven back into the valleys whence it had sought to extend itself; the reformation of Huss and Wicliffe cannot strictly be said to have ever been suppressed, it tarried until the greater light came. It compelled the Church of mediævalism to take cognisance of its wants, it forced the Council of Constance to seal its proceedings with its approbation; and that Council, in the very act of condemning the leader, was unconsciously supporting the movement which he led. Even when Luther came, the work of Wicliffe had not ceased; there were still abuses to be redressed, there were still corruptions to be exposed. But by that time the work of Wicliffe had no glory, by reason of a glory that excelled it. It had become patent to the heart of Christendom that mere negation would not regenerate the world. The movement of Wicliffe, in so far as it was a reform, had not passed the limits of a protest against additions to the Catholic faith. It had been content to accept the principles of mediæval Christianity, purified only from the servitude of Papal absolutism and the corruptions of a licentious age. But the age of Luther was no longer content in any form to accept mediæval Christianity; it wanted a new element of life. It felt that the moral nature of man would never be regenerated by the simple process of breaking down the walls and barriers to human progress. It felt that if the soul would be great and noble, it must study not so much what it ought not to be, as what it ought to be; that all prohibition of wrong was included in the sense of right. It felt, above all, that to implant a new principle of religious faith was the only course which would give permanence to the desire of reformation, the only course which would transform that desire from a violent and fluctuating impulse into a calm and stedfast resolve, and give it a motive for action higher than mere opposition to the men and measures of a passing age. That was the work of Luther. All who went before him only cleared the ground. It was their task to tear the old barriers from the field, and make room for the entrance of the spiritual seed; it was the task of Luther to plant the seed itself, and people the vacant field with new forms of life and beauty.

We have said that between the two periods of the negative and the positive reformation there was interposed a third or transitional age, and it is at this age that we have now arrived. The spirit of Christianity has completed its school-life, it has burst the trammels of scholastic education, it has proclaimed to the world that it has reached its majority. But its manhood has not yet dawned. It believes, doubtless, that manhood *has* dawned; but the belief is a delusion, and will be found to be a delusion. The spirit of Christianity is in that stage between the school-boy and the man— the stage of youth. All youth tends to over-estimate itself; it can scarcely do otherwise. Its aspirations are very high, and all aspiration is the prophecy of power; what wonder that youth should frequently mistake the prophecy for the realization ? Yet the aspirations of youth outrun its capacities; it is not really equal to the work it assigns itself to do. It forms a transition between two worlds—the world of school-life, and the world of manhood; and therefore, while it points to the possibilities of the man, it retains somewhat of the imperfections of the school. So was it emphatically with the spirit of Christianity as it emerged from the Council of Constance. It came forth in many respects a changed existence. The chains of outward authority which so long had bound it had been broken, and the spirit of Christianity was free. It looked out for the first time upon the vast world before it, it looked in for the first time upon the vast possibilities within it. It felt itself to have the promise of a great destiny, and the joy of that promise was the joy of youth. Yet the spirit of Christianity had not wholly lost the impress of earlier years. The mere striking off of the outward chains could not instantaneously emancipate it from the mental and moral imperfections which are fostered by a lengthened servitude. Its actual strength was not equal to what it believed it to be. It was over-confident in its present power to work out that destiny which dawned before it, over-persuaded of its present ability to carve out a road to its attainment of perfect happiness. In all this it was consistently the spirit of youth, for the spirit of youth is essentially the spirit of independence. It sees not the intermediate difficulties; it beholds only the goal, it believes not in the steepness of the mountain; it keeps its eye only on the summit bathed in light.

CHAPTER XXXV.

THE INDEPENDENCE OF YOUTH.

THERE are two powers which youth appropriates as peculiarly within its province; the power to secure riches, and the power to win immortality. We do not say that these desires always or even commonly reside in the same mind. He who seeks wealth is generally indifferent to posthumous fame; he who seeks posthumous fame is not seldom indifferent to wealth. Yet these desires, although not often conjoined in the hearts of the young, are possessions common to the spirit of youth, the two forms under one or other of which youthful aspiration clothes itself. There is an analogy between the buoyancy of youth and the joy of childhood, but their difference is deeper than their analogy. Childhood is joyous, from the predominance of the present over the future; youth is buoyant, from the predominance of the future over the present. Youth lives and moves and has its being in the future; this is 'the light of its common day,' 'the master light of all its seeing.' And not only so, but youth sees the very future it desires to see. Goethe says that man weaves for God the garment by which he beholds Him; that is just what youth does for the future. It clothes it in bright colours—the colours in which its own hope has painted it; and it falls down and worships the idol of its own creation, and consecrates to its service its labour and its life.

Now this was precisely the position in which mediæval Europe found itself at the close of the Council of Constance. The heart of Christendom was bounding with youth, vibrating with that hope of a great destiny which youth inspires, and pulsating with that conviction of power to realize it which is ever born of the prophecy of greatness. There was nothing vague or dreamy in this hope of Christian Europe; it pointed to two definite objects, the same which we have seen to be the objects of individual aspiration—the desire for wealth, and the desire for immortality. The future of mediæval Europe, like the future of youthful man, was decked in two colours—the golden and the green. The two objects of its ambition were to be ever rich and to be ever young. Nor did it pursue these objects as one pursues a castle in the air, by idle dreams and reveries. Strange to say, it sought them not only practically, but through the most practical sources. It looked out upon the different metals,—the gold, the silver, the mercury, the iron, the lead, the tin,—and it asked whether between these there were any bond of connection? There was a link which bound man to man in the moral world, and by that sympathetic link one human being could be assimilated to another. And was there no corresponding affinity in the objects of material nature? was there no sympathetic link by which the base iron and lead could be transmuted into the precious gold? Was it not possible that these substances, so different in their outward appearance, were in reality only the modifications of one substance which underlay them all? The light which is reflected by sea and shore bears a different aspect to the light reflected by the sky, yet the light of sea and shore is one with the light of the sky. The iron, the lead, and the tin were very different in aspect from the silver and the gold; yet might it not be that the aspect alone constituted the difference, and that the precious substance which had formed the gold was to be found in all the baser metals? And if so, if there were even a hope, a chance, a possibility of such a great discovery, should it not be the business of the world to seek out its source and to unearth its secret? If there were in the base copper all the preciousness of the yellow gold, if there were in the common tin all the value of the polished silver, why should not humanity discover it? Why should not chemistry by its varied analytic labours refine away the dross until it reached the pure ore, eliminate those accidental elements which made the apparent difference between the comparatively worthless and the transcendently valuable, until it arrived at last at the one substance sleeping underneath the many forms, the one common life which had animated such a variety of features? Then, indeed, would the world possess a philosopher's stone which would transmute whatever it touched into gold. Each man would carry within the palm of his hand the potential wealth of all the world, for he would bear that talisman which could conjure up the riches of untold ages, could create more wealth than had ever yet been united in the richest land, and could place the sons of daily toil on a height of affluence level with the luxury of kings.

But the Utopian dream of mediæval youth did not stop with the desire of boundless wealth; it wanted also boundless life to enjoy it. The philosopher's stone would have been little without the elixir of life; to have every want supplied would have been but a poor privilege, if the satisfaction were cancelled at last by the great negation, death. And so the independence of mediæval youth sought not only the means of living, but the means of living for ever; and this, too, it sought by an appeal to the order of nature. Was there no element of life in nature? This universe was not surely a dead mechanism; it was instinct with vitality, with force, with intelligence. And if so, must there not be a special substance in which this force resided? Did not all life inhabit a locality? Had not all life its seat in some material form, and must there not in the great organism of nature be some material form which was as it were the brain of the universe, the seat of its life, and the centre of its power? Might not this too be sought for? Might not the source of life as well as the source of gold be found? nay, was there anything impossible in the thought that the source of life might itself be the source of gold? might not the two secrets of happiness be reduced to one? Such was the reasoning of mediæval Europe, and it sought to reduce its reasoning to practice. It sought the talisman of eternal life through the same chemical process by which it had endeavoured to find the element of universal riches. It is difficult to see how, even if found, it would have been equally available. A man who had discovered the substance common to all the metals, might well be able to transmute the base into the precious, to transform the copper into the gold. But even if a man should discover a substance which contained the very essence of life, it is not at all easy to perceive by what means he could have that essence transferred into his own nature. The philosophers of mediæval Europe proposed to boil it into a fluid, and take it as an elixir. After having discovered it, such a process would indeed not be difficult; but even after the elixir had been taken, it is by no means clear to Protestant minds that it would produce the desired effect. We say to Protestant minds, for we must not forget that the men who promulgated this doctrine were firm believers in transubstantiation, nor must we forget that the believer in transubstantiation could find no special difficulty here. A Protestant is unable to see how, even conceding the change of the bread and wine into the body and blood, the partaking of that body and blood could produce any effect on the recipient; the Catholic does see this. He, therefore, in relation to this matter, stands on a totally different platform from the Protestant. The idea that a divine life could, through a material medium, be received into human nature, so as to become a portion of itself, was one with which he had been long familiarised by his solemn sacrament of communion, and he was accordingly in no position to reject as inherently absurd, the doctrine that the elemental life of nature might, if discovered and appropriated, become the perpetual life of man.

The science by which mediæval Christendom sought to work out these problems was called alchemy. It was not new to the Christian world ; nay, it belonged to the pre-Christian world. Its home was in Egypt; it passed thence into Greece and Rome, and from the Greeks and Romans it was received by the Arabs. When the Arabs conquered Spain, they brought it into Christian Europe, and in Christian Europe it found not altogether an uncongenial soil. There was so much about it which pointed to progress and human development, that it arrested and fascinated the activity of the western mind. It is a remarkable fact, that the periods when this science had its most brilliant epochs were those times of revolution in which the school-life struggled to be free. These were the seasons in which the coming independence of youth seemed to foreshadow itself, and anticipate its future boldness. Three times did the science of alchemy absorb the attention of the learned world, and each of them was a period of scholastic revolution. In the eighth century, it blazed out in the chemical work of Gebir. In the thirteenth, it shone forth in many phases of scholastic life, and was dignified by the patronage of many illustrious names — of Roger Bacon, of Albertus Magnus, of

Thomas Aquinas, of Raymond Lully. It was forbidden by one of the pontiffs of the Babylonish captivity; but the Council of Constance loosed the chain of all Papal prohibitions, and in the fifteenth century, the science of alchemy emerged into new life with Basil Valentine. From that time its course knew no pause, until the Lutheran Reformation had become an established fact; and little more than a hundred years after the meeting of the Council of Constance, it had attained its culminating triumph in the speculations of the great Paracelsus.

It may seem very strange that, in a region so religious as mediæval Europe, speculations in their origin so pagan, and in their character so dubious, should have found acceptance and countenance. It is true, the hierarchical party were unfavourable to them, and most of them owed their safety to the secrecy of those monastic retreats in which they were perpetrated. But the hierarchical party were not really the spiritual party; their prohibition was dictated by that selfish policy which found security in surrounding ignorance. What we want to know is, why men of undoubted spirituality, of sincere piety, of earnest life, and of upright aim, should have lent themselves to a practice which apparently partook so much of the nature of irreverence. Perhaps we ought to bear in mind, that what is irreverent in mature age, may admit in youth of a softer name. The characteristic of youth is the spirit of independence, and the spirit of independence presupposes the sense of self-sufficiency; the belief in its ability to break through all barriers, to traverse impassable paths, and to tread forbidden ground. Yet it is not too much to say, that had this been the sole aspect of the subject, it never would have found favour with the heart of Christian Europe. That heart was daring and venturesome, but it was always daring and venturesome in a spiritual direction, and with a spiritual end. It is clear, therefore, that beneath the seeming irreverence of this science of alchemy, it must have discovered something that was good and true. Can we, looking back from this distance, recognise any such element; can we find beneath these fantastic speculations any glimmerings of genuine light,—light that has consumed the very systems which enshrined it, but which still remains as a monument of their power? We think it must be evident that the speculations of the alchemist did indeed point to an eternal truth. In attempting to find in one object the source of all metals, and the source of all vitality, he was groping after an idea which theology approves, and which science is more and more confirming; the idea that there is but one plan of creation, and that if we only knew it, it is a very simple plan. The unity of God had been greatly obscured by image-worship; here was a scientific protest in favour of the unity of God. It declared that this universe with all its varied forms, and with all its complex laws, had sprung from one source, and issued from the simplest plan. Polytheism, and that image-worship which was the reflex of polytheism, was no longer possible to intellectual minds. The changeless had been seen amidst the mutable; God was one, and His universe had one law. Strangely have the aspects of modern science corroborated and confirmed that truth after which the alchemist of old was groping. We no longer hear, indeed, of the transmutation of metals, but we hear much of the correlation of forces. We no longer say that lead may become gold, or that copper may become silver, but we say constantly that light may be changed into heat, and that heat may become electricity. Modern science has reproduced on a higher plane, and on a wider scale, the question which was debated centuries ago. It has taught us as the alchemist sought to teach us, and with a certainty which the alchemist never attained, that all the forces of nature are but the varied forms in which man beholds the presence of the one inscrutable force, and that beneath these changing and fluctuating appearances, there resides one immutable, incomprehensible life. It has enabled us to transfer into the realms of material nature that thought which our English poet has portrayed in the realms of spirit:

> 'Our little systems have their day,
> They have their day, and cease to be;
> They are but broken lights of Thee,
> And Thou, oh Lord, art more than they.'

We have already pointed out, in the chapter on mysticism, that in the hands of the mediæval world the science of astronomy was being subjected to a similar treatment. Every science at the beginning of its course is youthful and romantic; it assumes a form adapted to the intellectual life of a nation which is only rising into manhood. Chemistry began with alchemy, and astronomy began with astrology. We have seen that mediæval astrology was actuated by the same motive which impelled mediæval alchemy. It wanted to bring the universe into unity, to find a meeting-place between these cold, apparently unsympathetic stars, and the warm, earnest, stirring lives of men. It desired to see heaven and earth joined together, to believe that the destinies of this world were not too small to attract the starry firmament, to read in that starry firmament the proofs of a sympathy with the fate of man. And we have seen that the astrologist, like the alchemist, was groping after the great truth of modern science — groping after the golden chain that holds the worlds in unity. It was peculiarly natural, that in the mediæval world this scientific idea should take the form of a handwriting on the heavens of man's future destiny. Modern science tells us that the existence of our earth is bound up with the existence of all stars and planets; but modern science does not tell us that all stars and planets exist only in order that earth may live and shine, only in order that they may foretell the fates of men. The reason lies in the fact that we are living under the system of new heavens. The mediæval world believed that earth was the centre of the universe; we have how learned that earth is only one amidst a myriad of stars, whose common centre is unknown. Yet who can fail to see how peculiarly the former belief was adapted to the spirit of youthful independence? Mediæval Europe, emerging from its school-life, cast its buoyant gaze over the starry realms of space, and declared them to be all its own; the sense of vast possession fitly followed the sense of boundless freedom. Were not all the worlds, and the glory of them, made for man? Were they not appointed to rule the day and the night of human destiny? Were they not designed to give light upon the earth to all dark places and to all dark circumstances, to enable the human spirit to pierce the surrounding clouds, and discern its promised land? And in the message of the stars, it was, indeed, a promised land that the youth of Christendom discerned; the land promised by its own hope, the land of boundless gold, and the land of endless life. What earth predicted with its subterranean metals, heaven foretold with its exalted stars, and earth and heaven alike shouted in the ear of Christendom one jubilant song of future glory, honour, and immortality. It was a thought born of the independence of youth, and it fostered that independence which gave it birth. With all the stores of earth below, with all the wealth of heaven above, the youthful heart of Christendom felt itself overflowing with joy, realized more and more its self-sufficiency and its power, and looked higher and higher for the consummation of its glory.

There is another point to which we have alluded in the chapter on mysticism, but which perhaps finds its most prominent illustration here. It was in this fifteenth century that the course of geographical discovery may be said to have systematically begun. It was this century which was to witness the boldest efforts that had hitherto been made in the cause of navigation. It was to see Giovanni Cabot breasting the waves of the Atlantic in search of lands unknown. It was to see Sebastian Cabot reaching the shores of Labrador. It was to see Vasco de Gama with his Portuguese sailors doubling the Cape of Good Hope, and penetrating to the East Indies. It was to see Christopher Columbus discovering Hispaniola and Cuba, the first-fruits of a new world. The completion of these events lies beyond our chronological limits, and the details of them belong not to our province; but we cannot but point out once more that relation, which we have already indicated, between the thirst for discovery and the waking sense of freedom. The independence of youth tempted it to seek a large sphere. The old confines were too small for it; it wanted wider fields to traverse, and vaster scenes to contemplate. And, as we have said, these scenes in the mind's vision were all prospectively glorious; youth was in this again true to its own nature. The same eye of hope which enabled it to behold boundless treasures in the earth, and boundless prophecies of glory in the stars, enabled it to see on the map of the world, lands brighter than the sun, and more luxuriant than the summer. There it might find the realization of its dreams. There it might discover a race of men on whom the golden shower had been perpetually pouring, whom poverty, privation, and toil had passed by on the other side, whom affluence, comfort, and luxury had crowned with their precious fruits. There at last it might meet a people who had found the secret of everlasting life, whose spring-time of existence never faded, and whose autumn never came; a people who had partaken of the blessed elixir, and thereby had received the bloom of immortal youth, the brightness of eternal noonday, the glory of perpetual joy. Such were the dreams which mediæval Europe wove around that paradise which lived only in the realms of its imagination; yet who shall say that these dreams were not the prolific sources of great and deathless realities? It was these dreams which stimulated the mariner to brave unheard-of dangers, to bear appalling privations, to confront terrific trials. Beyond sight of all land, he saw ever this land of his dreams; beyond reach of all aid, he beheld ever this haven of his rest; in the perpetual presence of danger and of death, his eye was ever riveted on the vision of a country where danger and death were unknown. It is true the vision was a delusion, but the power which it exerted was no delusion. That which the mariner accomplished was not that which he meant to accomplish, but it was far better. He wanted to reach a paradise of fadeless earthly joys; and had he reached it, he would have gained only a source of personal and selfish gratification. But all the time his vision, delusive to himself, was working out for humanity a real and a permanent good, was leading him unconsciously and involuntarily to become the benefactor of mankind. For what was it that the mariner was really doing while he was traversing the seas in search of a delusion? He was doing what the alchemist was doing, what the astrologist was doing, what the course of history was doing—bringing the world into unity. He was helping to unite races which as yet were ignorant of each other's existence, to join hand in hand those who had been separated by vast tracts of land, and by vaster expanse of sea, to restore that sense of a united brotherhood which humanity had lost in proportion as it had wandered from its parental home. The mariner of mediæval Europe was to the nations which he sought, what the missionary had formerly been to the Gentile world; a messenger of peace, and a pioneer of progress. He planted amidst savage tribes the seeds of Western civilisation; and the Western civilisation of the fifteenth century exhibited the highest outward culture which humanity had yet attained. And as, at the close of the Roman Empire, the barbarous tribes of Europe, by the very spontaneity of their wild nature, had been fit subjects for the reception of civilising impressions, so the savage tribes of the newly-discovered lands were, by the very simplicity of their untutored nature, well prepared to receive the imprint of European culture. The mariners of the fifteenth century were the messengers sent to proclaim the unity of the race of man, and to establish the sense of a common brotherhood, by imparting to distant realms the privileges of a common civilisation.

But the development of the age would have altogether mistaken its province, if it had sought for the brotherhood of humanity merely in distant realms. There was lying at the very door of civilisation a region which might be called an undiscovered land;

a region whose boundaries were contiguous to every great city, and whose representatives were found in the proudest centres of civilisation and refinement—the region of the unlettered poor. In such cities as Venice and Florence there might be seen the meeting of the extremes of civilisation; the culture which no age has surpassed, and which few ages have equalled, side by side with the superstition and the barbarism which no period of the world hopes again to see. The cities of Italy, nay, all learned cities of every land, exhibited a conjunction of light and darkness which made the light and the darkness alike more conspicuous by contrast. It is true that the ranks of the unlettered poor had been gradually thinned by a succession of recruits into the army of the learned. The decline of slavery had done much, the progress of social freedom had done more, the rise of the universities had done most of all, to diffuse the culture of the upper classes amongst the inhabitants of the villages. The translation of the Gospels which Peter Waldo gave to the Waldenses, and the translation of the entire Bible which John Wicliffe gave to the English people, circulated as these came to be from shore to shore, must have powerfully contributed to expand the limits of the unlettered mind. It was clearly a literature which to that mind was the desideratum. It wanted something higher than itself to rouse it into emulation, and to inspire it with a lofty ideal. Yet, hitherto, for the masses, such a literature had not been found. The Bible would indeed, to them, have supplied all the purposes of the greatest works of antiquity; the difficulty was not to find the book, but to find the means of making it known. The transcription of manuscripts was of necessity slow, and the number of manuscripts which could be transcribed was, in comparison to the need and the demand, limited in the extreme. What was wanted was a medium which could economise time and labour; a medium which could compress into days the work of months, and issue in hundreds those copies of standard books which had once come forth in tens. Such an apparatus would greatly equalise the advantages of men, and would place the materials of human knowledge at the disposal of all who had the mind and means to use them. In the absence of such a medium, there was clearly a greater difficulty in reaching brotherhood at home than could ever be found in establishing brotherhood with newly discovered lands. The savage tribes, as we have said, were impressible by their very spontaneity; but the unlettered peasantry had become rigid by the long disuse of natural powers. Their minds, moreover, had been paralyzed by hierarchical terrors. These terrors had once filled the world, they lingered still in the world's lowliest spots; cramping the spontaneous efforts of the human spirit, and making the gulf between the ignorant and the learned wider than the farthest separation between the European and American continents.

But it was just at this era that there was discovered that very medium which was wanted to circulate amongst the masses the results of scientific research and literary culture. We allude to the invention of that art, which perhaps more than all other mediæval influences has contributed to enlarge the limits of the human mind and to widen the domain of human investigation—the art of printing. Two nations contend for the honour of its birth—Holland and Germany. Holland assigns the merit of the contrivance to her countryman, Laurence Coster, of Haarlem; Germany attributes its glory to Johann Gänsfleisch, a member of the Gutenberg family. It is difficult, at this distance of time, to decide between the claimants; much can be said in favour of each. There seems no reason to doubt that, apart from the question who was the first in the field, the discovery on the part of each was original and spontaneous. That was an age in which the spirit of youth breathed everywhere, and the spirit of youth is ever the spirit of invention; its very sense of independence impels it to contrive. The art of printing, though new to the world as an object of discovery, was not new to the world as an object of desire. Men had long craved for a means of communicating thought similar or analogous to this. They had craved for it, and they had groped after its attainment in regions far remote and in ages long gone by. The Assyrians and the Chinese alike had seen this day afar off; dimly, imperfectly, unsatisfactorily, but prophetically still. Is it surprising, then, that at a period of intense literary fervour, at a time when thought was everywhere in action, and when the passion for the new dominated all, two minds, richly imbued with the spirit of their age, should without collusion light upon the same secret. Columbus discovered Hispaniola and Cuba five years before Cabot reached the shores of Labrador, yet we are not quite sure that the fame of Columbus' discovery had reached the ears of Cabot. In this case, though the priority in time must assign the glory to the former, the personal merit of the latter must be allowed to rank on equal ground. So, in like manner, it would seem that Coster claims the chronological priority; yet we have no reason to believe that his work was known to Gutenberg, and no reason to deny to both the merit of originating genius. It was not long before this new art passed from the mind of its originators into the possession of the united world. It found its earliest exercise at Haarlem, Mayence, and Strasburg; but in the course of a few years it travelled beyond the scenes of its nativity. It came to Rome, the centre of the Catholic world, to Venice, the home of merchandise, to Florence, the picture gallery of the earth, to Paris, the seat of the most liberal of universities, to Tours, almost the nursery of mediæval education, to Britain, unquestionably the nursery of national mediæval reform. Speaking from centres of such venerable fame, the new art could not fail to rule.

Scarcely had the last echoes of the triumph died away, when a storm was heard in the East; a storm which shattered the oldest dynasty of the Christian world, but which bore upon its blast new seeds of intellectual life. Since the days when Charles Martel had rolled back the Mohammedan wave from France, the Musulman power had ceased to be the assailant of Europe. The West had assumed the offensive, and the Mohammedans had been content merely to defend themselves. The assaults which Mohammedanism had made on mediæval Europe had up to this time been intellectual assaults, and we have seen how powerfully the mind of the East had dominated and moulded the intellect of the West. Yet, during all these ages, the Musulman had never for a moment lost sight of one object of ambition—the conquest of the Greek Empire. Great as had been the triumphs of the Mohammedan power in Asia and Africa, it had effected little in Europe. It had conquered Spain, but its conquest of Spain had contributed rather to advance its intellectual than its temporal dominion, and had brought it no nearer to the realizing of that project which in the European world was the goal of all its aspirations. Constantinople, the last monument of a world which had passed away, the last relic of that mighty power which once had filled the earth with its 'glory, had lingered behind for centuries as the ghost of the departed. Around it were woven all the associations of pagan greatness, around it were entwined the memories of that hour when Christianity first became the professed religion of the pagan great. Yet its grand political associations and its hallowed Christian memories had not been able to preserve it from corruption and decay. Whatever the union of Church and State may have been to the West, it had proved paralysis to the East. Rarely throughout the mediæval centuries had the Church of Chrysostom flashed forth into that spirit of independence which would have revealed its parentage. The image-controversy had at one time seemed to promise a revival of Eastern Christianity, but the gleam died away in deeper night, and the mind of Eastern Europe assumed an attitude not altogether dissimilar to the mind of China; an attitude of rigid movelessness and of waveless apathy. From intellectual apathy physical power cannot flow; the repression of thought does not strengthen the arm. Constantinople was as weak in empire as it was lifeless in religion, and the imperial weakness was in great measure owing to the want of religious life. For centuries it had dragged out an existence unworthy of the name, but the time had come when even that must be surrendered. The spirit of Mohammedanism seemed to be renewing its youth. It appeared once more to have revived its thirst for conquest, and the prize on which it fixed its eye was the venerable city of Constantine. On the throne of the Ottoman Empire, at the middle of the fifteenth century, sat a man well qualified to execute its schemes of ambition; a man who in some respects represented the Mohammedan religion of every age. Mohammed II., whom posterity has styled 'The Great,' was at this period a youth of three-and-twenty, yet even at that early age he exhibited all the leading features which have characterised the successive phases of eastern development. He had the fire, the impetuosity, the courage, the enterprise, and the cruelty which marked the first era of the Mohammedan religion. He had the intellectual acquirements which distinguished its second epoch; he was master of four languages, he was conversant with the natural sciences, he was familiar with ancient history, he had studied somewhat those facts of geography which Arabian enterprise had early made accessible to his forefathers. Amidst his unquestionable cruelty there were not wanting occasional gleams of generosity and chivalry, and these, perhaps, he had caught from the ages when the Musulman armies had stood face to face with the hosts of crusading Europe. He had the sagacity, the policy, the statesmanship of an age which had ceased to be warlike, and had become blunted to the sense of military glory; and he had, last of all, that practical knowledge of the fine arts, which by its intense power of representation tends to reproduce all ages in one. Such was the man who resolved to renew the military strength of the Crescent, and to retaliate upon Europe the injuries of the crusading wars. And his preparations were equal to his abilities for using them. These preparations occupied an entire year, and at the end of that time there was gathered an army of 258,000 men and a fleet of 320 vessels. With this formidable support from land and sea, the successor of the great prophet approached the walls of Constantinople.

Thus, on the 6th of April 1453, Europe and Asia met face to face once more; met after long years, and after many changes, resolved to decide that great question which had long been pending between the East and West,—the question whether the Eastern or Western civilisation should dominate the mind of the future world. And though Europe was assailed in its weakest point, it made an admirable defence. Sometimes, shortly before death, the strength of a man seems to revive; so was it with the city of Constantine in its dying hour. It had more glory in its hour of death than in all the centuries of its life which had followed the second Nicene Council. Beset by a multitudinous host by land, barricaded by a mighty fleet by sea, assailed by the most powerful artillery which that age could command, the garrison, aided by 2000 Genoese strangers, under the heroic Justiniani, struggled long and fiercely to preserve their liberty and their name. Seven weeks the engines battered the walls, and seven weeks they battered in vain. At last a great assault was made; land and sea alike and simultaneously poured forth their armies. The combat was long and deadly. At length the Greeks prevailed; the seamen were driven back to the ships, the troops were driven back from the ramparts, and Constantinople stood a victor on the field. But it was a victory which had all the effect of defeat. The brave Justiniani was wounded, the flower of the Grecian ranks had perished, and all felt instinctively that in resisting further they were resisting for honour alone. A panic spread amongst the defenders. The courage, which had nerved them in the hour of emergency, forsook them in the season of momentary reaction. The Sultan saw his opportunity, and seized it. He led back his beaten troops. The Janizaries made a dreadful charge, and the Greeks step by step gave way. At last their emperor himself died fighting in the breach, and with him died the only surviving representative of a world which was no more. Over the corpse of him who had filled the last throne of the Cæsars the victorious Musulman armies poured into the devoted city.

The capture of Constantinople produced important effects, both physical and literary. It was the foundation of Turkish power in Europe, and as such it brought the Crescent and the Cross into immediate proximity and into direct antagonism. For some time it seemed as if the Crescent were about to supplant the Cross. The fall of Constantinople was followed by a succession of triumphs; quick, brilliant, and decided. Belgrade, indeed, stood firm, and the Hungarians displayed that spirit of patriotism which has since continued to characterise them. But if the Mohammedan power was foiled here, it had ample compensation for the failure. The Morea, the Crimea, the kingdom of Epirus, the kingdom of Trebizond, and the kingdom of Servia went down before it. The Genoese were deprived of Caffa; the Venetians were stript of Friuli, Istria, Negropont, and Lemnos; and Italy was forced to part with Otranto. It was not till seventy years later that its appalling course was stayed, and its victorious march arrested, before the walls of the Austrian capital.

But it is with the literary effects of this revolution that we have chiefly to do. To the eyes of any contemporary who beheld the destruction of the great Greek Empire, the catastrophe must have seemed to be an unparalleled blow inflicted on Christian literature. And yet it was to Christian literature one of the greatest boons which the fifteenth century, prolific as it was in benefits, ever conferred. On this occasion it was not the influx of the Mohammedans which proved the boon; it was the dispersion of the Greek Empire. The Greeks had never been deficient in learning, and had never wanted a roll of illustrious literati. Their deficiency in later years had lain in the lethargy which had crept over them. They had been content to remain self-contained and isolated,—content to occupy the rear of human progress, and to derive all their glory from the memories of their past. Their learning had thus been of no service to humanity; their exclusive nationality had led them to contribute nothing to the welfare of mankind. It was clear that no greater boon could befall mankind than the breaking up of this exclusive nationality; and that benefit was unconsciously conferred by the armies of the Turkish Sultan. Turkey broke down the walls, and the imprisoned life ran free; ran over that world from which it had long been isolated, and enriched it, fertilized it, glorified it. The Grecian sages, driven from their homes, and exiled from their country, wandered over the length and breadth of the earth in search of a new home and a new country. They bore along with them the atmosphere of ancient learning, and they carried more than an atmosphere. As in days of old the eastern sages of Asia had brought the gold, the frankincense, and the myrrh to lay at the feet of infant Christianity, so in mediæval days the eastern sages of Europe brought to the more developed Christian spirit gifts more precious still. They conveyed into the centres of civilisation many of those writings of the illustrious dead which, by the great mass of mankind, had been for ages overlooked and forgotten; manuscripts dusty, moth-eaten, age-worn, bearing externally the marks of that long descent which made them venerable, but which yet, on the wings of the new printer's art, were to renew their youth, and to be wafted far and near. The fall of Constantinople was to the fifteenth century what the fall of imperial Rome was to the fifth, and what the fall of ancient Jerusalem was to the first. Each of these catastrophes was the death of a nation, but each of these deaths was a life added to the world beyond the nation. The walls which constituted its national embodiment were destroyed, but that national spirit which lived behind the walls went forth to people future worlds; it was expedient for humanity that these empires should pass away.

We have now reviewed those sources which supplied the first stimulus to the independence of mediæval youth. We have seen that this independence was chiefly manifested in weaving the vision of an imaginary future. It becomes now natural to ask whether, amidst these fancied anticipations, there were to be found no anticipations of that future which was really coming. It is the nature of youth to be prophetic. It is the boundary-line between two worlds, and if it bears somewhat the imperfections of that which is gone, would we not expect it also to prefigure somewhat the glories of that which is drawing near? There are two directions in which we must seek in mediæval youth for a process preparatory to approaching manhood; there must be a moral and there must be an intellectual preparation. We intend in the two following chapters to exhibit each of these successively. In the course of these chapters we shall find it necessary to mention individual names which overlap in order of time the limits of this work, to consider the works of men which were chronologically subsequent to the birth of Luther. But if the lives of the Italian renaissance overlap the birth of Luther in order of time, they all precede it in order of thought; their work was preparatory to his work, and therefore with reference to religious development their lives were ideally earlier than his. Before entering, however, upon the survey of the great moral and intellectual preparation, it may be well to ask, What is that which mediæval youth is preparing for? Mediæval youth itself had clearly no notion that it was preparing for anything, or that it had anything left to desire. It appeared to have reached the climax of all its wishes, and to have arrived at the summit of all its perfections. It believed itself to be already partaker of the spirit of manhood, and it was this belief that induced it to give such pre-eminence to its assertion of independence. It seemed to stand upon a watch-tower, and survey beneath its feet a whole world of possessions. It had power over the land. It had command over the sea. It had the prospect of boundless wealth. It had the hope of immortal bloom. It had access to the treasures of the human mind in the past. It had a destiny in the future, watched over by the stars of heaven. With such privileges in hand, and with such glories in anticipation, why should it esteem itself at less than the highest value? Why should it look forward to a time when it must yield up its stage of development and become the servant of a higher life? Did not all objects point to the conclusion that it had reached the ultimate height, and seen the furthest expanse over which the human mind could travel. With such beliefs as these the exhortation to progress would have seemed an impossible command, and the idea that this mediæval glory was after all but a point of transition, would have sounded in the ear of the youthful world as a jest or a fable. Yet such was in reality the case. Mediæval youth had fallen short of the spirit of manhood through that very sense of independence, which it mistook for the evidence of manhood. There are two ideas which youth is specially apt to confound— the sense of independence and the sense of individual responsibility. There is one point in common between them; they both imply the possession of freedom, or at all events the belief in such possession. He who feels himself to be independent believes himself to be free; he who feels himself to be responsible believes that he has the power over his own actions. But there the agreement ends and the difference begins. A man's sense of independence is the belief in his freedom to act for himself; a man's sense of responsibility is the belief in his freedom to act for a higher power. The one is essentially will-worship; the other is distinctively the depression of the individual will, and the recognition at once of its duty and its ability to serve a mandate higher than its own. This was what mediæval youth did not see, this was what the future must compel it to see. In the revelation of this neglected truth was to lie the secret of that great preparation by which the heart and the intellect alike of mediæval Europe were to be prepared for the entrance into a higher life. It was necessary that the pride of its youth should be depressed, in order that the sense of its responsibility might be exalted. It was essential that the feeling of its independence should be shaken, in order that it might learn the existence of a nobler freedom; a freedom which should find its glory in self-surrender, and which should reach the proudest consummation of its strength in attaining the power of a voluntary service.

CHAPTER XXXVI.

THE MORAL PREPARATION OF YOUTH.

LET us here ask, What is that train of experiences which we would consider best adapted to further the moral development of Europe as it now stands? We see it in the flush of youthful ardour, impressed above all other sentiments with the sense of its own independence; its ability in its own strength to accomplish all ends. It is this sense of independence which constitutes at once its danger and its weakness. It over-estimates its power, it underrates its frailty. As long as this sense of independence endures, the conviction of responsibility cannot come, for the false idea of freedom repels the true. The heart of Christian Europe is as yet too much turned inward upon itself to contemplate any object higher than itself; and without such contemplation of the higher, the feeling of responsibility must be dead. It is clear that, before Europe can emerge from the false freedom of self-exaltation which is youth, into the true freedom of self-surrender which is manhood, the belief in its independence must be shattered and dispelled. It must be taught that, so far from being able to do everything, it cannot even direct its own moral life; that, so far from being adequate to the sovereignty of the universe, it is incapable of ruling the passions of its own nature.

It follows, then, from this, that the best moral preparation for the heart of mediæval Europe was the increasing prevalence of its corruption. It was necessary that the sense of independence should be broken; and in order to be broken, it must be proved to be delusive. Its delusiveness must be shown through the increase of those moral evils which the self-will, if it could, would have averted. It must be shown in the inability to find rest which would never have existed, had the independence of youth been real. It must be shown in the growing dissatisfaction with all those objects and attainments which youth had originally esteemed its perfection and its goal; and it must be shown in that craving for a nameless good, that aspiration after an unknown joy, that longing to find a light that shines not on sea or land, which is ever the certain proof that man is not an end to himself. These were the experiences which were best fitted morally to prepare the youth of Christendom, and these were the experiences through which the youth of Christendom was to pass. It is a singular historical fact, that in the prominent nations of Europe, the close of the school-life was followed by a period of political and social decline,—a decline which would be unaccountable if we did not view it as itself a species of school training, destined to break the pride and to curb the self-will of youth. We intend in the course of this chapter to take a rapid view of the circumstances of some of these nations. We shall find the study somewhat discouraging,—discouraging, that is, from the world's own standpoint. We shall fail to discover any realization of those high hopes which had throbbed in the heart of youthful Christendom; we shall fail to see any fulfilment of those magnificent dreams which had peopled the future with starry forms. We shall find, on the contrary, many tokens of retrogression, many evidences of a fading glory, many signs of a declining day. Yet in these very discouragements we shall be able to trace the preparation for a real development. We shall see in them the breaking down of the old ruins preparatory to the building of a new temple, the destruction of the fabric of human pride preliminary to the rearing of a structure whose foundation will be deeper than the life of self.

We begin with that nation which, as a united people, had always shown itself the most active in the cause of religious reform—the kingdom of England. At the very moment when the Council of Constance was emancipating the school-life from the restraints of outward authority, England was stamping out the last fires of Lollardism. These unfortunate followers of Wicliffe had fallen upon evil days. They had been subjected to bitter persecution at the hands of a new king, and that king the son of the very Duke of Lancaster who had been the leading supporter of Wicliffe's doctrine amongst the aristocracy. We are not quite sure that Henry IV., in so far as he had any religious leanings, was not himself a Lollard; we are perfectly sure that his motive for persecuting them was not horror of their religious tenets. His position was somewhat peculiar. He had broken the long line of hereditary descent, and had by a violent revolution placed himself on the throne. His title was more than doubtful, his tenure far from firm; any moment might sweep the sceptre from his hand. His conscious insecurity made him tenacious of authority; he acted despotically in proportion as he feared his right to act at all. He dreaded all popular ferments, and he dreaded whatever promoted these. He remembered how strongly the English people had been influenced by that religious movement patronised by his father, and he remembered how close upon the rise of that movement had followed the dangerous political revolution of Wat Tyler and the populace. He naturally connected them, and transferred to the religious movement the odium of the political revolution. He resolved to suppress Lollardism; not, however, as a religious sect, but as a species of rebellion; it was in this light, and in this light alone, that he disliked and feared it. Not the less on that account did the cause of Wicliffe suffer. At the close of Henry's short reign, the sect was almost extinguished, and in the persecution continued by his son and successor it altogether expired. With the fall of Lollardism, the spirit of the English people seems itself to have sunk, and for a time that feudalism which had been greatly diminished, appears to have asserted itself once more. Throughout that long and bloody period, known as the Wars of the Roses, the history of

England is the history of the English barons. Feudalism rose from the grave in the person of the Earl of Warwick, and with him, on the field of Barnet, it went down to the grave again. It was but a temporary resurrection; yet it lasted long enough to roll back by several generations the development of the English people. The aristocracy of the land exterminated themselves, but they first exterminated the aspirations of the middle classes, tore up from the national soil those seeds of freedom which the centuries had sown. When the carnage of Bosworth field extinguished the miserable struggle, and when the Tudors came into possession of the English throne, they came into possession of a kingdom approaching nearer to the appearance of an absolute monarchy than any English sovereign had ever previously known. We say the appearance of an absolute monarchy, for it was not so in reality. The English constitution had not been altered, the privileges of the people had not been really impaired. But the people had no longer a heart to assert their privileges. Had they possessed such a heart, they might have risen to greater power than ever. The feudal barons had been swept away, and between them and the crown there was no intermediate class; it was clear that now was the time in which either king or people might make themselves supreme. But the people had not the spirit to seize the moment; that spirit had been crushed out of them by the temporary revival of feudalism, and the second death of feudalism could not bring back their life. And what the people had not the heart to do, the new house of Tudor did; it seized the reins of empire, and became practically despotic. It was not that the Tudors beat down the will of the people; the people for the most part had no will to beat down. In any conflict between public opinion and the desire of the crown, the desire of the crown must have yielded; but in the age preceding the Lutheran Reformation, no such conflict arose. The popular voice was silent, the voice of public opinion was silent, the voice of religious reform was silent; and those who had once aspired to political freedom, lifted up their eyes with awe to the majesty of the throne. If during this period the idea of Papal headship somewhat revived, it was precisely for the same reason. The Council of Constance had freed religious England as effectually from an absolute Papacy, as the House of Commons had freed secular England from the danger of an absolute monarchy. If, in defiance alike of its own religious and constitutional privileges, England still persisted in relinquishing its secular and its sacred rights, it could only be because its moral degeneracy had made these privileges no longer dear.

There arises here another point which is highly suggestive. It is a remarkable fact that the darkest period of English history, since the days of the Norman Conquest, is that period which intervenes between the opening of the Wars of the Roses and the accession of Henry Tudor. When we say the darkest period, we do not mean that it was the bloodiest, the most cruel, or the most superstitious; we mean something far more remarkable. We refer to the fact that nowhere are the annals so bare, nowhere the records so meagre, nowhere the statements so inconsistent and irreconcilable. And this is in the age of discovery, in the age of scientific investigation, in the age which witnessed the invention of printing, nay, in the age when the art of printing was introduced by Caxton into England itself. Why should the period of greatest literary light be marked by the densest obscurity in the materials of historical knowledge? Now in answering this question we must bear in mind the source whence historical knowledge had hitherto flowed. That source was the monastery. The monks had been the earliest chroniclers of English history. To them we are indebted for nearly all the historic light which has been thrown over the early and mediæval annals of our country. It will be found, we think, that in periods of religious fervour these annals are most full, that in seasons of religious decadence they are comparatively meagre. On this principle it will follow that, in the age which elapsed between the opening of the Wars of the Roses and the accession of Henry Tudor, the monastic life was passing through a stage of spiritual decadence. And this, indeed, is in strict keeping with all the facts of the case. It is not denied, even by the admirers of monastic life, that in the period preceding the Reformation the monasteries had become intensely corrupted. No one will suspect Mr. Froude of an undue bias against mediævalism, yet Mr. Froude has in the strongest terms declared this to be his conviction. We do not for a moment suppose that the monasteries of England had become worse than the monasteries of other lands. There are two reasons why the immorality of the English monasteries has furnished a favourite text to Protestant writers. The first is, the fact that in England monastic life more than Papal life was the source of the national religion. The second is, the fact that in England, through political circumstances, the corruption of the monasteries was detected in a way that it could not be on the Continent. Neither of these facts, however, would warrant us in concluding that the decline of English monasticism was anything more than one part of a universal decline; one illustration of a great decadence of monastic life which was taking place throughout the whole world. Nor, if the matter ended here, would we be disposed to lay immense stress upon it. We have already pointed out in an earlier part of this work, that in the period preceding the Lutheran Reformation the monasteries had ceased to be the schools of the Christian spirit, that by this time they had long since served their day, and existed only as survivals of a past culture. When institutions are suffered to exist after they have served their day, and after they have no further work to do, we cannot expect that they will exist in a healthy state, or that their existence will contribute to the moral health of the community. It will not therefore surprise us, that the English monasteries of the fifteenth century had become the homes of moral disease; nor shall we be disposed to infer from that fact alone, that the entire Catholic system had become debased. The monasteries were no longer the representatives of that system, and Catholicism must now be judged by another standard. When, however, we search for that standard, we shall be convinced that not only was the decline of the English monasteries the phase of a universal monastic decline, but that the monastic decline itself was only one phase of a wider decadence extending to the whole moral fabric. It will be found that when institutions professedly sacred become secularized, institutions professedly secular become time-serving. The monasteries affected the universities. The universities, indeed, had borne to the monasteries a very close relation in the order of historical development. When the sacred tuition of the school-life had closed, they had become its secular teachers. It is true, even the universities were no longer to be the boundaries of the Christian intellect, but they were still to be the tributaries to that intellect, and as such it was imperative that their waters should be pure. We find, however, that if the universities had not partaken in the glaring vices of the monasteries, they had been infected by the monasteries with a moral lethargy. It is true of all nations, it is pre-eminently true of the English nation, that periods of moral lethargy are unfavourable to mental expansion. The times when the English universities poured forth their greatest students, were the times of moral fervour, if not of religious enthusiasm. The fourteenth century had filled the English firmament with literary stars, the sixteenth century was to fill that firmament with literary stars again. But the intermediate period was almost starless. There is perhaps no epoch of British history which presents in every department or literature such an absence of illustrious names. The age of Chaucer was past, and the footsteps of the new poetic age were not yet heard approaching. The days of Wicliffe were gone, and the days of Tindal and of Latimer had given no sign of their coming. Had the universities been full of their wonted life, there would have been no such dearth of greatness; and had the universities been pervaded by their wonted spirit of moral earnestness, their intellectual life would have been full to overflowing. The English mind is so eminently practical, that it can neither reason, study, nor investigate, unless in that study and investigation it can discern a practical good; and where it has ceased to care for the practical good, where it has ceased to be animated with a moral motive, its intellectual aspirings will be lukewarm, and its intellectual efforts will be feeble.

But it is when we cross the Channel, it is when we pass from England into France, that we are most impressed with the decay of university life. The Sorbonne of Paris had been unquestionably the greatest theological faculty in the world; it had contained life in itself, and it had been a source of life to all other schools of learning. One great cause of this had been its moral disinterestedness. It had sought truth for its own sake; fearlessly, uncompromisingly, devotedly, and often in the face of great opposition. But the period of the Council of Constance is, strange to say, the period of its decline. It is not that subsequent to that council the University of Paris lost its influence on the nation. On the contrary, after that date it rose to a height of influence which it had never occupied before. But it obtained this proud position by deserting its own legitimate sphere,—obtained it, not as a university, but as a political institution. There was indeed room in France for a new political institution. Here, as in England, the fifteenth century presents the darkest period which had yet marked the national history. Never had there been witnessed in the past, only once has there been witnessed in the future, an age of such complete anarchy as that which immediately followed the Council of Constance. A lunatic king, a profligate queen, an abandoned court, a disorganized society, a perpetual reign of terror resulting from the alternate domination of rival factions, all contributed to weaken and degrade the life of the French people. The Dukes of Orleans and of Burgundy strove for the reins of government, and scrupled at no means by which they might attain their end. Open war, brutal violence, deliberate murder, and secret assassination, were alike in turn resorted to. The butchers and the carpenters ranged themselves on different sides. The fact is highly significant, as it indicates the growing power of the middle classes. But what was a source of political exaltation to the butchers and the carpenters, was a source of moral degradation to the University of Paris. That university ought to have remained as a city set upon a hill, conspicuous by its height, and luminous by its literary glory. Instead of that, the University of Paris came down into the heat of the fray, and identified its interests with the interests of the political struggle. The result was what might have been expected. An institution so influential throwing the weight of its authority into the scale could not do otherwise than secure vast political power, but it secured that power at the expense of that disinterested morality which in former years had been its crown. Its students became soldiers, its professors took the lead in city brawls, or became in public harangues the champions of those who did so. The university was no longer searching for truth, it was searching for empire. It was no longer seeking to benefit humanity, it was seeking to support a very inferior section of mankind. It was no longer advocating the freedom of the French people, it was advocating the liberty of one faction to fetter the hands of another. By and by there came a cloud which for a time swept the whole spectacle from view,—king, queen, court, university, and rival factions. The intestine war was swallowed up and lost in a far more tremendous struggle; a struggle which prostrated the French monarchy, and destroyed for a season the national independence. In the great war with England, France was brought to the verge of ruin. Her armies were beaten, her strongholds were dismantled, her capital was conquered, and the crown was torn from her brow; for a few years an English king nominally and virtually occupied the French throne. And though recovery came, it was slow and painful. The beginning of her recovery was the revival of her spiritual life. It was when she had been bruised and broken, when her pride had been humbled in the dust, when her sense of independence had been transmuted into a sense of nothingness, that the spirit of religion began to dawn once more. The flower which is crushed gives forth its perfume; and the mind, whether national or individual, which has been crushed by adversity, emits the fragrance of a broken and a contrite spirit. France woke up to spiritual fervour in the hour of her utmost outward exhaustion, and it was the power of her spiritual fervour that bore her back to her place amongst the nations. Those armies which, under the command of the first generals of their age, had been beaten and shattered, were now content to march under the generalship of a peasant girl, because they believed that in that peasant girl there dwelt the inspiration of the divine life. It was that belief which led them on to victory. It emboldened their hearts with the confidence of a divine mission, and it paralyzed the hearts of their enemies with the terror of a divine judgment. It carried them from city to city, and from fortress to fortress, until at last they stood as conquerors upon the liberated soil of their native land. There have been many instances in history of the power of religious faith. The annals of Judaism supply one national example, and the annals of Mohammedanism furnish another. But we doubt if in all history there is to be found so striking an instance of the power of faith as is that spectacle of a mediæval army led from the depths of despair back to victory and freedom by the belief in the divine mission of the Maid of Orleans.

If we pass now to Holland and Germany, we shall find a more promising aspect of affairs. It is to be remarked that, in general, the nations of the north were more ripe for a positive reformation than those of the south. The Teutonic mind had always retained something of its primitive spontaneity, and was incapable of being permanently moulded by mediæval forms of culture. Nevertheless, at this period the attitude of Holland and of Germany towards the reformation was by no means identical. Both of these nations claimed a share in the invention of the art of printing, yet to each of them the new art was valuable on different grounds. To Holland it had a speculative, to Germany it had a practical, importance. It is singular that the German mind, which ultimately immersed itself in speculation, should in the period preceding the Reformation have been desirous only of practical progress, have sought only for the light in order that it might have a guide to its footsteps. The Germany of the fifteenth century and the Holland of the fifteenth century differed from the rest of Europe in this respect, that they were both dissatisfied; neither of them could be charged with the pride of self-independence. Yet they were each dissatisfied in a different way. Holland wanted speculation, Germany desired action. Holland wanted theological thought, Germany desired religious work. Holland wanted the power to investigate, Germany desired the liberty to believe. Holland wanted the emancipation which flows from culture, Germany desired the freedom of religious truth. Holland wanted an Erasmus, Germany desired a Luther.

But it must not be forgotten, that however promising the aspect of Germany may have been, its influence was almost neutralized by its subsequent and long-continued union with a country which was destined to be the mainstay of the most rigid Catholicism. Spain, in the fifteenth century, was only emerging into distinct nationality; but in the course of that century it was to attain a prominent place amongst the nations. It may seem strange, that a people whose nationality was so young should thus early have begun to exhibit the germs of a religious spirit; severe, morose, exclusive, narrow and bigoted. Youthful nations are generally more prone to spontaneity than to rigidity. But we must remember the peculiar circumstances in which Spain had stood for centuries. It was divided into separate kingdoms, and in the midst of them there was one which belonged not to the Cross. The Moors had from the eighth century obtained a footing in Spain, and had manifested the singular spectacle of a Mohammedan power in the very heart of Catholic Europe. It will be found that wheresoever a nation has been called to battle with extreme opinions, its own opinions have been carried to an opposite extreme. It was so with Spain. That country had for centuries stood face to face with a religion which in all its aspects was peculiarly opposed to the spirit of Catholicism. It is not wonderful that, in its recoil from the vision of the false Prophet, Spain should have become more Catholic still; more rigid, more austere, more formal, more devoted to the letter of hierarchical law, and more resolved to maintain the integrity of mediæval worship. Every man is partly the result of his age, and every nation is partly the product of the external influences which surround it. It is not surprising that the Spain of the fifteenth century should have been rather hardening than softening; but it would have been surprising in the extreme, if that hardening of its moral nature had proved a favourable omen for the great Reformation.

If we pass now to that land which was the very head and centre of the Catholic life, we shall see the spirit of youth at once in its glory and in its shame. Italy bounded from the Council of Constance, as a slave bounds from the chain. Nowhere did the youth of Europe display such intense consciousness of the joys which awaited it, and of the possibilities which lay before it. The heart of Christendom, long restrained from self-expression, burst forth into exuberant delight, and forgot everything but the rapture of the hour. It was in Italy that the spirit of youth found its special home, it was in Italy that it abandoned itself to its deepest dissipations. It plunged into the glare and glitter of the gorgeous cities, it stole the delights of life from flower to flower. It had long been denied liberty, and it indemnified itself by licence; it had long been compelled to strain at the gnat, and in compensation it swallowed the camel. There are two periods of mediæval history in which the life of Italy has exhibited intense moral corruption. The first is that period familiarly known as the Dark Ages; the second is the age immediately preceding the Reformation. Between these epochs of history it would indeed not be easy to choose. Alexander VI., at the close of the fifteenth, was equal to the worst pontiffs of the tenth century. Nevertheless these similar effects were the result of vastly different, even of contrary causes. The corruption of the tenth century sprang from the lethargy of life, the corruption of the fifteenth originated in the fact that life was overflowing. The debasement of the tenth century proceeded from the absence of self-respect, the degeneracy of the fifteenth resulted from the recklessness of an exaggerated self-esteem. The sensualities of the tenth century sprang from the predominance of brute instinct, the moral impurities of the fifteenth had their source in the overweening power of a brilliant and unbalanced imagination. There was indeed in this latter epoch everything which could contribute to feed and foster such an imagination. In Republican Florence, one family, that of the Medici, had risen to almost regal power by the wealth and the munificence it had showered upon the city. Its immense riches had been the enrichment of Florence, and the enrichment of Florence was the beautifying of Italy. Through the opulence, the generosity, the literary taste, and the æsthetic culture of that family, the city of Florence directly, and all the cities of Italy indirectly, were basking in a sunshine of artistic glory. All that eye had seen, all that ear had heard, all that it had entered into the heart of man to conceive, had been gathered into one blaze of splendour within the central home of Catholic life. All nature had poured its treasures at the feet of Italy. Her ocean had spread its blue waves before her, inviting enterprise, and tempting the spirit of discovery. The skies had spread their serenest canopy above her, to lift her thoughts into the region of creative beauty. Wealth had poured its treasures into her bosom, to enable her to add the triumphs of art to the gifts of natural beauty. The poetic muse had gifted her with a soul susceptible to the impressions of that loveliness which surrounded her, and had empowered her to wed the harmonies of nature to the harmonious utterances of the human spirit. It is not surprising that, in the first awakening to her resplendent position, her eyes should have been dazzled by the glare. It is not wonderful that, when the first flush of youthful independence was added to the knowledge of such boundless treasures, her heart should have forgotten that spirit of self-sacrifice which is itself the spirit of Christianity. Indisputable it is that the eyes of Italy *were* dazzled, and that her heart *was* rendered worldly. Her preparation for the great reform was also to be the lesson, that the sense of independence is spiritual death.

And the more the fifteenth century advanced, the more was that lesson borne home upon the heart of Italy. The remarkable experience in her case is, that while she had greater outward advantages than any other nation of Europe, she was of all the nations of Europe furthest removed from happiness. In proof of this, we have only to appeal to the fact that the Italian renaissance of the fifteenth century was the sphere in which the Roman hierarchy reaped the largest profits from the sale of indulgences. Prevalent as that practice had been in former days, it attained in this country, and in this century, a prevalence and a power which hitherto had been unknown. And here we must repeat a remark which we made in a former part of this work. We there said that the matter to be accounted for was not the supply but the demand. The hierarchy would never have issued indulgences if there had not been in the public mind a want felt for these, or for something equivalent to these; and the very avidity with which the indulgences were purchased by the men of that generation, is a proof how strong must have been the want, and how deep must have been the craving. But the question which suggests itself is this, Why should there have been such a want? In Italy, the home of the renaissance, the palace of the beautiful, the throne of art, the capital of commerce, the abode of all luxury and refinement, where could room be found for the admission of an ungratified desire? Yet it was in this Italy so beautiful and so favoured, so rich in worldly wealth and so full of mental glory, that the worst symptoms appeared of that old unrest which had proved a source of gain to the priesthood of former days. The worldly riches and the mental glory had failed to reach the needs of the spiritual nature, had failed to remove from the soul the sense of its separation from the divine life, had failed to answer the question by what means the spirit of man could become united to the Spirit of God.

It may be said, indeed, that these cries for indulgences were not sent up by the same class who revelled in the glories of the renaissance, that they came chiefly from the poor, who were unable to appreciate the advantages of the present world, and were forced to fix their thoughts upon the possible joys and the possible sorrows which might await them in the future. No doubt, to a certain extent, this is true. The sale of indulgences was most effectual amongst primitive minds. Excessive culture is apt to blunt the spontaneity of feeling, and in an age of inherent corruption the sense of sin was not likely to be most keenly felt by those who were immersed in speculative studies. Yet it by no means follows, that where the sense of sin was blunted there was an absence of all unrest. The unrest of the Italian renaissance showed itself for the most part in the sense of a nameless voyage; undefined, indefinable, conspicuous only by the blank it left in the soul. If the desire for indulgences found its peculiar sphere amongst the uncultured, the unrest which knew not what to desire found almost its exclusive sphere amongst the sons of the great literary revival. It was not long before Italy was to receive a striking illustration of this. It was to come not from the valleys, not from the haunts of poverty, not from the homes of ignorance. It was to be manifested in the life of one who, by birth, by education, and by circumstances, occupied the heights of society, and dwelt in the very blaze of Italian glory.

Jerome Savonarola was beyond all question the most remarkable man of the fifteenth century. His life was bounded by three worlds,—a world which was dead, a world which was living, and a world which was coming,—and by each of these he was distinctly influenced. It is by the combination of these different influences that we shall be best able to arrive at a true portrait of the man; a portrait which has been variously painted, and which, in the varieties of its delineation, has not always been allowed to preserve the golden mean between the traces of flattery and the touch of depreciation. Savonarola cannot be separated either from the present, the past, or the future; and if we would see him as he was, we must consider what his life derived from each of these sources. From that present into which he was born he received a high social position, and all the advantages which such a position affords. He came into the world when the spirit of Christianity was in the bloom of its youth, and in the full conviction of its strength of independence. He came into a part of the world where the spirit of Christianity had intimately associated itself with the spirit of culture, of discovery, and of investigation. He was born at a season peculiarly favourable to the development of intellectual life. Just one year after his birth, occurred that great catastrophe which sank an empire in the dust, and sent forth its life to vivify other shores—the capture of Constantinople. In no land were the fugitive strangers so warmly received as in Italy, in no city so warmly welcomed as in Florence, by no family so ardently patronised as by the Medici. The result was, that they gave back more than they received, and rendered Italy more rich, from the riches it had showered on them. The world which was contemporary with Savonarola, was a world in which the spirit of ancient Greece had revived, and in which the learning of ancient Greece had become the recognised standard of erudition. The classical had taken the place of the mediæval, and for a time the pagan models seemed to have supplanted the Christian. And with the revival of Greek learning had been increasingly fostered that thirst for freedom which had peculiarly belonged to the ancient Greek spirit, before that spirit had been curbed by the iron yoke of the Byzantine power. In this world of Greek resurrection Savonarola spent his earliest years, drank of its streams and gazed on its beauties, and travelled over its paths; nor did there seem any reason which should prevent him, with his talents and his opportunities, from becoming in after life one of its leading citizens.

But while, in outward circumstances and in intellectual characteristics, there was no such restraining reason, there was in the heart of Savonarola an obstacle more potent than any outward circumstance, or than any intellectual disqualification could have been. That obstacle was the sense of a spiritual void,—a void which the Greek renaissance could not even meet, much less supply. Influenced as he was by his own age and surroundings, the shadows of a coming age seem to have fallen upon his path, darkening his present enjoyment, and imparting to all objects a pensive shade of sadness. What was this world of revived paganism contributing to the soul of man? What was it doing for his spiritual nature? What was it adding to that immortal element which hungered within him? Was it not really destroying human spirituality by a new species of image-worship? —the worship of those objects which the tempter had offered to the Master of old as worthy of adoration,— the lust of the flesh, the lust of the eye, and the pride of life. Was not all Italy repeating the sin of ancient Judea,—bowing down to the golden calf, and paying abject homage to the work of its own hands? And ought not the spirit of man to revolt against this image-worship of paganism as strongly as it had revolted against the image-worship of Christianity? Nay, was not this new evil the worse pestilence of the two? The images of saint and martyr had at least evoked a sense of religious emotion; but the images of wealth and rank and sensuous magnificence could only evoke the deepest selfishness of the soul.

It was these questionings which led Savonarola to become the forerunner of Luther. He failed to find satisfaction in the world which surrounded him, and he cast his eyes forward to that world which was coming. Not that Savonarola ever attained, or eve claimed to attain, the rank of a positive reformer. At no time did he contemplate a separation from the Church of his fathers, and in his last awful hour, when he was called to pass through his baptism of fire, he professed himself a true adherent of the Catholic faith. The position of Savonarola was not unlike that of the Waldenses; he sought, like them, a worship more primitive in its simplicity, and a faith which manifested its fruits less in the form and more in the life. There was, indeed, one marked difference between the Waldenses and Savonarola,— they objected to vanities they had never enjoyed; he repudiated these vanities after he had tasted all their pleasures. Savonarola's dissatisfaction with the world came from a personal proof of its inadequacy. He found that it could not meet the wants of his deepest nature. The discovery was made at the age of twenty-two,—a period when human life in general is absorbed in the interests of the passing hour. If thus early he could pronounce an unfavourable verdict on the world, it was not likely that such a verdict would be softened by the gravity of maturer years. Savonarola seems to have felt this; he accepted the decision of his youth as a final decision. With him there was no pause between resolve and action; the moment his heart had condemned the world, he prepared to leave it. He withdrew himself from its pomp and its vanity, from its learning and its glory, and retired into the seclusion of the cloister. There the experience happened to him which had befallen Hildebrand in the monastery of Cluny. There fell upon his soul the conviction of a great work given him to do, the sense of a heavenly mission, the power of a call from God. He must regenerate this abandoned Italy; must wake it to a sense of danger; must open its eyes to behold the dreadful precipice on whose brink it revelled. He must proclaim anew the thunders of Mount Sinai; must tell the world that life was short, and that after life was judgment; must rouse mankind into a perception of the awful responsibility of existence, and the terrible trust involved in the keeping of one human soul. Fired with this sense of a heavenly mission, Savonarola in a few years appeared once more in the world of men, no longer to be its votary, but to be its adversary, and, if possible, its conqueror. His appearance as a public preacher was in that year which immediately preceded the birth of the great German reformer, as if the star of Savonarola were not to set until the star of Luther had dawned to fill its place in the future. But it seemed at first as if the Italian preacher had over-estimated his strength and mistaken his destiny. Seldom has subsequent oratorical eminence been inaugurated by so ominous a beginning. Nature had denied to him all those gifts which form the popular orator. His harsh voice, his unmusical intonation, so rare amongst his countrymen, his ungainly delivery, so repulsive to the men of every country, all contributed to deprive his words of that force which they really contained. He failed, and he covered his failure by a new retirement. For a few years we lose all sight of him, and when next he appears before us, it is in a world where all is changed. He is no longer the despised orator, resorted to by few, and listened to long by none. He is the observed and the admired of all, the centre of applauding crowds, and the point of attraction where rest the eyes of myriads. What has effected the transformation? What has brought thousands to hang on the lips of a man whom a few years ago none cared to patronise? Is it that Savonarola has improved his defective utterance, or is it that his piety and zeal have kindled him into yet greater fire? Perhaps, to some extent, both of these causes may have operated; yet we think both of them combined will not suffice to explain the change. That change, if we mistake not, lay not in Savonarola, but in society. The gay circles of Florence had during his absence caught the spirit of the reformer, been seized with that vague dissatisfaction which had been to him the beginning of life. To them also the world had lost its charm, upon them also the world's pleasures had begun to pall. It was this more than any actual increase in Savonarola's power which lent to his second ministry so terrible a force. Never since the days of apostolic fervour were human words attended with so startling an effect. The public square was crowded with ladies of the highest fashion; ladies whose lives had been one scene of uninterrupted gaiety, whose thoughts had been bounded by the vanities of the day and hour, whose hearts had been hardened by perpetual contemplation of self-interest. They came now, laden with their costliest jewels, and bedecked with their most precious ornaments; but they came in order that in this thoroughfare, which had been the scene of their vanity, they might renounce that vanity for ever. They came with their jewels that they might cast them away before the eyes of multitudes, throw them on the highway like useless lumber, and leave them to be trodden under the feet of man and beast. Such a spectacle could not have been produced by the passing impression of any sermon; it must have been the last result of meditative years. In front of the cathedral was to be witnessed a spectacle not less startling, and not less significant. There were gathered there some of the foremost writers of the age, and they came to consume their writings in the flames. The gallant brought his licentious love-songs, the novelist carried his immoral works of fiction, even the grave philosopher brought his pagan treatises to burn them. Still less than in the former case could such a scene have been produced by the preaching of an hour. It must have been the final voice of a long dissatisfaction, the last utterance of a protracted spiritual unrest which had tasted all the pleasures earth had to give, and had found their taste to be the gall of bitterness.

We have seen Savonarola in relation to two worlds: that of the living, and that of the coming age. But Savonarola was also influenced by the world of the dead. He shared in that mediæval dream which had haunted the heart of the Catholic hierarchy — the dream of a revived Jewish theocracy. He looked forward to the establishment of a great republic, whose only king should be God, and whose only law should be the gospel; and the city of Florence was that spot where he hoped to see his vision realized. It did not seem to strike Savonarola that the establishment of such a republic would be the restoration to the hierarchy of all that it had lost. It did not seem to strike him that it would be purchased by the total subordination of the secular to the priestly power, and therefore by the surrender of everything which Savonarola himself held dear. But there was one evil consequence of this republican dream which Savonarola did see, and for which we regret to say he must in great measure be held responsible. He knew that Florence could only receive such a constitution at the point of the sword; yet he did not shrink from that knowledge. On the contrary, he invited the arms of France to the invasion of Italy, and he hailed Charles VIII. as the national saviour. In all this we do not doubt the sincerity of Savonarola. We do not doubt that his politics were subordinate to his piety, and that he desired the invasion of foreign enemies only that he might transform his country into a visible kingdom of God. Nevertheless, we are glad that we are not called to follow him through his closing years. Strange to say, we like him better in his self-denying life than we do in his martyr's death. We are made painfully conscious that his was, after all, only a political martyrdom. Savonarola never suffered death for his religious opinions; he met the fate of one who had conspired to subvert the constitution of his native land. He died, not for the cause of Christian truth, but for the sake of a Utopian dream,—of a dream of theocratic empire, which never could have been realized on earth, and which, if it had been realized, would have ended in the re-establishment of an absolute Papacy. On these grounds, we shall prefer to think of Savonarola as he was in his youth and freshness, shall prefer to associate his name with the days when his religion dwelt apart from his politics. We shall raise to him a monument in our hearts, but we shall place that monument, not in front of the French invading army, nor yet in front of those awful flames in which his form was consumed to ashes. We shall raise it in the public square of Florence, and shall fashion it after his attitude in that day when he stood proclaiming in words of terrific power the vanity of earth, and the nothingness of worldly joys.

We have now completed our review of the moral preparation of youth for the stage of approaching manhood. We say that at best it was only a negative preparation; when it had revealed the sense of dependence, its work was done. All that it could do was to show the inadequacy of the world to bring rest. But during all this time, through the channel of youthful imagination, there was going forward a great intellectual movement,—a movement which was preparing the mind of Christendom for a higher life than it had ever enjoyed before, and was leading the footsteps of human progress right into the promised land. This movement, which forms in our view the true intellectual transition to the age of Luther, will be the subject of our attention in the following chapter.

CHAPTER XXXVII.

THE INTELLECTUAL PREPARATION OF YOUTH IN ITS RELATION TO ART AND THE REFORMATION.

WE have observed, in the course of mediæval history, an increasing demand for adequate forms to express the Christian spirit. We have found that, while the school-life was forced to represent the truths of Christianity by outward images or symbols, it was never able to rest long satisfied with any of these; for the spirit was perpetually outgrowing the form, and the thought ever leaving the representation far in the background. We have seen how the simple engravings were superseded by the statues, and we have marked how the statues themselves were ultimately inadequate to meet the longings of the Christian heart. They were too cold, too lifeless, too unimpassioned to represent the objects of eternal adoration, and the Church had been compelled to institute a higher mode of expression, in which the forms of the sacred dead should be seen to live and move. Accordingly, the miracle-plays and mysteries had arisen, and men for a time found the images of the past reproduced in all their freshness, and exhibited in all their power. But the spirit of

Christianity had since these days expanded further still, and the form had again become too small to contain the thought. Men wanted to see more than even life or action; they wanted to behold the evidences of a human soul. They desired to gaze upon the forms of the sacred dead, not as mere forms, nor yet merely as forms in motion, but as forms which expressed the voice of a soul, which revealed the depth of love, and the warmth of passion, and the strength of enthusiasm, which suggested an infinitude of power which they were unable to portray, and lifted the eye of the beholder beyond their own visible representations to that invisible and spiritual world which they strove faintly to prefigure. It was such images as these that the spirit of Christianity desired when it arrived at the days of its youth; images which should reveal in form and feature not only what the eye could see, but what the heart could feel; not only what the sense could admire, but what the soul could love; not only what the hand could reverently touch, but what the spirit could silently adore.

And it was in answer to this demand that Italian art arose. In the triumphs of the canvas, image-representation reached its highest possible perfection, and mediævalism reached, we believe, the nearest approach it ever made to the standard of Protestant theology. It is on this account that we have called art the intellectual preparation of youth. We regard it as the real point of transition between the intellect of mediæval and the intellect of Protestant Europe, and it is in this light alone that we propose to view it.

With art in itself, with the rules of the painter and the intrinsic beauties of the paintings, we have here nothing to do. We want to know what was the relation of art to the spirit of Christianity, what was that special want in mediævalism which it was designed to meet, and what was that special contribution which it furnished to the development of the human race?

There is one thought which has run like a thread through this whole historical narrative, and that is the divorce in the mind of the mediæval world between the divine and the human Christ. We have repeatedly directed attention to the fact that, from the days of Gnostic speculation, divinity was regarded as something inharmonious with and opposed to humanity. We have seen that, from that time, that which was human in the person of the Master ceased to occupy any large share in the thoughts of men. The Christ on whom the mediæval world fixed its eye was a Christ outside the range of human nature; a Christ so supernatural that He was inapproachable, and so transcendent that He had no meeting-place in His being for the wants of lower life. He was a Christ whose works were all on a large scale, and for whom it would be degradation to operate in minute details. He atoned not for petty sins, but only for such sins as merited eternal death. He came not into immediate connection with the course of human history; His province was only to sum up that history in a final act of judgment. Hence between Him and humanity there was a chasm; a chasm which must be filled up, lest the very memory of His presence should be banished altogether. We know how the mediæval world attempted to fill up that chasm. We know how it sought to bridge the distance it had created between earth and heaven, by interposing a ladder of communication, on which the angels of God ascended and descended. We know, above all, how it endeavoured to supply the void it had made, by the creation of an ideal of human purity, the apotheosis of the Virgin Mother. We have already pointed out that, in this reverence for the Virgin, the spirit of Christianity was seeking the living among the dead, was trying to discover in the forms of its own imagination that portrait of human beauty which had been perfectly delineated in the earthly side of the Master's character. Gradually, as the years rolled on, there had crept over the heart of Christendom the conviction that, in lending to a creation what belonged to the veritable Master, it was denuding that Master of one-half of His glory. In the desires of Francis of Assisi to receive the impress of the wounds of Jesus, we see already a reaction from the contemplation of a Christ who was purely supernatural. Yet not even with Francis of Assisi did the world reach the true estimate of the humanity of Jesus. He deified the wounds of the Master, yet the wounds were only physical, and even these were to him invested with a supernatural or magical significance. That region of Christ's nature which had not been appropriated by the world was the region of the pure human soul: distinct from the supernatural on the one hand, and from the physical on the other; and therefore removed at once from that transcendentalism which overleaps humanity, and from that materialism which degrades it. Man wanted communion with God, and that communion he had hitherto failed to find. He had failed to find it, because God, even an incarnate God, had been represented as a being foreign to his soul, distinct from his nature, separate from his humanity. He had made frantic efforts to scale that tremendous height, on whose summit the mediæval world had placed the supernatural. That the supernatural was at the door of nature, and had manifested itself through nature, had not entered into the thoughts of that world, and so man had to climb in search of that which was touching the very threshold of his being. And he did climb, manfully and courageously. He heaped Pelion on the top of Ossa, that he might reach the dizzy height which transcended human thought, and distanced human nature. He climbed on the head of angel and archangel, striving by an ever-ascending series of gradations to attain the wondrous summit. He reached at last that form which was divided by no other from the divine life of the Master,—the image of the Virgin Mother. But here bitterest disappointment awaited him. He found that, although no intermediate form divided the human virgin from the divine Christ, they were separated by an impediment more terrible than any intermediate form—a gulf of boundless distance. And then slowly the conviction forced itself upon his reluctant mind that he was searching for an impossible good, that if the divine were incompatible with the human, he could never attain it until he had laid down his humanity, that as long as he remained a finite individual he must wander at an infinite distance from the promised land, and that communion with God was a boon never to be reached below.

It is not difficult to see what was wanted to dispel such a delusion. It had originated in an error, it could be eradicated by the removal of that error. Let but the truth be borne home upon the human spirit, that the divine was not antagonistic to the human; let but the mediæval world be convinced that the earthly side of the Master's portraiture was itself the mediator between God and man, and in an instant the whole intermediate paraphernalia would be swept away. Virgin, angel, archangel, relics of martyrs, tombs of saints, consecrated images of wood and stone, would cease to have any value as possible avenues to the divine, when one short and certain avenue had been opened through the human soul of the Master. The question was, How such a thought was to be presented to the mediæval world? We know that with the Lutheran Reformation it burst upon the mind with startling power, but it would never have proved so effective if the mind had not been partially prepared for it. What was the source of this preparation? Mediæval youth could not be reasoned with; logic was too slow a process to enlist the attention of its buoyant spirit. Nor would mediæval youth consent to be taught and disciplined;

it was too conscious of its independence, and too confident in its strength. One course alone remained. It must be approached through its own nature, through that very channel of youthful imagination which it held to be its peculiar glory. The mediæval world must be taught, without knowing that it was taught. It must be instructed by a voice professing only to amuse, moulded by a hand claiming only to caress, dominated by a power pretending only to minister to its selfish desires. That voice, that hand, that power was art. Art was to be to the mediæval world what the poet is to all worlds ; an unconscious teacher, an educator whose design is not to educate, but only to please; an elevator of the moral nature who yet has aspired to be no more than a minister to human imagination. Art came to be the servant of the mediæval world, and it became its master; came to amuse its leisure hours, and became the guide of its greatest moments. It imparted a new truth to the world, that truth after which it had been vainly groping for ages. It brought, for the first time, before the Catholic mind, the full vision of the Master's human glory, withdrew the curtain which for centuries had shrouded the earthly hemisphere of His being, showed to the eyes of men how beautiful, how sublime was that humanity which He bore, and how sublime is all humanity because it was borne by Him. It revealed in language swifter and more eloquent than words, that truth which lies at the basis of Christianity, and which all paganism before and since had ignored, the truth that self-sacrifice is the highest strength, and that the glory of suffering virtue excels the glory of conquering power.

This, then, we believe to have been the peculiar province of art, in so far as art related to the development of the Christian spirit. It was to bring into prominence that element which had been long neglected—the vision of Christ's humanity; and it was thus to open for the heart of man a door of direct communion with the life of God. This tendency of Christian art towards the representation of a human Christ had already prefigured itself in the previous age. All revolts of the school-life were anticipations of the spirit of youth, prophetic of its coming, and suggestive of its message. In that great poetic outburst of religious life which was inaugurated by the visions of Dante, Christian art, for the first time, lifted its voice in the praise of the human soul. We have seen how Giotto of Florence was imbued with the spirit of Dante, and we have seen how powerfully he expressed in painting that love of purity which Dante expressed in song. With Giotto, the purity had a different incarnation; it was enshrined, not in the heart of an imaginary Beatrice, but in the human soul of the living Master. In his work the Catholic world, for the first time, beheld what might be called the apotheosis of Christ's humanity; the lifting up to the highest heaven of that which hitherto had been esteemed too lowly for reverence. He was the first who painted the crucifixion as an expression of love. Before his time that scene had been indeed depicted, but it had been depicted chiefly in its aspects of physical terror; with Giotto, the centre of all the spectacle is the human soul of Jesus. The eye ceases to linger upon the merely physical agonies, and rests no more upon that preternatural darkness which covered His dying hour, for it is arrested and riveted by that light of His human countenance which even the darkness cannot dim — the light of a love that passeth knowledge.

It was not to be supposed that the new attitude assumed by mediæval art would all at once be consistently maintained. Giotto was rather prophetic of the future than representative of the present. He owed his superior power partly to that intellectual outburst which marked the transition of the renaissance from France into Italy; the same outburst which had inspired the soul and tuned the voice of his friend and companion, Dante. Both these men were in advance of their time. They were the representatives of a real stage of humanity, but that stage had not yet come. Their mission was a prophetic and an anticipative mission; they had been sent to spy out the promised land, and to bring back into the world of the present, specimen fruits of the world which was coming. Accordingly we are not surprised that, after the first impulse of the Italian renaissance had subsided, the world fell back somewhat upon its original position. In the age immediately succeeding that of Giotto, art especially appears to have experienced what may be called a theological relapse. When we say so, we do not mean that it became in itself less artistic, we do not mean that its touch was more coarse, or its delineation less vivid. It is not in the mode of expression, but in the thought which is expressed, that we observe a relapse. Mediævalism seems to recoil once more from the exaltation of the human soul of Jesus. As an example of this, we may take the very striking representation of the Last Judgment, by Andrea Orcagna. It is conceived in the true spirit of Catholicism. The dead, small and great, stand before God awaiting their final sentence; on the right are the souls of the sanctified; on the left are the spirits of the unregenerate. Two thrones stand in the centre; one is occupied by Christ, the other by the Virgin Mother. Nothing can be more unlike than the attitude of these heavenly personages. Christ, true to the mediæval conception, is delineated in all the terrors of majestic power. His countenance bespeaks mingled authority and anger; conscious majesty, and the indignation of outraged honour. He turns to the left; His thoughts bent upon the gloomy side of the picture, and His aspect wearing the impress of the gloom. He uncovers His wounded side, to remind the trembling host of the unregenerate that they are looking upon Him whom they pierced. His hand is raised with a menacing gesture, to tell them of His power and His determination to use it; and the sentence of condemnation, 'Depart from me,' is expressed more vividly in His look than if it had been uttered by His voice, or written by His hand on the face of heaven. Far different is the attitude of the Virgin Mother. All that ought to have been contemplated in the human Jesus is here transferred to her. Unlike her divine Son, she loves to dwell upon the hopeful view. She turns her eyes to the right, that they may rest upon the army of the saved, and also that they may hide themselves from the vision of the lost. There is discernible in her averted countenance the horror with which her pitying soul beholds the condemnation of multitudes, and mingling with that horror there is seen the look of unspeakable tenderness that would fain recall the erring within the pale of salvation. There is no need to point the moral of this picture; like all true art, it points its own moral. Volumes would not have expressed so clear a comment on mediæval morality as is furnished at a glance by this one painting. Orcagna certainly did not intend it for a satire; but had he so intended it, he could not more forcibly have portrayed the truth that mere supernatural power is powerless to win love, that divinity divorced from humanity is divorced from human sympathy, and that a heaven repelling earth must be repelled by earth in turn.

This painting of Orcagna, however, may be regarded as the last outburst of the older mediævalism, the last strong effort to maintain the worship of a Christ separated from human nature. The spirit of Giotto was still alive, and there were causes at work older than the spirit of Giotto. The gradual diffusion of learning, and the steady advance of the renaissance, had raised the dignity of man in his own estimation, had led him insensibly to the conclusion that humanity was, after all, not so mean a gift. He became less timorous in attributing to the Master that which he felt not ignoble in himself; he began to dwell more habitually and more endearingly on the human soul of Jesus. Accordingly the age which followed Orcagna was a regress to the age of Giotto. In the paintings of Masaccio, the human soul beams forth once more, and in the works of Fra Angelico it shines with even greater lustre. Whatever Fra Angelico portrays is eminently human. Whether it be the Virgin Mother, or the images of the saints, or the forms of the celestial hierarchy, we feel that the portrait is drawn by the touch of a sympathetic man. And when he seeks to unfold the divine image of the Master, he clothes that divinity in all that is best in human nature; clothes it in the calmness of a restful heart, in the purity of a sinless soul, in the self-sacrificing devotion of one in whose being all other beings live and move. It might be said that such a treatment of the subject had its chief ground in the nature of the man, did we not see the same course of thought manifested in the art of his contemporaries. While Fra Angelico in Florence was painting the crucifix surrounded by adoring saints, the four members of the Van Eyck family were jointly delineating in Flanders their great picture, the 'Adoration of the Lamb.' Here we have the same transition into the reverence for the gentler attributes, the discovery of the glory of self-sacrifice, and the recognition of the majesty which may reside in suffering weakness. If we pass now to Venice, we shall find art passing through a similar experience, only in an intensified degree. The portraits of Christ by Gian Bellini exceed in moral grandeur all that had gone before them, and are unsurpassed by any that follow them. It is the moral element in these paintings that makes them grand. Not only is there no effort at adventitious ornament, but there is a very strenuous effort to suppress such ornament. It had been customary to surround the head of the Saviour with a halo of glory, which was called a nimbus. In the portraits of Bellini, the Saviour stands forth with no nimbus encircling His head, with no outward glory enshrining His form. He stands with no adornment but that which comes from within. The light which transfigures Him, is the light which irradiates His countenance from His own pure spirit; the glory which attracts all eyes, is the glory which emanates from a heart of perfect love; the beauty which transfixes the gaze, is the beauty which shines transparently from a sinless human soul. Can we fail to perceive that in the very conception of such a portrait humanity has already risen from its self-abasement, has learned those glories that are slumbering within it, has awakened to those infinite possibilities which lie before it? It no longer fears to attribute to the object of its worship a nature kindred to its own. It glories in such an ascription, it rejoices to behold the Christ clothed in that garb familiar to its sense and to its spirit, and it paints Him in the chambers of its imagination, no longer as a giant of portentous power, but as one who was found in the fashion of a man.

And now there rise in the firmament of art four resplendent stars,—stars which were sent to shed their light upon that age which ushered in the great Reformation, but whose light through all the ages was to know no setting. Their names have become familiar to us as household words; they are Leonardo da Vinci, Titian, Michael Angelo, and Raphael. In Leonardo da Vinci we find the pursuance of that same ideal which Fra Angelico had sought, and which Gian Bellini had attained—the ideal of a Christ whose glory was His perfect humanity. His great picture is a description of the Last Supper, in which the leading thought is that mutual human love which binds together the disciple and his Lord. The Master sits at a long table, and on either side of Him there is seated a group of His disciples. The ages of these disciples are marked in their countenances, and we can trace the gradation of their years, from the youthful face of John to the grave maturity which marks the visage of Peter. The Master is uttering the words: 'One of you shall betray me,' and the reply to that utterance is a crowd of different emotions, rising in the hearts and beaming out in the faces of His auditors. On the one side we see doubt, incredulity, the sense of impossibility; on the other we discern the glance of suspicion, which indicates the fear of treachery. Here we have the expression of boundless astonishment; there we see depicted the utmost indignation which the human heart can feel: the words of the Master bring out the respective characters of His disciples. That Master Himself remains calm; He who knew what was in man, is not shaken by the deceitfulness of the human heart. His countenance expresses perfect resignation. It is not the resignation of stolidity; the clear presentiment of death is written on that brow. It is not the resignation of impassiveness; in His look there is infinite pain, only it is pain not for Himself but for His betrayer. It is the resignation of a heart which is capable of suffering deeply, but whose sufferings are all impersonal, and whose sense of individual sorrow sinks into utter nothingness, when weighed against that load of human sin and misery which it is longing to remove.

Titian of Venice is not essentially a religious painter. It is true, in his picture of the entombment of Christ, he shows that he has caught the spirit of his age, and is in harmony with the tendency to exalt human nature. He who makes the entombment of Christ a subject for the canvas, has ceased to dissociate human sacrifice from divine strength. Nevertheless, the genius of Titian is essentially secular, and tends rather towards the beautiful than the moral. Venice was always more disposed than Florence to expatiate on the glories of light and colour; a fact which makes the purely moral grandeur of the portraits of Bellini all the more remarkable, and all the more significant. Titian followed his countrymen in their ordinary practice of bowing down to physical beauty, and it was perhaps on this account that he found a more congenial field in pagan than in Christian subjects. Yet the paintings of Titian are by no means confined to the delineation of outward form and colouring. Forms and colours there are, but these are the vesture of a spirit which dwells within them, and that spirit is the life of the Greek renaissance. It is here that Titian comes into union with the general preparation for reform. Living in the days of the Greek revival, he had caught the glow of freedom which that revival had kindled. The study of Grecian literature had inspired him with the breath of Grecian freedom. True, it carried his heart rather back to the past than forward to the future, yet the very desire to retrace his steps indicated dissatisfaction with the present. His past was, after all, a Utopian past — a future in disguise. He invested it with a freedom which it never really held, except in the fond imaginations of its poets and its sages; and while he sought a paradise in the revival of a world which was dead, he was unconsciously forecasting his gaze on that world which was about to be.

When we consider Michael Angelo and Raphael in their relation to Christianity, we find it necessary to view them not separately, but in combination. They are the two halves of one whole. Raphael is the counterpart of Michael Angelo; Michael Angelo is the complement of Raphael. Angelo exhibits Christianity in its strength; Raphael shows it in its gentleness. Angelo portrays the Christ in His grandeur as the head of humanity; Raphael delineates Him in His beauty at the lowest stage of human frailty—the stage of infancy. Angelo reveals the majesty of Christian truth; Raphael paints the loveliness of Christian purity. Angelo exhibits the Christ in His power to convict; Raphael sets Him forth in His power to attract. Angelo is the Dante, Raphael is the Petrarch of Christian art. Angelo is John the Baptist standing in the moral wilderness of the world, and crying in a voice of thunder: 'Repent, for the kingdom of heaven is at hand;' Raphael is John the Evangelist leaning on the bosom of the Master, and seeking, by means of contact, to catch the impress of His divine gentleness. Yet, while they are thus contrasted, they are not wholly separated. There are points in which the difference between them seems to be bridged over, and each lends to the other a portion of his own life. Angelo is generally the stern reformer, denouncing the vices of his age, and exhibiting the judgment on these vices in figures of terrible wrath. Yet, who will deny that, mingled with the severity of his portraits, there lurks an unmistakeable touch of sadness, which reveals beneath his frown a yearning for humanity? Raphael, on the other hand, is generally the very incarnation of gentleness, so absorbed in the love of the beautiful, that he has seldom leisure to turn his gaze upon the darker sides of human nature. Yet, occasionally, even his gentleness flashes out into the fire of the reformer, and he becomes one with Michael Angelo in his mission of purifying mankind. There is one picture in which he describes the union of heaven and earth. They are united by a sacramental altar, on either side of which are groups of saints and angels. Amongst these groups Raphael has the moral courage to place the figures of two men who had been peculiarly the objects of Papal and hierarchical displeasure; the one was the poet Dante, who had spent his life in exile; the other was the reformer Savonarola, who, only ten years before, had closed the life of a nonconformist with the death of a martyr. We have said that to do this required moral courage; in truth, it required more. It presupposed in the heart of Raphael the possibility of righteous anger, the capability of warming into passion in beholding the spectacle of human iniquity, the power of rising up in revolution against the prevalence of vices whose long continuance had given them the weight of social conventionalities. Raphael and Angelo here met side by side.

Let us now glance for a few moments at each of them in turn. It was not possible that the paintings of Michael Angelo could fail to exhibit the evidences of the great Reformation struggle. He lived and moved and had his being in that struggle. His long life of eighty-eight years witnessed the preparation for it, the beginning of it, the progress, middle, and end of it. He was born eight years before the birth of Luther, and he died long after Luther and the greater part of his illustrious band had passed to their rest. The world into which he was born was not the world in which he died. The light rose upon him when the Italian renaissance was in its glory, and his sun went down in death when the Italian renaissance was beginning to fade into the light of Elizabethan England. Living thus amid the struggles of a changing society, it was inevitable that he should be affected by the severity of the atmosphere which he breathed; and we find that his latest work, the picture of the Last

Judgment, is impregnated with that severity. As, however, it is the production of his old age, it lies far beyond our historical limits. The work of Michael Angelo, which expresses our present stage of development, is one which belongs to the days of his youth, and which has generally been esteemed his masterpiece; it is the ceiling of the Sistine Chapel. It bears fewer marks of the contemporary conflict than most of his other works; indeed, it is essentially rather conciliatory than polemical. Its leading idea seems to be the ingathering of the whole world under the headship of Christ; and it is the contemplation of this headship as a direct object of worship which here places Michael Angelo amongst the ranks of the reformers. The ceiling of the Sistine Chapel contains the representation of some of the principal events recorded in the Old Testament; but these are all contemplated in their relation to the great event of the New. In one compartment we see the ancestors of the Virgin leading up to Christ; in another we are confronted by figures of the prophets and the sibyls foretelling the approach of the Son of man. It is the thought expressed in this second compartment which especially strikes us. The union of the prophets and the sibyls is a very bold conjunction. It indicates the meeting of Judaism and heathenism; and therefore it implies a conviction that there is a basis of Catholic truth underlying and permeating both. The joint prediction of the prophets and the sibyls is also a remarkable and suggestive circumstance. It indicates that in the mind of Michael Angelo there was a deep persuasion that all the religions of the past had a divine mission to fulfil; that heathenism, like Judaism, was contributing to the development of mankind, and leading the world upward to the summit of the sunlit hills. Above all, in this picture of Michael Angelo there is seen an exaltation of Christ which the mediæval world had never witnessed before. The Son of man stands before us as the head of all humanity, as the goal of all progress, as the consummation of all earthly glory. He is the 'sum of the thoughts of God;' the realization of the dreams alike of prophet and of sibyl; the unconscious object of worship in all heathen temples and in all pagan aspirations, and the light in whose resplendent beams are blended the unities which bind the hearts of men, and eliminated the differences which hold their hearts asunder. The ceiling of the Sistine Chapel is the most eloquent of all sermons on the immediate communion of Christ with a whole united world.

The life of Raphael, unlike that of Angelo, was not spent amid struggle. He was born in the same year as Luther, and he died at the early age of thirty-seven, before Luther's distinctive work can be said to have begun. His life was therefore passed in a comparative calm. He lived amidst the glories of the renaissance, and he did not survive to witness that social disorganization which followed the outburst of Lutheranism. His works, accordingly, are in keeping with the atmosphere which surrounded him. Perceiving no anarchy in the affairs of men, he does not contemplate Christianity in its aspect of authority over men. He portrays Christ, not as the head of humanity, but as the member of a human family; not in His earthly sovereignty, but in His earthly sonship. Michael Angelo had contemplated the Redeemer as He appeared in the fulness of time, Raphael preferred to look upon Him as His life dawned in the days of infancy. We would almost imagine that a presentiment of his own short life had prompted him to measure the strength of the divine existence rather by the intensity than by the duration of its years. We would think so, did we not know that in the gay heart of Raphael there were no presentiments. Seldom has a human life exhibited fewer traces of sadness. Enjoying the pleasures of the hour, he disturbed himself not with anticipations of the future. He was too gentle to ruffle others, too placid to be easily ruffled by them, and too hopeful to be troubled by imaginary calamities. And being joyous himself, he loved to think of all others as joyous, and strove to paint all others in the colours of his own joy. It was this, we believe, which attracted him peculiarly towards the infancy of Jesus. That life of suffering humanity, which succeeded to the child-life of the Master, was too awful to be contemplated by the gentle soul of Raphael. His heart was too tender to dwell long upon such a vision, and without dwelling on the vision he could never on the canvas have realized it. But in the child-Jesus he found a congenial theme; perfect humanity, perfect beauty, perfect sinlessness, unaccompanied as yet by one shade of sorrow. And so Raphael fastened on this spectacle, and made it his own. His portraits of the child-Christ mark a new era in the history of art. It is not that the child-Jesus was absent from the works of previous artists; Raphael was by no means the earliest who sought to depict the first days of the Son of man. But he was assuredly the earliest who perfectly succeeded. The portraiture of the child-Jesus is his distinctive work; not because he was the first who tried it, but because he was the first who finished it; the first who gave to the infancy of the Redeemer the full tribute of beauty which art could lend. Men hitherto had been too exclusively bent on the Madonna; here the Madonna was not forgotten, but she had to share her glories with the child. We do not mean to say that, in his descriptions of the infant Saviour, even Raphael reaches the purely human standpoint. Artistically, his portraits of the child-Christ are perfect; theologically, we should still like a little less of the preternatural, less of the effort to find the man in the child. We shall see this by a single illustration. Here is a brief sketch of one of his finest Madonnas. John the Baptist is represented in boyhood as capturing a goldfinch, and bringing it in triumphant glee to the infant Jesus, who is standing between His mother's knees, with His foot resting upon hers. The infant Christ lays His hand upon the bird, and as He does so the aspect of His countenance is striking. It bespeaks at once the majesty of a creator and the love of a preserver, the conviction that the creature is in His power, side by side with the desire to ward off any injury which may befall it. The bird remains passive under His touch, as if the consciousness that it lay in its Creator's hand dispelled all fear. Over against this picture of Raphael, let us, by way of contrast, place another. It is that in which the Virgin Mother is represented in all her youth and beauty, seated on a low chair, and clasping to her breast the infant Jesus, who is overcome with weariness. We do not ask, Which of these portraits is the finer picture? that is a question for the art critics, and amongst these we do not claim to rank. We profess to deal with art only in so far as it relates to the dawning spirit of the Reformation. We shall therefore put the question in another form, and ask, Which of the pictures marks the highest Christological development? To describe creative majesty in the face of the infant Christ may require a greater stretch of genius than merely to represent the infant in that attitude of weariness which is natural to all infancy. But is an infancy which manifests in its countenance creative majesty as perfect as that infancy which is subject to the weariness of so fragile an age? We feel assured it is not. We are convinced that every preternatural attribute added to the infant Jesus detracts from the perfection of His infant years, makes Him no longer a child, but a man in the disguise of a child, and robs Him of that human interest which the evangelist endeavoured to create, when he described Him nineteen centuries ago as growing in wisdom and in stature. It was not, indeed, surprising that mediævalism should not all at once have emancipated itself from its dominating idea—the idea of a superhuman Christ. We mention the fact not to detract from the great painter, but merely to show that the conception of a glorified humanity was still in a stage of development. Let us acknowledge, however, with gladness, that the step which mediævalism had already attained was a step of real progress. It had found in the child-Jesus a meeting-place for the grandest thoughts of the human soul, and the very effort to render that childhood preternatural was an unconscious striving to exalt humanity. It was groping after a proclamation of the truth that the divine can stoop to the very level of the human, and that the human, without the aid of images or of angels, may rise immediately into communion with the divine.

It seems to us, however, that even in the department of art, the real transition into the age of the Reformation is made not by Italy but by Germany. The development of German art had been of far later origin and of far slower growth than that of Italy; and the cause lay partly in the difference of their respective natural surroundings, and partly in the difference in the character of the national mind. Northern and Southern Europe were originally strongly contrasted in their characteristic features. The North, the home of the barbarous tribes, was more active than receptive, more disposed to leave on surrounding objects the imprint of its presence, than to be itself impressed and moulded by these objects. The South, the abode of classical refinement, was, in later days at least, more receptive than active, less prone to alter the aspect of the world, than to be itself moulded and dominated by that world of beauty which environed it. Accordingly the South received with avidity all impressions of the beautiful, until it became naturally, and almost spontaneously, the very soil of poetry and art. The North, on the other hand, resisted long the influence of culture, and made the very spontaneity of its existence an obstacle to the reception of foreign impressions. But if the reader will refer to the concluding portion of the seventeenth Chapter, he will find that we there anticipated a time when the bald North would be clothed in the luxuriance of the sunny South, and when the stern spirit of the religious reformation would be refined and softened by its union with the spirit of the Italian renaissance. At that time we have now arrived. We have come to a period when Germany was to catch the glow of Italy, and when the art of the South was to be transported into the rugged North. Nay, the time had come when the North was to accomplish by art what the South had never done—the direct transition into a new age. Italy had revealed the human Christ in all the glorious colours which its luxuriant imagination could command, but Italy had rested when the work of imagination was done. Germany was also to reveal the imagination of a human Christ, but it was to pass from a creation of the fancy into an active longing of the soul. Italy was content to picture, Germany desired to find the picture a reality.

The man whom Germany sent forth to be the

representative in art of that reformation spirit which Luther was to inaugurate in religion, was Albrecht Dürer, of Nuremberg. He had this in common with Michael Angelo and Raphael, that he was impressed with the spirit of his time. But we have seen that Angelo and Raphael had each caught a different phase of the age; Angelo had received the sternness of its reformers, Raphael had imbibed the softness of its culture. Dürer, on his part, was affected by his time in a different way from either. If Raphael was rendered gay, if Angelo was made stern, Dürer, by the contemplation of the surrounding world, was forced to be sad. There is no finer proof of the fact, that similar men may behold the same object with different eyes. Dürer looked at the world from the German side. The character of his nation was grave and serious; his own individual bent was towards solemn contemplation, and the natural tendency had been fostered by the outward circumstances of a somewhat sad domestic experience. The same cause, therefore, which repelled Raphael from dwelling on the portraiture of the sorrowful Christ, impelled Dürer to make the life of the Man of Sorrows the peculiar object of his study. He may be said to have reached in his delineations the deification of human suffering. There is one of his woodcuts which embraces this thought in a single figure. It is that which represents the Redeemer bearing the cross along the Dolorous Way, and fainting under the weight of His burden. Here we arrive at the grand truth, that divine greatness can exist in union with the utmost human pain.

We see the portraiture of the Master, not merely in the innocence of infancy, but in the conscious frailty of manhood. Nor alone do we see the portraiture; we are compelled to adore it. We are constrained to bow down with reverence before the image of a Christ who has divested Himself of the awful majesty, and stooped to the servant's form. We are arrested and riveted by a gaze whose claim to admiration is not the dazzling lustre which transcends humanity, but the very pain of humanity itself. We rise for the first time into perfect communion with the divine life; for we see that life for the first time depicted in its perfect communion with ourselves, touching our nature at its lowest base, meeting us in the utmost frailty of that weakest of all hours, the hour of death. The Master, fainting beneath the load of His burden, annuls the worship of a Christ who transcends the human, and dismisses the intermediate host of intercessors, by standing Himself on a level with the suffering soul.

When Dürer deals with the infancy of Jesus, he manifests the same absence of the preternatural. There is another of his woodcuts called the Repose in Egypt, where the Virgin Mother spins beside the cradle of the sleeping babe, around whom beautiful angels hover in the attitude of worship. The angelic worship expresses with sufficient strength the thought of the potential majesty, yet that majesty is not manifested in the infant; His attribute is the common attribute of infancy; He sleeps in human frailty. Nor does it seem to Dürer that the spinning in which the Virgin is engaged, is an occupation too unpoetic for the painter's art. He knows that it should be the aim of all art to make all things beautiful, to lift the mean into the glorious, to turn the water into wine. In raising up the human, he raises up the earthly; in exalting the soul of man, he ennobles the commonplaces of man's life.

But in the works of Dürer there is something more than imaginative portraiture; there is active longing. He represents here the spirit of his nation; he is not content to paint, he desires to see his painting realized. He has expressed that desire in one of the most remarkable engravings on which the eye of man has ever gazed. It purports to be a description of Melancholy, which it represents as a sorrowful winged woman; sorrowful amidst prosperity, and destitute amidst abundance. She stands surrounded by all the implements of the philosopher, the man of science, the artist, and the mechanician—the keys to all the avenues of nature. The book is there, as the representative of the treasures of literature. The chart is there, to indicate the triumphs of discovery. The lever, the plane, and the hammer are there, to suggest the progress of architecture. The crystal and the crucible are there, to tell of the researches of alchemy. And amidst them all the woman stands sorrowful still, with the great void in her heart speaking through her eyes. The picture is evidently allegorical. It is more than a mere representation of Melancholy, it has evidently a historical significance. The interpretation of the parable has been much disputed, yet it seems to us that its meaning is not veiled. The winged woman is the spirit of mediævalism; the wings express the spirituality, and the sex expresses the ideal type of the Catholic world. That world whose glory had been the exaltation of womanhood, stands in the bloom of her youth resplendent and dissatisfied. Around her are the trophies she has won by land and sea. All the beauties of art encircle her, all the triumphs of literature do her homage, all the voices of the newly-discovered lands ring her praises across the ocean. But her eyes rest not on the trophies, her ear listens not to the plaudits; her eye is far away in a future of her own dreams, her ear is strained to catch a music she has never heard. The past and the present have poured their treasures into her bosom; but where her heart is, there alone can her treasure be. And her heart is not here. It pants for holier joys, it throbs for diviner beauties; it vibrates with the anticipation of a more celestial life. Mediævalism has exhausted all her pleasures, drained all her cups, admired all her pictures, traversed all her worlds, and the verdict she has written at the close, is the verdict of Israel's ancient preacher: 'Vanity of vanities; all is vanity.'

CHAPTER XXXVIII.

THE DAWN OF A NEW DAY.

WE have heard a prolonged cry going up from the heart of mediævalism; a cry which had been swelling through the years, and which had now at last become articulate in the voice of Albrecht Dürer. That cry was an unmistakeable revelation that the days of youth were beginning to melt into the age of manhood; that youthful independence had lost the confidence in its own powers, which for a time had blinded it to the coming future. The spirit of Christianity, emancipated from the authority of school, was longing for the guidance of a new authority; a power on which its helplessness might repose, and on whose supporting arm it might pursue its journey. The sorrowful winged woman in the portrait of Albrecht Dürer, revealed to the world that a new age was coming, for her sorrow was the evidence of a spiritual enlargement, and her dissatisfaction was the prophecy of higher heights to gain.

What, then, were those objects for which the world waited? What were those wants, in the mediæval heart, which all the mediæval pleasures had failed to fill? What were those unsatisfied desires which had wrung forth that prolonged and bitter cry? It seems to us that they may be summed up under three heads. There were three distinct objects which the world was waiting for. First of all, it wanted a great indulgence. It had been seeking to find rest in a series of successive pardons. At the repetition of every flagrant sin, it had repaired to the hierarchy to obtain the assurance of forgiveness. But it was weary of going daily up to the mount of blessing. It was weary of those partial resting-places, where it could find repose only for a brief hour, and which at every fresh transgression it must leave to seek a fresh pardon. It wanted a final act of indulgence; an indulgence which would not only forgive, but would forgive once for all, which would not only free from the punishment of the latest sin, but would liberate by one great pardon from the punishment of all sins—past, present, and future. The world desired to be forgiven, but it desired to be forgiven no longer by instalments, but in full. It wanted a cancelling of the past, but it wanted that past to be cancelled no longer by the repetition of the words of mercy at each closing day, but by the proclamation of one great indulgence, which should cover all the days of life: 'Thy sins, which are many, are all forgiven thee.'

But again, the world wanted more than a great indulgence; it desired a great sacrifice. It sought an indulgence which would pardon sin without making light of sin. The mediæval world felt that a mere act of indemnity would not elevate its moral nature. It longed for such a forgiveness as would pardon the offender, without diminishing the guilt of the offence. This was what the hierarchy had failed to do. They had told the suppliant that his sin was forgiven, but the comfort which they had imparted to him had been purchased at the price of blunting his moral sense. The world asked forgiveness; but it asked forgiveness not as a mere act of divine condescension, but as an act which was grounded on the fact of expiation. It desired to believe not merely that sin was pardoned, but that sin had received an atonement; an atonement which had fully revealed its heinousness and its horror, and had fully confessed the misery of its thrall. It sought to rest upon an indulgence which reposed on sacrifice; a sacrifice enfolding all ages and all climes; a sacrifice for universal sin, temporal or eternal, mortal or venial; a sacrifice which covered all donations, embraced all penances, and rendered the struggles of individual life requisite no more.

But there was a third requirement of the mediæval heart, and that the most important of all. It wanted a direct and immediate communion between the human and the divine. The great indulgence and the great sacrifice were only the preliminary steps to this highest good. The sacrifice was to blot out the terrors of a past which seemed to cry for vengeance; the indulgence was to grant forgiveness for a future which seemed filled with the clouds of impending wrath; but both were only steps leading to the temple, not the door of the temple itself. That door was the communion of the soul with God; the communion of peace and joy which followed the removal of the enmity; and it was this that most of all the weary Church desired. To meet face to face with the Eternal; to be granted a direct approach into the holy of holies; to be suffered to pass by the intercessory host of angel and archangel, cherubim and seraphim, saint and martyr; to be allowed an entrance into the divine presence, unaccompanied even by the Virgin Mother, and without the need of being aided by her prayers; to stand at last on equal ground of communion with Him whose paradise had long been guarded by the flaming sword of judgment, was now the dearest desire of the heart of Christendom. It had toiled for it, it had longed for it, it had struggled for it; last of all, in the delineations of the canvas, it had sought to portray it, and the very portraiture of its fondly cherished vision was bringing more near the possibility of its fulfilment.

The time, indeed, had now arrived when all these desires were about to be accomplished. The great indulgence, the great sacrifice, and the great communion, were each and all on the eve of proclamation. From land to land there was to spread the message of a forgiveness which included in its benevolent range all acts of sin that were, or are, or shall be. As the ground of that forgiveness, there was to be proclaimed a sacrifice commensurate with all time, which would prevent the sin-stained soul from asking indulgences any more. Finally, as the fruit of both the forgiveness and the sacrifice, humanity was to be invited into direct and immediate divine communion,—a communion unassisted by celestial spirits, unsupported by earthly intercessions, but resting on the union of the human soul with the human life that dwelt in the heart of God.

We have said that the time had come for the accomplishment of these desires; in truth, their accomplishment had already begun. That great movement which was to usher in the Church's manhood was, unconsciously alike to Church and world, rising silently from the valleys. Like all great movements, it had dawned in the life of one individual soul. While Raphael and Michael Angelo were still in the days of their boyhood; while Albrecht Dürer was preparing in the stages of school-life to be in the world of art the greatest of religious reformers, there was born in the village of Eisleben a life whose work and destinies were to change the course of history, and impart a new impulse to the development of the human soul. On the 10th of November 1483, Martin Luther saw the light of that world which he was to guide into a light more resplendent still. It is beyond the limits we have assigned to this volume to trace the experience of the great reformer; the subject is too large to be entered upon with justice at so late a stage. For the present, we must leave him in the dawn, trusting that hereafter we may be able to resume the history of the march of mind. Yet, standing as we are in the grey light of morning, we cannot but remark how marvellously the destinies of this man converged toward the accomplishment of his great mission. Luther was to be the founder of a new religious world, and he who would attain that pre-eminence must find his preparation for it in a life of wide experiences. No man can be the centre of a world who has not within himself a meeting-place for all types of human character; no man can attract the common mind who has not within his soul something common to all minds. It is this extreme difficulty of finding a many-sided nature which has caused the number of world-reformers to be few. There have been multitudes who have made a figure in their age, few who can claim the suffrages of all ages; multitudes who have been adored by their party, few who have been acknowledged as the benefactors of mankind. In this latter light, Martin Luther must be allowed to stand. His work went far beyond his party. He not only imparted a positive character to the life of Protestantism; he brought a reforming influence over the very life of Catholicism. He forced the Catholic world to take notice of the moral elements it had neglected, and to strengthen the faith which was ready to vanish away. Luther's Reformation, though it was distinctively Protestant, was in truth a reformation of all Europe, and it was so because Luther the reformer was himself a world-wide man. It is the unconscious preparation of his life for becoming the meeting-place of the nations, that causes us to marvel as we stand in the dawn. It would seem as if in that life were to be recapitulated once more all the stages through which the spirit of Christianity had already passed, in order that by the experience of all, it might be able to deal with all. We see the son of the poor miner, born in obscurity, bred in poverty, growing up amid the neglect of the surrounding world, and we are reminded of that early time when all Christianity was poor, despised, neglected. We see him in the school of Mansfeld, his self-will absolutely crushed beneath the cruel lash of a stern task-master, his days become a burden, and his nights a weariness, and we feel that here he is repeating the experience of mediæval Christendom. We see him in the University of Erfurt, immersed in the studies of the schoolmen, and recapitulating the university-life of the whole Christian spirit; its outbursts of freedom, its struggles for emancipation, its weariness of the old, its efforts after the new, its doubts of all that once had been cherished truths, its straining to compensate for the weakness of religious life by a strong life of culture and refinement. Then we see that befalling him which had befallen the spirit of Christianity at large; dissatisfaction with all the efforts, inability to find rest in all the culture. We behold him, like the winged woman of Albrecht Dürer, throwing aside the works of the schoolmen and the memorials of classic literature, and seeking, as the Franciscans had done before, to reach a purer life by penance and abnegation. Once more, like the Christendom of the fourteenth century, he emerges from the cloister, and stands forth in the face of day, but, like that Christendom also, it is no longer as the pupil, but as one who aspires to be the teacher. In the University of Wittenberg, he repeats the experience of Wicliffe and of Huss; he arrests the students by his boldness, and he holds them bound by the spell of his eloquence. Last of all, we find him at Rome, in the heart of the great renaissance, striving to preserve his reverence for the sacred city, in the vision of its frightful corruptions, and with all his veneration striving in vain. From that hour the life of Luther becomes identified with the religious life of Europe.

Here, then, in the history of a single man, we have what may be called a microcosm of the whole history of Christianity, a repetition of the successive and varied stages through which the collective Church had to pass in the process of its development. And can we fail to perceive that this widely diffused experience inevitably gave to Luther a widely diffusive power? He sprang from the lowest ranks of society, and that alone placed him on vantage ground as a reformer. He spoke not, like Tauler, to the philosophers; he spoke not, like Savonarola, to the politicians; he spoke to the people, and the people heard him gladly. They knew his voice, and he knew their wants. He knew that, first of all, they wanted the one great indulgence and the one great sacrifice; and therefore, first of all, he proclaimed redemption by the cross. Yet Luther was more than the man of the people; he was the man of the universities too. He had read much, and pondered more. His was no faith which believed on mere authority; he had a reason for the hope that was in him. If he held the beginning of religion to be the sense of sin forgiven, he held its joy and crown to be the personal communion with the divine light. Tauler himself, in this respect, was not a greater mystic than he. Nor would Luther allow any man to lead him to the light. All the scepticism of the universities lingered in his nature; his own eyes must see, or his heart would not believe. But the wideness of Luther's range did not end here. He was not only the popular preacher proclaiming man's need of redemption, he was not only the university professor asserting man's right of private judgment; he was the social reformer aspiring to be the elevator and the renovator of human society. Catholicism had dealt with society in two ways: by caresses and by frowns. In the renaissance of France and Italy, it had pandered to its vices; in the rigid austerities of monasticism, it had sought to ignore its very existence. Luther repudiated both courses. He had stood in the streets of Rome, and he had recoiled with horror from the spectacle of a city given over to the worship of its own corruptions; with a society thus constituted, his soul refused to have fellowship. But Luther would not therefore conclude that man ought to shun the contact with his brother man. If he had seen the corruptions of Rome, he had also seen the corruptions of the cloister. He had lived for three years in the isolation of the convent, striving to find rest, and struggling by forgetfulness of others to crucify the passions of his own nature. And he had found that experience of monasticism to be the experience of bitter failure. He had found that the concentration of thought upon himself had narrowed his sympathies, and restrained the warm impulses of his heart; that forgetfulness of the interests of others had rendered his very virtue a form of selfishness. Therefore Luther emerged from the convent resolved to battle through life with monasticism and monastic vows, resolved to defend and maintain man's right to be a social being. He felt that the system which called itself Catholic, sacrificed the catholicity of human nature, presented to God the offering of a maimed and a mutilated humanity, and purchased the redemption of the human spirit by the captivity and the slavery of the human body and the outward life. Luther claimed for Christian manhood what manhood alone can claim—the right of a perfect brotherhood, the unfettered intercourse of soul with soul, the privilege of appropriating the world, and making it sublime.

Thus marvellously were the events of this man's life converging towards his great mission as the religious regenerator of Europe. But there was another side of the picture. All the time that the destinies of Luther were weaving for Europe, the destinies of Europe were equally weaving for Luther. The civilised world was gathering fast into unity. Its unity was essential to the success of any reformation; it was necessary that the blow which struck one part should reverberate over all. Accordingly, in preparation for a united manhood, Europe was rapidly becoming a politically united continent. Spain was expelling from her dominions those followers of the Crescent who long had held sway upon her soil. Germany was entering into a union with Spain which was to blend together the most Catholic and the least Catholic of European lands. Italy was to find herself overshadowed by the Empire of Germany, incapable of self-action, and governed by imperial rule. France, before the united power of Spain, Italy, and Germany, was to sink for a time prostrate, and yield her king a captive. Nay, the new world itself—that world which Columbus had recently found—was to be partially overshadowed by the great German Empire. Spain was to enter Mexico and Peru with fire and sword, carrying desolation and horror into the heart of the trans-Atlantic world; a cruel, a bloody, and unhallowed warfare, yet a warfare which was the source of much moral gain. The legions of Spain thought they were engaged on a mission only of conquest and rapine; they believed that when they had subjugated the new lands, and appropriated the new treasures, they had fulfilled that work which was assigned them to do. But in truth, unconsciously to themselves, there had been assigned to them a greater, a nobler, a more enduring work. While they imagined that they were merely overpowering the Mexican and Peruvian tribes, they were in reality stretching across the Atlantic an electric wire of sympathy, on which the current of the reformation-life would bound from the European to the American continent. Thus, in various forms and in diverse manners, by the power of the sword or by the force of political expediency, the nations of the earth were being drawn into one. The many families were becoming one family. Papal unity had fallen, and with it the glory of Catholicism had passed away; but Protestant unity was rising, and its centre was the heart of Protestantism. It was around Germany that all the nations clustered; by a singular concurrence of circumstances, the land of Luther had become the focus of the earth. The throne of Charles v. was the political centre of the world. It prompted the counsels of Wolsey, the Prime Minister of England; it subjugated the imperious will of Francis the First of France; it dominated the fairest provinces of Italy; it held in absolute subjection Clement the Seventh of Rome; it stretched its empire over Spain, and, in enfolding Spain, it embraced an immense tract of the new world of America. When Luther proclaimed the German Reformation, he proclaimed the Reformation of the united earth.

Thus we have brought the world to the very threshold of modern times. We have carried it to the verge of that boundary line which divides the mediæval ages from those ages which we proudly call our own. Standing on the frontier between the old and the new, we see mediævalism everywhere fading, its forms melting, its shadows vanishing, its life dying. Yet its death is no sudden convulsion, no violent explosion, no abrupt catastrophe; it is a transition so silent and gentle, that we are not at once conscious of the change. The life of mediævalism quits not the old tenement until it has caused that tenement to be swept and garnished and prepared for the entrance of the new and higher spirit. The past parts not in anger from that future which has met it face to face;

it is content to be the forerunner of the greater light, and it makes haste to prepare its way. And now, ere the vision of that past has quite faded, let us cast back our eye once more over the long course through which we have travelled. We have been engaged in a lengthened pilgrimage. Has it led us to any permanent resting-place? Have we reached, as the result of this historical inquiry, the scientific determination of any eternal truth? Let us marshal once again the testimonies of the past. We have seen the mind of man sleeping profoundly in China, dreaming wildly in Brahma, reposing restlessly in Buddha, half-waking in Persia, fully conscious in Egypt, strongly active in Greece. Then we have seen the life of strength taken up into the life of sacrifice, the power to do transmuted into the power to suffer, and paganism fading in the light of Christianity. Christianity itself we have beheld rising from very small beginnings: first, the infant that could only wonder; next, at the Pentecostal outpouring, the child learning to speak; then, in the home associations of Jerusalem, the child learning to feel. By and by we have seen these home associations broken, and Christianity driven forth to seek an enlarged sympathy and a wider brotherhood. We have seen the child's first guesses at truth, its first experiences of worldly contact, and its first dreams of worldly ambition. We have marked how these dreams were disappointed in the very act of their fulfilment, and how the attainment of childhood's goal was the death of childhood's joy. Then we have followed the spirit of Christianity from the life of childhood into the life of school, have seen it first trained under the abbot, and afterwards under the rod of the Roman bishop. We have observed the gradual yet steady development of that scholastic life from its beginning in the representation of truth by images, to its glorious consummation in the incarnation of truth in art. We have marked how, at each successive stage of development, the school-life became more and more dissatisfied with school, and how, as the spirit grew larger than the form, the form became increasingly repulsive to the spirit. We have traced the violent revolutions by which that repulsiveness was manifested, from the image-controversy of the East to the rising of Wicliffe in the West. At last, in the Council of Constance, we have beheld the close of the school-life, and the entrance into the age of youth. We have followed Christianity through its youthful Utopian dreams, have seen the castles of its fancy and the lands of its imagination beyond the sea, and have heard the proud boast of independence by which it asserted its newly found freedom. And we have seen how the castles crumbled into ruins, we have marked how the lands faded into empty space, we have heard how the proud boast was transformed into a bitter cry — the cry of disappointed hope, the cry of unsatisfied desire. We have seen, finally, how the conscious helplessness of youth was to be the regenerative hour of manhood, joining together the long-separated elements of individual freedom and individual responsibility; the power of self-action and the necessity to act for God.

Thus far we have journeyed, and we need journey no further in order to reach the great conclusion that this world is not a chaos, but a cosmos; not a series of chances, but a grand moral order. It is not that here and there in the history of the past we observe the outburst of great practical movements. It is not that in some apparently isolated events the historian can succeed in tracing a deep connection; such facts would be powerfully suggestive, but they would not necessarily be persuasive. But here is a river of life, never diverted, never broken; a river sometimes corrupted in its waters by the soil it is passing through, sometimes retarded in its course by the artificial embankments raised by man, yet through all corruptions and through all retardations swelling surely onward to the mighty sea. The course of humanity has been an onward course. Individual men have gone back, individual nations have gone back, but humanity itself has never receded. And wheresoever Christianity has breathed, it has accelerated the movement of humanity. It has quickened the pulses of life, it has stimulated the incentives to thought, it has tuned the passions into peace, it has warmed the heart into brotherhood, it has fanned the imagination into genius, it has freshened the soul into purity. The progress of Christian Europe has been the progress of mind over matter. It has been the progress of intellect over force, of political right over arbitrary power, of human liberty over the chains of slavery, of moral law over social corruption, of order over anarchy, of enlightenment over ignorance, of life over death. As we survey that spectacle of the past, we are impressed that the study of history is the strongest evidence for God. We hear no argument from design, but we feel the breath of the designer. We see the universal life moulding the individual lives, the one will dominating the many wills, the infinite wisdom utilizing the finite folly, the changeless truth permeating the restless error, the boundless beneficence bringing blessing out of all. We do not say with Leibnitz, 'This is the best of possible worlds;' but we do say, that for such a world as this, the course of past development has been of all others the best.

And what shall we say of the future? We do not mean the future of the sixteenth century, but all the futures of all the centuries. Does this reflected light of the past cast any prophetic lustre upon the days to come? To us, indeed, it seems unquestionable that all our hope for the future must reside in the teachings of the past. There are days in the depth of winter, when the mid-day sun is hidden in folds of impenetrable gloom, but we do not therefore conclude that the sun will not rise on the morrow; we fearlessly repose in the uniform experience of nature, and our confidence in the future rests in our knowledge of the past. There are frequent fogs in the spiritual world, causing night where the eye expected noonday; hours of darkness, hours of coldness, hours that are impregnated with an unhealthy moral atmosphere. But we will not therefore conclude that the sun of human progress will appear no more; we will fearlessly repose in the uniform experience of mind. We trust the laws of physical nature when they tell us that that which was shall be, yet the laws of the human soul are at least as invariable as those of nature. Tracing these laws in the past, we find that the life of mind has been a life of progress. Have we any reason to believe that the course of the moral universe will be altered by a miracle, that thought will cease to expand, that humanity will cease to grow? There have been those in our age, as in all ages, who have seen in the future only the blackness of desolation; clouds without silver, nights without star, winters without prophecy of spring. We know not how much of that gloom may belong to the actual surroundings, we know not how much may have been lent to them by the melancholy eye of the beholder. Ours is a position in some respects analogous to that of the mediæval world; the landmarks of the past are fading, the lights in the future are but dimly seen. Yet it is the study of the landmarks that helps us to wait for the light, and our highest hope is born of memory. In the view of that retrospect we cannot long despair. We may have moments of heart-sickness, when we look exclusively at the present hour; we may have times of despondency, when we measure only what the eye can see. But, looking on the accumulated results of bygone ages, as they lie open to the gaze of history, the scientific conclusion at which we must arrive is this, that the course of Christianity shall be, as it has been, the path of a shining light, shining more and more unto the perfect day.

INDEX.

ABELARD, Peter, ii. 87.
Adonis, i. 34.
'Adoration of the Lamb,' ii. 362.
Adrian, i. 148.
Alaric, the Goth, i. 276.
Albertus Magnus, ii. 299.
Albigenses, ii. 120, 134-145.
Alchemy, ii. 299-302.
Alcuin, i. 364 ; ii. 250.
Alexander the Great, i. 37.
Alexander Severus, i. 179.
Alexander II., ii. 59.
Alexander V., ii. 265.
Alexander VI., ii. 338.
Alexandria, i. 201.
——, Church of, i. 110, 124-129.
Alexandrian Clement, i. 7, 144.
Alexandrian library, Burning of, i. 341.
Alexandrian school, ii. 191.
Alfred the Great, i. 371 ; ii. 27.
Andrea Orcagna, ii. 360.
Angelo, Michael, ii. 364-370.
Anselm, Archbishop, ii. 86.
Antioch, Church of, i. 205-209.
Antoninus Pius, i. 148, 159.
Apollos, Party of, i. 108.
Apostolic Constitutions, i. 182.
—— Canons, i. 182.
Aquinas, Thomas, ii. 300.
Architecture, ii. 34.
Arianism, i. 209.
Arius, i. 209, 235-240.
Arles, Council of, i. 300, 302.
Armagh, Richard of, ii. 242.
Arnold, Matthew, ii. 35.
Arnolf, Archbishop, ii. 39.
Artevelde, Jakob von, ii. 241.
Artillery, Introduction of, ii. 245.
Astrology, ii. 217.
Astronomy, ii. 216.
—— Ptolemaic theory of, i. 326.
Athanasius, i. 222, 234-240, 248.
Athenagoras, i. 144.
Augustine, i. 7, 66, 145, 250, 268, 285.
——, The monk, i. 311.
Augustus, Philip, ii. 143.
Aurelian, i. 179, 217.
Aurelius, Marcus, i. 160.

BACON, Roger, ii. 299.
Barbarossa, Frederic, ii. 117.

Barcochba, i. 124.
Basil Valentine, ii. 300.
Basilides, i. 133.
Baur, i. 201.
Becket of Canterbury, ii. 117.
Bede, i. 362-364 ; ii. 250.
Belisarius, i. 295.
Bellini, Gian, ii. 362.
Benedict of Nursia, i. 305.
Benedictine monasteries, Foundation of, i. 303.
Berengarius, ii. 58.
Bernard of Clairvaux, ii. 86, 191.
Bertram, ii. 20.
Boccaccio, ii. 241, 256.
Bolingbroke, i. 5.
Bonaventura, ii. 191.
Boniface VIII., ii. 221-236.
Bradwardine, ii. 242, 249.
Brahm, i. 51.
Brahminism, i. 23-26.
British feudalism, Decline of, ii. 92.
Buddhism, i. 27-29, 145.
——, Chinese, i. 21.

CABOT, Sebastian, ii. 305.
Cædmon, i. 361 ; ii. 250.
Cæsar, Tiberius, i. 117.
Caracalla, i. 179.
Carlyle, i. 291 ; ii. 102.
Carthage, Church of, i. 191.
Celsus, Epicurean, i. 148.
Cerinthus, i. 133.
Charlemagne, i. 366-375 ; ii. 7-16.
Charles V. of Germany, i. 367.
—— VIII., ii. 349.
Chaucer, ii. 256.
China, i. 19, 23, 44.
Christ, Party of, i. 108.
Church and State, Earliest disruption between, ii. 61-65.
Claudius of Turin, ii. 46, 126.
Clement V., ii. 236.
Clement VI., ii. 261.
Clement of Rome, i. 116, 285.
Clementine Homilies, i. 154-182.
Clovis, i. 311.
Coalitionists, i. 124.
Columba, i. 311.
Columbus, ii. 305.
Confucius, i. 208.

Constance, Council of, ii. 272-282, 332.
Constantine, i. 208.
Constantine, Copronymus, i. 357.
Constantinople, i. 230; ii. 312-316.
Constantius Chlorus, i. 223.
Continental poetry, Birth of, ii. 82.
Copernicus, i. 342.
Corinth, Church of, i. 108.
Crusaders, The, ii. 73-98.
Cyprian, i. 179.

DANTE, ii. 179-182, 222, 241, 256, 358.
Dark Ages, The, ii. 23-50.
Darwin, i. 20.
Dean Milman, ii. 52-143.
Dean Milner, i. 2; ii. 122.
Dean Stanley, i. 351.
Decian persecution, i. 179.
Decius, i. 217.
Diocletian, i. 217-224.
Diognetus, Epistle to, i. 143.
Dionysius, ii. 191.
Diospolis, Synod of, i. 265.
Döllinger, ii. 258.
Dominic, ii. 152.
Dominicans, ii. 162-164, 170-172.
Domitian, i. 131, 147.
Donatism, i. 264.
Draper, i. 292; ii. 39.
Duns Scotus, ii. 242.
Dürer, Albrecht, ii. 376-379.

EARL OF WARWICK, ii. 326.
Easter, Observance of, i. 124.
Ebionism, i. 124, 134.
Eckart, ii. 192, 198, 211.
Edward I. of England, ii. 224.
Egbert, i. 371.
Egypt, i. 19, 34.
Elixir of life, ii. 297.
Emerson, ii. 14.
England, ii. 324-331.
English poetry, Birth of, i. 360.
Ephesus, Council of, i. 322.
Epiphanius, i. 198.
Erasmus, i. 109.
Erigena, i. 372; ii. 20, 191.
Essenes, i. 62-65.
Eusebius of Cæsarea, i. 219-223, 235-240, 288.
Everlasting gospel, The, ii. 173.

FENELON, ii. 52.
Feudal system, The, ii. 18.
Feudalism, ii. 326.
Florence, ii. 178, 338.
Foundling hospitals, Rise of, i. 299.
Fra Angelico, ii. 362.

France, ii. 331.
Francis of Assisi, ii. 164-170, 354.
Franciscans, ii. 164, 170-178.
Frankfort, Council of, i. 372; ii. 7.
Frederic II. of Germany, ii. 143, 156-158.
Frederic II. of Prussia, ii. 157.
Froude, i. 291; ii. 328.

GALERIUS, i. 224.
Galileo, i. 342.
Gänsfleisch, ii. 310.
Gebir, ii. 299.
Geographical discovery, ii. 304.
Geography, ii. 217.
Gerhard, ii. 174.
Germany, ii. 335.
Gerson, ii. 274.
Gibbon, i. 8, 271.
Giotto, ii. 182, 358.
Giovanni, ii. 305.
Gnosticism, i. 132-146, 164, 183.
Goethe, ii. 294.
Goths, i. 243.
Greece, i. 19-38, 164, 183.
Gregory XI., ii. 260.
Grostete, ii. 242.
Guiraut Riquier, ii. 82.
Guiscard, Robert, ii. 70.
Guizot, ii. 149.

HARDWICKE, i. 5.
Hegel, i. 20, 21.
Heliogabalus, i. 179.
Hellenism, i. 134.
Hengstenberg, i. 291.
Henry II. of England, ii. 117.
Henry IV. of England, ii. 324.
Henry IV. of Germany, ii. 65-70.
Henry VIII., ii. 254.
Heruli, i. 243.
Hildebrand, ii. 51-72.
Holland, ii. 335.
Hospitals, ii. 97.

IGNATIUS, Age of, i. 143.
Images, i. 315-329.
'Imitation of Christ,' ii. 192, 214.
Incarnation, Doctrine of, i. 16.
India, i. 19, 24-26.
Infanticide, Abolition of, i. 298.
Innocent III., ii. 142-145, 150, 156, 160.
Inquisition, The, ii. 149-155.
Investiture, Ceremony of, ii. 62.
Irenæus, i. 6, 66, 156-159, 173, 203, 285.
Irene, i. 357; ii. 7.
Isidore of Seville, ii. 20.

Isidorian Decretals, ii. 20.
Isis, i. 34.
Italian art, Rise of, ii. 352.
Italian renaissance, ii. 340-350.
Italy, ii. 337.

JAMES, i. 285.
Jerome, i. 198; ii. 267-271, 274-279.
Jerusalem, Synod of, i. 264.
Jerusalem, Council of, i. 102-107.
John, Life of, i. 6, 125-129.
John of England, ii. 143.
John Oliva, ii. 175.
John Tauler, ii. 192, 198, 203, 211, 214.
John Wicliffe, ii. 250-260, 264, 267.
John Huss, ii. 264-271, 274, 279.
John XXIII., ii. 269, 273.
Judaic Christianity, i. 112-129.
Judaism, i. 31-34, 43.
Judea, i. 36-39, 56.
Julian, i. 244-249, 254.
Jury, Trial by, ii. 28.
Justin, i. 253.
Justin Martyr, i. 6, 144, 285.
Justinian, i. 295-305.
Justiniani, ii. 315.

KNIGHTS TEMPLARS, ii. 79.
———, Suppression of, ii. 236-238.

LADISLAUS, ii. 265.
Lanfranc, ii. 58.
Languedoc, ii. 134.
'Last Judgment,' ii. 360.
Lateran, Council of, 1215, ii. 155.
Laurence Coster, ii. 310.
Leckie, i. 292.
Leibnitz, ii. 395.
Leo the Isaurian, i. 357.
Leo IV., i. 357.
Leo, ii. 149.
Leonardo da Vinci, ii. 364, 365.
Llorente, ii. 149.
Lollardism, Fall of, ii. 325.
Lollards, ii. 255, 324.
Louis the Meek, ii. 14.
Lunatic asylums, Rise of, i. 346.
Luther, i. 109; ii. 203-205, 285-293, 384-391.
Lyell, Sir Charles, i. 20.
Lyons, Poor men of, ii. 130.

MACARIUS, i. 372.
Macaulay, i. 291; ii. 134.
Magi, i. 86.
Manichæans, i. 256.
Marcion, i. 133.

Marcion, Followers of, i. 6.
Mariner's compass, ii. 218.
Mariolatry, i. 322-326.
Martel, Charles, ii. 311.
Martin V., ii. 274.
Masaccio, ii. 362.
Max Müller, i. 81.
Maxentius, i. 224-225.
Maximian, i. 179, 224.
Medici, The, ii. 338.
Merovingian dynasty, Fall of, i. 336.
Middle Ages, Church of, i. 141.
Milan, Edict of, i. 267.
Miracle plays, ii. 110.
Mohammed, i. 330-346.
Mohammed II., ii. 313.
Mohammedanism, i. 334-337.
Monasteries, ii. 328-331.
Monasticism, i. 249.
Monnica, i. 253.
Montanism, i. 161-172, 176-183.
Montanus of Phrygia, i. 161.
Muratori, ii. 38.
Mysticism, ii. 194-216.

NARSES, i. 295.
Neander, i. 83.
Neo-Platonism, Age of, i. 143.
Nero, i. 119, 147, 160.
Nestorians, ii. 40.
Newton, i. 342.
Nice, Council of, i. 233, 237, 372; ii. 7.
Nicephorus, i. 358.
Nominalists, ii. 104-107.
North Africa, Church of, i. 7.
Novatian, i. 191.
Novatus, i. 189.

OCCAM, ii. 242.
Orders of Chivalry, Rise of, ii. 78.
Orientalism, i. 134.
Origen, i. 144, 145, 198, 202, 285; ii. 191.
Orleans, Maid of, ii. 335.
Osiris, i. 34.
Otho III., ii. 47.
Otho the Great, ii. 33, 46, 47.

PAPACY, Rise of the temporal, ii. 4.
Paracelsus, ii. 350.
Paris, University of, ii. 332.
Parsism, i. 29-31, 46, 47, 135.
Pascasius Radbert, ii. 20.
Patricius, i. 252.
Paul, i. 6, 97-124, 285; ii. 1, 4, 74.
———, Party of, i. 108.
Pelagianism, i. 264-266.
Pentecost, i. 82-84.

Pepin, i. 366.
Persia, i. 19, 51.
Peter, i. 285.
——, Party of, i. 108.
Petrarch, ii. 241, 256.
Pharisees, i. 61-70.
Philip the Arabian, i. 180.
Philip 'the Fair' of France, ii. 224-241, 286.
Philo, i. 38-40.
Philosopher's stone, ii. 296.
Phœnicia, i. 34.
'Piers the Ploughman,' ii. 252.
Pisa, Council of, ii. 265.
Pitt, William, ii. 60.
Platonism, i. 48-51, 258.
Praxeas, i. 141.
Printing, Invention of, ii. 310.
Provence, ii. 134.

RANKE, ii. 149.
Raphael, ii. 364-368, 370-374.
Raymond Lully, ii. 300.
Raymond of Toulouse, ii. 134.
Realists, ii. 104-107.
Recognitions, The, i. 153, 182.
Religious scepticism, Birth of, ii. 84.
Rheims, Synod of, ii. 39.
Roman Empire, Desolation of, i. 281.
Rome, Burning of, i. 118.
Roses, Wars of the, ii. 325.
Rouen, Council of, i. 299.
Ruysbroek, ii. 192, 198, 211.

SABELLIANISM, i. 209.
Sadducees, i. 62-65.
Saul of Tarsus, i. 174.
Savonarola, ii. 342-350.
Sbinko, Archbishop, ii. 269.
Schelling, i. 18.
Schlegel, i. 19.
Schleiermacher, i. 291.
Schola Palatina, i. 369.
Scholasticism, i. 229; ii. 103.
Secular education, Diffusion of, ii. 89.
Sermon on the Mount, i. 44.
Shiva, i. 51.
Sigismund of Germany, ii. 273.
Spain, ii. 336.
Sphinx, i. 34.
St. John, Knights of, ii. 79.
St. Mary, Teutonic Knights of, ii. 79.
Stephen of Rome, i. 192-197, 265, 287.
Stilicho, i. 276.
Stoics, i. 49.
Strauss, i. 201.

Swero, ii. 143.
Swevi, i. 243.
Sylvester II., ii. 47, 73.

TAINE, M., ii. 100.
Tatian, i. 6, 144.
Tertullian, i. 7, 66, 173-178, 183, 203, 285.
Teuton, i. 278.
The 'Black Death,' ii. 248.
Theatre, Rise of, ii. 109-111.
Theodora, i. 358.
Theophilus, i. 144.
Thomas à Kempis, ii. 192, 216.
Tindal, i. 5.
Titian, ii. 364-366.
Toulouse, Council of, 1229, ii. 155.
Tours, Council of, ii. 57.
Trajan, i. 148.
Transubstantiation, Doctrine of, ii. 20, 57-59.
Trinity, Doctrine of, i. 16, 50-52.
Troubadours, The, ii. 82.
Tübingen, School of, i. 201.
Tudors, The, ii. 326.
Tyre, Council of, i. 240.

ULLMANN, ii. 192, 216.
Ulphilas, i. 244.
Universities, Rise of, ii. 89.
Urban II., ii. 65.
Urban VII., ii. 261.

VALENTINIAN, i. 278.
Valentinus, i. 133.
Valerian, i. 217.
Valerian's persecution, i. 195.
Vandals, i. 243, 277.
Van Eyck family, ii. 362.
Vasco de Gama, ii. 305.
Venice, ii. 113-117.
Victor, i. 159.
Vishnu, i. 51.

WALDENSES, ii. 120-135, 289.
Waldo, Peter, ii. 127-132.
Wat Tyler, ii. 254.
Western schism, ii. 261-264.
William of Poitiers, ii. 82.
Woman, Influence of, ii. 41-43, 80.

ZOSIMUS, ii. 265, 266, 287.

Dr. LUTHARDT'S WORKS.

In three handsome crown 8vo volumes, price 6s. each.

'We do not know any volumes so suitable in these times for young men entering on life, or, let us say, even for the library of a pastor called to deal with such, than the three volumes of this series. We commend the whole of them with the utmost cordial satisfaction. They are altogether quite a specialty in our literature.'—*Weekly Review.*

APOLOGETIC LECTURES
ON THE
FUNDAMENTAL TRUTHS OF CHRISTIANITY.
Fourth Edition.
By C. E. LUTHARDT, D.D., LEIPZIG.

'From Dr. Luthardt's exposition even the most learned theologians may derive invaluable criticism, and the most acute disputants supply themselves with more trenchant and polished weapons than they have as yet been possessed of.'—*Bell's Weekly Messenger.*

APOLOGETIC LECTURES
ON THE
SAVING TRUTHS OF CHRISTIANITY.
Third Edition.

'Dr. Luthardt is a profound scholar, but a very simple teacher, and expresses himself on the gravest matters with the utmost simplicity, clearness, and force.'—*Literary World.*

APOLOGETIC LECTURES
ON THE
MORAL TRUTHS OF CHRISTIANITY.
Second Edition.

'The ground covered by this work is, of course, of considerable extent, and there is scarcely any topic of specifically moral interest now under debate in which the reader will not find some suggestive saying. The volume contains, like its predecessors, a truly wealthy apparatus of notes and illustrations.'—*English Churchman.*

Just published, in demy 8vo, price 9s.,

ST. JOHN THE AUTHOR OF THE FOURTH GOSPEL.
By PROFESSOR C. E. LUTHARDT,
Author of 'Fundamental Truths of Christianity,' etc.

Translated and the Literature enlarged by C. R. GREGORY, Leipzig.

'A work of thoroughness and value. The translator has added a lengthy Appendix, containing a very complete account of the literature bearing on the controversy respecting this Gospel. The indices which close the volume are well ordered, and add greatly to its value.'—*Guardian.*

'There are few works in the later theological literature which contain such a wealth of sober theological knowledge and such an invulnerable phalanx of objective apologetical criticism.'—*Professor Guericke.*

Crown 8vo, 5s.,

LUTHARDT, KAHNIS, AND BRÜCKNER.
The Church: Its Origin, its History, and its Present Position.

'A comprehensive review of this sort, done by able hands, is both instructive and suggestive.'—*Record.*

Just published, Second Edition, demy 8vo, 10s. 6d.,

The Training of the Twelve; or, Exposition

of Passages in the Gospels exhibiting the Twelve Disciples of Jesus under Discipline for the Apostleship. By A. B. BRUCE, D.D., Professor of Divinity, Free Church College, Glasgow.

'Here we have a really great book on an important, large, and attractive subject; a book full of loving, wholesome, profound thoughts about the fundamentals of Christian faith and practice.'—*British and Foreign Evangelical Review.*

BY THE SAME AUTHOR.

In one volume 8vo, price 12s.,

The Humiliation of Christ in its Physical,

Ethical, and Official Aspects. (Sixth Series of Cunningham Lectures.)

'Not only does Dr. Bruce's work put a great many theological questions in a very clear and intelligible form—this would be something—but its merits are much higher. The writer gives evidence of extensive and accurate theological learning in the topics of which he treats, and he shows that he has theological grasp as well as learning.'—*Church Bells.*

'We regard this volume as a substantial contribution to the best school of constructive scriptural theology amongst us.'—*British Quarterly Review.*

'The author has given us a book that will really advance the theological understanding of the great truth that forms its subject.'—*British and Foreign Evangelical Review.*

Just published, in one large 8vo volume, Eighth English Edition, price 15s.

A Treatise on the Grammar of New Testa-

ment Greek, regarded as the basis of New Testament Exegesis. Translated from the German [of Dr. G. B. WINER]. With large additions and full Indices. Second Edition. Edited by Rev. W. F. MOULTON, D.D., one of the New Testament Translation Revisers.

The additions by the Editor are very large, and will tend to make this great work far more useful and available for *English* students than it has hitherto been. The Indices have been greatly enlarged, but with discrimination, so as to be easily used. Altogether, the Publishers do not doubt that this will be the Standard Grammar of New Testament Greek.

Just published, in demy 8vo, Third Edition, price 10s. 6d.,

Modern Doubt and Christian Belief: A

Series of Apologetic Lectures addressed to Earnest Seekers after Truth. By THEODORE CHRISTLIEB, D.D., University Preacher and Professor of Theology at Bonn. Translated, with the Author's sanction, chiefly by the Rev. H. U. WEITBRECHT, Ph.D., and Edited by the Rev. T. L. KINGSBURY, M.A., Vicar of Easton Royal, and Rural Dean.

'We recommend the volume as one of the most valuable and important among recent contributions to our apologetic literature. . . . We are heartily thankful both to the learned author and to his translators.'—*Guardian.*

'All the fundamental questions connected with revealed religion are handled more or less fully. The volume shows throughout intellectual force and earnestness.'—*Athenæum.*

Just published, price 7s. 6d.,

ON CHRISTIAN COMMONWEALTH.

TRANSLATED AND ADAPTED (WITH THE REVISION OF THE AUTHOR)

From the German of
Dr. HENRY J. W. THIERSCH.

'The book is brilliant in style, and does not read heavily, as such books mostly do. It is lighted up in almost every page by an abundance of historical allusion and illustrations, and will be read both with profit and pleasure.'—*Literary Churchman.*

In demy 8vo, price 7s. 6d.,

SERMONS TO THE NATURAL MAN.

By WILLIAM G. T. SHEDD, D.D.,
Author of 'A History of Christian Doctrine,' etc.

'These sermons are admirably suited to their purpose. Characterized by profound knowledge of divine truth, and presenting the truth in a chaste and attractive style, the sermons carry in their tone the accents of the solemn feeling of responsibility to which they owe their origin.'—*Weekly Review.*

Recently published, in demy 8vo, price 7s. 6d.,

THE MIRACLES OF OUR LORD
IN RELATION TO MODERN CRITICISM.

TRANSLATED FROM THE GERMAN OF

F. L. STEINMEYER, D.D.,
ORDINARY PROFESSOR OF THEOLOGY IN THE UNIVERSITY OF BERLIN.

'This work vindicates, in a vigorous and scholarly style, the sound view of miracles against the sceptical assaults of the time.'—*Princeton Review.*

'We commend the study of this work to thoughtful and intelligent readers, and especially to students of divinity whose position requires a competent knowledge of modern theological controversy.'—*Wesleyan Methodist Magazine.*

In demy 8vo, price 12s.,

INTRODUCTION
TO
THE PAULINE EPISTLES.

By PATON J. GLOAG, D.D.,
Author of a 'Critical and Exegetical Commentary on the Acts of the Apostles.'

'Those acquainted with the Author's previous works will be prepared for something valuable in his present work; and it will not disappoint expectation, but rather exceed it. The most recent literature of his subject is before him, and he handles it with ease and skill. . . . It will be found a trustworthy guide, and raise its Author's reputation in this important branch of biblical study.'—*British and Foreign Evangelical Review.*

'A work of uncommon merit. He must be a singularly accomplished divine to whose library this book is not a welcome and valuable addition.'—*Watchman.*

'It will be found of considerable value as a handbook to St. Paul's Epistles. The dissertations display great thought as well as research. The Author is fair, learned, and calm, and his book is one of worth.'—*Church Bells.*

Just published, in crown 8vo, price 6s.,

SERMONS
FOR THE
CHRISTIAN YEAR.
ADVENT—TRINITY.
BY PROFESSOR ROTHE.

Translated by WILLIAM R. CLARK, M.A. Oxon.,
Prebendary of Wells and Vicar of Taunton.

'The volume is rich in noble thoughts and wholesome lessons.'—*Watchman.*

'The sermons before us are wonderfully simple in construction and expression, and at the same time ,remarkably fresh and suggestive. . . . It is a mind of real keenness, singularly pure and gentle, and of lofty spirituality, that expresses itself in these discourses.'—*Weekly Review.*

Just published, in two vols., large crown 8vo, price 7s. 6d. each,

THE YEAR OF SALVATION.
WORDS OF LIFE FOR EVERY DAY.
A BOOK OF HOUSEHOLD DEVOTION.
BY J. J. van OOSTERZEE, D.D.

'A work of great value and interest. To the clergy these readings will be found full of suggestive hints for sermons and lectures; while for family reading or for private meditation they are most excellent. The whole tone of the work is thoroughly practical, and never becomes controversial.'—*Church Bells.*

'The *very best* religious exposition for everyday use that has ever fallen in our way.'—*Bell's Weekly Messenger.*

'This charming and practical book of household devotion will be welcomed on account of its rare intrinsic value, as one of the most practical devotional books ever published.'—*Standard.*

'Massive of thought, persuasive, earnest, and eloquent.'—*Literary Churchman.*

'As might have been expected from so clear and vigorous a thinker, every passage is valuable either as an exposition or a suggestion.'—Henry Ward Beecher in *Christian Union.*

BY THE SAME AUTHOR.
Just published, in crown 8vo, price 6s.,

MOSES:
A BIBLICAL STUDY.

'Our author has seized, as with the instinct of a master, the great salient points in the life and work of Moses, and portrayed the various elements of his character with vividness and skill. . . . The work will at once take its place among our ablest and most valuable expository and practical discourses.'—*Baptist Magazine.*

'A volume full of valuable and suggestive thought, which well deserves and will amply repay careful perusal. We have read it with real pleasure.'—*Christian Observer.*

T. and T. Clark's Publications.

Just published, in demy 8vo, price 12s.,

THE SCRIPTURAL DOCTRINE OF SACRIFICE.
By ALFRED CAVE, B.A.

BOOK I.—PREPARATORY.

PART I. THE PATRIARCHAL DOCTRINE OF SACRIFICE.
Chap. I. The Origin of Sacrifice.
Chap. II. The Development and Significance of Patriarchal Sacrifice.

PART II. THE MOSAIC DOCTRINE OF SACRIFICE.
Chap. I. The Mosaic Injunctions.
Chap. II. The Essential Significance of the Mosaic Injunctions.
Chap. III. The Symbolic Significance of the Mosaic Injunctions.
Chap. IV. The Sacramental Significance of the Mosaic Injunctions.
Chap. V. The Typical Significance of the Mosaic Injunctions.
Chap. VI. General Review of the Mosaic Sacrificial Injunctions.

PART III. THE POST-MOSAIC DOCTRINE OF SACRIFICE.
Chap. I. The National Conception of Mosaic Sacrifice.
Chap. II. The Hagiographic Conception of Mosaic Sacrifice.
Chap. III. The Prophetical Conception of Mosaic Sacrifice.
Chap. IV. Other Theories of Old Testament Sacrifice reviewed.
Chap. V. The Transition.

BOOK II.—PLEROMATIC.

Chap. I. The New Testament Doctrine of Sacrifice generally considered.
Chap. II. The New Testament Description of the Work of Christ as Sacrificial.
Chap. III. The New Testament Doctrine of the Work of Christ.
Chap. IV. The Work of Christ as expressed in Sacrificial Language.
Chap. V. The New Testament Doctrine of Atonement.
Chap. VI. Critical Review of Theories of Atonement.
Chap. VII. The Theories of Bushnell, Campbell, and Dale.
Chap. VIII. The Atonements of the Old and New Testaments.
Chap. IX. Human Sacrifices in the New Testament.
Chap. X. Human Sacrifices under the New and Old Covenants.
Chap. XI. The Sacrifice of the Lord's Supper.
Chap. XII. A Review of other Views upon the Holy Eucharist.
Chap. XIII. Sacrifice in the Heavenly World.
Chap. XIV. The Scriptural Doctrine of Sacrifice.

Just published, price 9s.,

SAINT AUGUSTINE.
A POEM IN EIGHT BOOKS.
BY THE LATE HENRY WARWICK COLE, Q.C.
With Prefatory Note by the Bishop-Suffragan of Nottingham.

Just published, in crown 8vo, price 4s.,

OUTLINES OF BIBLICAL PSYCHOLOGY.
By J. T. BECK, D.D.,
PROF. ORD. THEOL., TÜBINGEN.
Translated from the Third Enlarged and Corrected German Edition, 1877.

Just published, in crown 8vo, price 5s.,

THE SYMBOLIC PARABLES
OF
THE CHURCH, THE WORLD, AND THE ANTICHRIST.
Being the Separate Predictions of the Apocalypse,
VIEWED IN THEIR RELATION TO THE GENERAL TRUTHS OF SCRIPTURE.
By Mrs. STEVENSON.

In one volume 8vo, price 10s. 6d.,

THE CONFESSIONS OF ST. AUGUSTINE.
AN ENTIRELY NEW TRANSLATION.
WITH COPIOUS NOTES, HISTORICAL AND EXPLANATORY, BY
Rev. J. G. PILKINGTON, M.A.,
Vicar of St. Mark's, West Hackney.

'The notes are the most complete we have seen, and the general appearance and getting-up of the volume are very superior to any edition now to be had, or, as far as we know, ever published.'—*Church Bells.*

'This edition is not a mere translation: the translator's notes are invaluable; and, in fact, without such notes, very much of the work would be unintelligible.'—*Nonconformist.*

'The most edifying book in all the patristic literature. . . . Certainly no autobiography is superior to it in true humility, spiritual depth, and universal interest.'—*Dr. Schaff.*

In two volumes 8vo, price 21s.,

THE THEOLOGY OF THE OLD TESTAMENT.
By Dr. G. F. OEHLER,
Professor of Theology in Tübingen.

'Crowded with fresh and keen suggestions upon all the difficult topics which occur to the student, a more timely and serviceable work has not appeared.'—*Churchman.*

'A treatise of rare worth, where there are many precious thoughts finely expressed.'—*Bibliotheca Sacra.*

In crown 8vo, price 5s.,

VOICES OF THE PROPHETS.
Twelve Lectures Preached in the Chapel of Lincoln's Inn, in the Years 1870-74, on the Foundation of Bishop Warburton.
By EDWARD HAMILTON GIFFORD, D.D.,
Formerly Fellow of St. John's College, Cambridge, and Head Master of King Edward's School, Birmingham; Rector of Walgrave; Honorary Canon of Worcester; Examining Chaplain to the Bishop of London.

'A valuable addition to the literature of prophecy. It is fresh, clear, learned, and interesting.'—*Church Bells.*

In one volume 8vo, price 10s. 6d.,

ST. AUGUSTINE ON THE TRINITY.
Translated by Rev. ARTHUR HADDAN, B.D.,
Hon. Canon of Worcester, and Rector of Barton-on-the-Heath.

'In giving this work to the English reader, Canon Haddan has left us another of those rich legacies which endear his memory as a scholar and real divine.'—*John Bull.*

In one volume 8vo, price 10s. 6d.,

ST. AUGUSTINE ON CHRISTIAN DOCTRINE; THE ENCHIRIDION (being a Treatise on Faith, Hope, and Love); ON THE CATECHIZING OF THE UNINSTRUCTED; ON FAITH AND THE CREED.
TRANSLATED BY
Professor J. F. SHAW and Rev. S. D. SALMOND.

'A valuable book for the theologian. In the four treatises which it contains, he will find, ready to hand, in a very excellent translation, the teaching of the great Augustine on questions which are fermenting in the world of religious thought at the present day, and challenge discussion at every turn. He will also meet with practical suggestions so fresh in tone, and so directly to the point, that they might have been the ideas of a contemporary speaking in view of existing creeds.'—*Church Bells.*

Just published, Second Edition, price 7s. 6d.,

AN INTRODUCTORY HEBREW GRAMMAR;

With Progressive Exercises in Reading and Writing.

By A. B. DAVIDSON, M.A., LL.D.,

Professor of Hebrew, etc., in the New College, Edinburgh.

'Well adapted for the instruction of College classes. The author has a firm grasp of the principles of Hebrew Grammar, and his mode of treatment is, on the whole, clear and correct.'—*Guardian.*

'This excellent little book supplies a want of which all who are interested in the cultivation of Hebrew studies by our students and ministers have long been painfully conscious. . . . As a system of Hebrew accidence, within the proper limits of the subject, the book is characterized by great completeness as well as simplicity.'—*British and Foreign Evangelical Review.*

In crown 8vo, Second Edition, price 4s.,

PRINCIPLES OF NEW TESTAMENT QUOTATION

Established and Applied to Biblical Science.

BY REV. JAMES SCOTT, M.A., B.D.

'This admirable treatise does not traverse in detail the forms and formulæ of New Testament quotation from the Old, nor enter with minuteness into the philological and theological discussion arising around many groups of those quotations—the author confines his attention to the *principles* involved in them. . . . An interesting discussion vindicating the method thus analyzed is followed by a very valuable summation of the argument in its bearing on the Canon, the originality of the Gospels, the internal unity of Scripture, and the permanence of Revelation.'—*British Quarterly Review.*

'In terse and well-ordered style the Author deals with a subject too little studied and less understood. He shows himself to be, in the best sense of the word, rational in his method and conclusions. . . . Strength, acuteness, sound judgment, and reason, chastened by reverence, pervade this book, which, with pleasure, we commend to all students of Holy Scripture.'—*Record.*

In two volumes 8vo, Subscription Price 14s.,

CALVINI INSTITUTIO CHRISTIANÆ RELIGIONIS.

CURAVIT A. THOLUCK.

Tholuck's edition of Calvin has been long very scarce, and the Publishers have, with the Editor's consent, reprinted it carefully and elegantly. It contains Dr. Tholuck's chapter headings and very complete indices, and the text has been carefully printed from the very accurate edition contained in the *Corpus Reformatorum*; so that, in point of completeness and accuracy, it excels any previous edition, and it is also exceedingly cheap.

'Printed from the most accurate edition of Calvin's great work, we are thankful to welcome it in a shape so accessible to students, and so handy for use.'—*British and Foreign Evangelical Review.*

Second Edition, in crown 8vo,

DAVID, THE KING OF ISRAEL:
A PORTRAIT DRAWN FROM BIBLE HISTORY AND THE BOOK OF PSALMS.

By F. W. KRUMMACHER, D.D.,
Author of 'Elijah the Tishbite.'

'This volume has all the characteristics of the Author's earlier productions— orthodoxy, and earnest piety and a lively, figurative style.'—*Rock.*

At the close of two articles reviewing this work, the *Christian Observer* says: space will not permit us to consider more at large this very interesting work, we cannot do less than cordially commend it to the attention of our readers. It gives such an insight into King David's character as is nowhere else to be met with, and is therefore most instructive.'

'This will be a pleasant household reading-book for many people.'—*Literary Churchman.*

BY THE SAME AUTHOR.

In crown 8vo, Eighth Edition, price 7s. 6d.,

THE SUFFERING SAVIOUR:
OR, MEDITATIONS ON THE LAST DAYS OF THE SUFFERINGS OF CHRIST.

'A book which has reached its eighth edition needs no introduction to the reading public. And yet the very circumstance of its repeated publication entitles it to popularity. There is a richness in these meditations which wins and warms the heart.'—*Nonconformist.*

'A book of inestimable value.'—*John Bull.*

'The reflections are of a pointed and practical character, and are eminently calculated to inform the mind and improve the heart. To the devout and earnest Christian the volume will be a treasure indeed.'—*Wesleyan Times.*

In crown 8vo, price 7s. 6d.,

THE FOOTSTEPS OF CHRIST.
Translated from the German of A. CASPERS.

'A very interesting and instructive book. Its style is quaint and antithetic; it abounds in bright thoughts, presents striking views of Scripture facts and doctrines, and is altogether eminently fitted to refresh and edify believers.'—*Family Treasury.*

'There is much deeply experimental truth and precious spiritual love in Caspers' book. I do not always agree with his theology, but I own myself much profited by his devout utterances.'—Rev. C. H. SPURGEON.

In crown 8vo, Third Edition, price 5s.,

LIGHT FROM THE CROSS:
SERMONS ON THE PASSION OF OUR LORD.
Translated from the German of A. THOLUCK, D.D.

'These sermons have already attained a third edition, and abound in passages calculated to stir up the deepest feelings of devotion, and to awaken the most careless of sinful souls.'—*Rock.*

In demy 8vo, price 6s.,

THE SERVANT OF JEHOVAH.

A COMMENTARY, GRAMMATICAL AND CRITICAL,
UPON ISAIAH LII. 13 – LIII. 12.

WITH DISSERTATIONS UPON THE AUTHORSHIP OF ISAIAH XL.-LXVI.,
AND UPON THE MEANING OF EBED JEHOVAH.

By WILLIAM URWICK, M.A.,

Of Trinity College, Dublin; Tutor in Hebrew, New College, London.

'This is a very able and seasonable contribution to biblical literature.'—*Watchman.*

'The commentary evinces the great ability, accurate and extensive scholarship, and admirable judgment of the author.'—*Weekly Review.*

'We can sincerely congratulate the author on the learning and fidelity with which he has executed his task.'—*Record.*

Recently published, in demy 8vo, price 9s.,

A CHRONOLOGICAL AND GEOGRAPHICAL INTRODUCTION TO

THE LIFE OF CHRIST.

By C. E. CASPARI.

TRANSLATED FROM THE GERMAN, WITH ADDITIONAL NOTES, BY

M. J. EVANS, B.A.

Revised by the Author.

'The work is handy and well suited for the use of the student. It gives him, in very reasonable compass and in well-digested forms, a great deal of information respecting the dates and outward circumstances of our Lord's life, and materials for forming a judgment upon the various disputed points arising out of them.'—*Guardian.*

'In this work the Author affords us the results of many-sided study on one of the most important objects of theological inquiry, and on a knot of problems which have been so often treated and which are of so complex a nature. The Author is unquestionably right in supposing that the so-called outworks of the life of Jesus have their value, by no means to be lightly esteemed. Their examination must be returned to ever afresh, until the historic or unhistoric character of the substance of the gospel narrative has been brought out as the result of scientific examination. . . . In conclusion, we believe we can with full conviction characterize the whole work as a real gain to the scientific literature of the question, and a great advance on previous investigations; not doubting that the most important positions maintained by the Author will in all essential points win the approbation of the student.'—*Jahrbücher für Deutsche Theologie.*

'An excellent and devout work. We can strongly recommend it.'—*Church Quarterly Review.*

In crown 8vo, Second Edition, price 4s. 6d.,

AIDS TO THE STUDY

OF

GERMAN THEOLOGY.

By Rev. GEORGE MATHESON, M.A., B.D.

'The Author has done his work well, and has given us a real help to the understanding of German theology.'—*Princeton Review.*

'A work of much labour and learning, giving in a small compass an intelligent review of a very large subject.'—*Spectator.*

'An excellent and modest book, which may be heartily recommended.'—*Academy.*

'A helpful little volume: helpful to the student of German theology, and not less so to the careful observer of the tendencies of English religious thought.'—*Freeman.*

'The writer or compiler deserves high praise for the clear manner in which he has in a brief compass stated these opinions.'—*Christian Observer.*

Recently published, in demy 8vo, price 10s. 6d.,

DELIVERY AND DEVELOPMENT
OF
CHRISTIAN DOCTRINE.

The Fifth Series of the Cunningham Lectures.

By ROBERT RAINY, D.D.,
PRINCIPAL AND PROFESSOR OF DIVINITY AND CHURCH HISTORY IN THE NEW COLLEGE, EDINBURGH.

'We gladly acknowledge their high excellence and the extensive learning which they all display. They are *able* to the last degree; and the Author has in an unusual measure the power of acute and brilliant generalization. He handles his array of multifarious facts with ease and elegance; and we must needs acknowledge (and we do it willingly) that the Lectures are a real contribution to the settlement of the vast and obscure question with which they are occupied.'—*Literary Churchman.*

'It is a rich and nutritious book throughout, and in temper and spirit beyond all praise.'—*British and Foreign Evangelical Review.*

Just published, price 5s.,

MESSIANIC PROPHECY:
Its Origin, Historical Character, and Relation to New Testament Fulfilment.

By Dr. EDWARD RIEHM,
PROFESSOR OF THEOLOGY, HALLE.

Translated from the German, with the Approbation of the Author,

By the Rev. JOHN JEFFERSON.

'Undoubtedly original and suggestive, and deserving careful consideration.'—*Literary Churchman.*

'Its intrinsic excellence makes it a valuable contribution to our biblical literature.'—*British and Foreign Evangelical Review.*

'The product of a well-balanced mind, which is able to weigh conflicting theories and to assign them their due proportion.'—*English Independent.*

'The subject is one confessedly of profound interest, and has been ably treated. . . . Even if his readers may not coincide with all his views, much valuable information will be gathered from the Author's lucubrations, which deserve careful consideration.'—*Christian Observer.*

Recently published, in crown 8vo, price 6s.,

THE SENSUALISTIC PHILOSOPHY OF THE NINETEENTH CENTURY CONSIDERED.

By R. L. DABNEY, D.D., LL.D.

'The volume is marked by discriminating criticism, and clear, strong exposition and defence of the intuitional theory of knowledge.'—*Daily Review.*

DUGALD STEWART'S WORKS.

In Eleven Volumes, demy 8vo, 12s. each.

The Collected Works

OF

DUGALD STEWART, Esq., F.R.S.S.,
PROFESSOR OF MORAL PHILOSOPHY IN THE UNIVERSITY OF EDINBURGH.

EDITED BY

SIR WM. HAMILTON, BART.

CONTENTS.

Vol. I.—Dissertation.

Vols. II., III., and IV.—Elements of the Philosophy of the Human Mind.

Vol. V.—Philosophical Essays.

Vols. VI. and VII.—Philosophy of the Active and Moral Powers of Man.

Vols. VIII. and IX.—Lectures on Political Economy.

Vol. X.—Biographical Memoirs of Adam Smith, LL.D., William Robertson, D.D., and Thomas Reid, D.D.; to which is prefixed a Memoir of Dugald Stewart, with Selections from his Correspondence, by John Veitch, M.A., Professor of Logic and Rhetoric, Glasgow University.

Vol. XI.—Translations of the Passages in Foreign Languages contained in the Collected Works; with General Index.

'This edition is one of great and permanent value. It has the incalculable advantage of being superintended by a man of greater genius than the author, and hence it possesses a double interest to the philosophical reader.'—*Church of England Quarterly Review.*

'Altogether the style of this edition leaves nothing to be desired. A more illustrious monument to the memory of a great man could not be raised, and the admirers of Mr. Stewart's genius, and indeed all the disciples of mental philosophy, must feel greatly indebted to Sir William Hamilton for the worthy service he is performing.'—*Eclectic Review.*

'This edition, with notes by Sir William Hamilton, is incomparably the best that has been published, and ought to find its way into every good library.'—*Christian Observer.*

Just published, in demy 8vo, price 9s.,

HIPPOLYTUS AND CALLISTUS;
OR,
THE CHURCH OF ROME IN THE FIRST HALF OF THE THIRD CENTURY.

By J. J. IGN. VON DÖLLINGER.

Translated, with Introduction, Notes, and Appendices,

By ALFRED PLUMMER, M.A.,

MASTER OF UNIVERSITY COLLEGE, DURHAM.

'That this learned and laborious work is a valuable contribution to ecclesiastical history, is a fact of which we need hardly assure our readers. The name of the writer is a sufficient guarantee of this. It bears in all its pages the mark of that acuteness which, even more than the unwearied industry of its venerated author, is a distinguishing feature of whatever proceeds from the pen of Dr. Döllinger.'—*John Bull.*

'We are impressed with profound respect for the learning and ingenuity displayed in this work. The book deserves perusal by all students of ecclesiastical history. It clears up many points hitherto obscure, and reveals features in the Roman Church at the beginning of the third century which are highly instructive.'—*Athenæum.*

'Dr. Döllinger's masterly volume..... The translator has not only given us an excellent version, in good and idiomatic English, but he has added notes, which are terse, brief, and thoroughly to the point, and has discussed in some excellent appendices, criticisms on writers who, having for the most part written since Döllinger, are not referred to in the original work.'—*Church Quarterly Review.*

Just published, in two volumes, demy 8vo, price 12s. each,

A HISTORY OF THE COUNCILS OF THE CHURCH.
From the Original Documents.

TRANSLATED FROM THE GERMAN OF

C. J. HEFELE, D.D., BISHOP OF ROTTENBURG.

VOL. I. (*Second Edition*), TO A.D. 325.
By Rev. PREBENDARY CLARK.

VOL. II., A.D. 326 TO 429.
By H. N. OXENHAM, M.A.

'The second volume strikes us as scarcely if at all inferior in importance to the first. The translation reads as if it were an original work.'—*Church Quarterly Review.*

'Of the thoroughness of Bishop Hefele's learning and eminent fairness as a historian it is needless to speak. He is acknowledged to be unrivalled in his own country as a scholar and a profound theologian.'—*Pilot.*

'This careful translation of Hefele's Councils.'—Dr. PUSEY.

'A thorough and fair compendium, put in the most accessible and intelligent form.'—*Guardian.*

'A work of profound erudition, and written in a most candid spirit. The book will be a standard work on the subject.'—*Spectator.*

'The most learned historian of the Councils.'—*Père Gratry.*

'We cordially commend Hefele's Councils to the English student.'—*John Bull.*

www.ingramcontent.com/pod-product-compliance
Lightning Source LLC
Chambersburg PA
CBHW050844300426
44111CB00010B/1119